A
SEPARATE
PLACE

A
SEPARATE
PLACE

A Family,
a Cabin in the Woods,
and a Journey of Love
and Spirit

DAVID BRILL

A DUTTON BOOK

DUTTON
Published by the Penguin Group
Penguin Putnam Inc., 375 Hudson Street, New York, New York 10014, U.S.A.
Penguin Books Ltd, 27 Wrights Lane, London W8 5TZ, England
Penguin Books Australia Ltd, Ringwood, Victoria, Australia
Penguin Books Canada Ltd, 10 Alcorn Avenue, Toronto, Ontario, Canada M4V 3B2
Penguin Books (N.Z.) Ltd, 182–190 Wairau Road, Auckland 10, New Zealand

Penguin Books Ltd, Registered Offices: Harmondsworth, Middlesex, England

First published by Dutton, a member of Penguin Putnam Inc.

First Printing, September, 2000
10 9 8 7 6 5 4 3 2 1

 REGISTERED TRADEMARK—MARCA REGISTRADA

LIBRARY OF CONGRESS CATALOGING-IN-PUBLICATION DATA

Brill, David.
    A separate place : a family, a cabin in the woods, and a journey of love and spirit / David Brill.
        p.   cm.
    ISBN 0-525-94497-4 (acid-free paper)
    1. Brill, David.   2. Divorced fathers—Tennessee—Morgan County—Biography.   3. Fathers
and daughters—Tennessee—Morgan County.   I. Title.
HQ756.B737 2000
    306.87—dc21   00-024127

Printed in the United States of America
Set in Sabon
Designed by Eve L. Kirch

This book is printed on acid-free paper.

For Challen and Logan—
the brightest points of light in my universe

And for Susan—
Our daughters bear evidence of the perfect moments
in an imperfect marriage

To yield is to be preserved whole.
—Lao-tzu, *The Way of Lao-tzu*

ACKNOWLEDGMENTS

This book and the experience on which it's based were influenced by many special people. Among them are:

My agent, Scott Waxman, who helped shape the book concept into a salable package and who made it possible for me to tell this story.

My editor, Jennifer Kasius, whose skillful guidance helped me transform a cathartic outpouring into a book.

My dear friend Constance Griffith, the best ambassador for Christ I know.

Mom and Dad, who remain my role models for how marriages are supposed to work—through good times and bad—and who laid aside judgment in accepting the outcome of things. Steve and Linda and Aunt Sue and Uncle Dan, for their support and perspective.

My friends Willow and Bob, Jimbuddy, John, Kit and Candy, Mike and Tammy, Russ, Kent, Dave, Dale, and Jeff, but especially Sam Jones and James J. Rochelle, who made this journey right beside me. I love you all.

Jack Barkenbus and Dennis McCarthy, who offered encouragement and forgave my lapses at work while I struggled with the end of my marriage.

My cosmic counselors Sarah C. and Julie B. and the other Prayer Meeting regulars at the Great Southern Brewing Company.

CONTENTS

A
SEPARATE
PLACE

PROLOGUE

Indulge me while I violate the tenets of good narrative writing and begin with the denouement: My family is a casualty of divorce, a common occurrence in a society where broken marriages are said to run neck and neck with those that endure. But statistics can't account for the emotional effects of the cataclysm, which becomes a defining experience for the children and parents, the brothers and sisters, and the grandparents of shattered families.

To my family, 1999 was a landmark year, maybe *the* landmark year, and I suspect that we will calculate the dates of lesser events by counting forward or back from this milestone.

It's said that divorce is a death. If so, I fear that it's a lingering one. There's no body to surrender to the nitrogen cycle. Friends who have passed this way before me say that the corpus of divorce festers but never completely rots. Try as you may, you can't tamp down the last shovelful of dirt and walk away. You gaze on the corpse all over again every time you look into your children's faces and think you see a callousness in their eyes that didn't exist before.

For the key players, even the reluctant ones who get dragged along by partners eager to end things, there's the undeniable guilt and shame of violating a sacred vow, or if not sacred, at least a legally binding one: "What therefore God hath joined together, let no man past asunder" (Matthew 19:6). The scriptures aren't particularly fuzzy on this point. Neither are the secular laws, which force divorcing couples to study closely and divide equitably shared assets and debts—a painful process that requires them to tabulate and review the many stages of their lives spent together.

If, in the following pages, I present my ex-wife, Susan, as a somewhat single-dimensional character, it reflects my reluctance to wag fingers. For every one of my wags, she could answer with two of her own, perhaps more. It also reflects my limitations as a writer. Susan is, in fact, a creature full of passion, energy, goodness, and, I suspect, greater depth than I ever had occasion to glimpse, in part because she opted not to reveal it to me. Toward the end of our relationship, the emotions I encountered most frequently in her were disappointment and anger, and anger casts a broad, obscuring shadow.

This is *our* story, but I am the one telling it, and I am fully aware of the responsibility and difficulty one encounters when he endeavors to capture in words the essence of a human being, particularly one who has fully infiltrated his cells. I long ago lost my fix on the point where Susan ended and I began; she and I are, and will always be, fused into *we*, even if we're no longer married.

The split has taught my daughters, Challen, ten, and Logan, eight, to regard with skepticism what appear to be sure bets. And it's ossified some of the places in our hearts that, I believe, God intended to stay soft and pliant. Perhaps that's the saddest effect of all. Our emotional margins have closed in; it will take us years to determine just how far.

Divorce has also forced us all to redefine the shape and form of our family and to settle into new roles, a process that still presents many awkward moments and has prompted more than a few tears.

As Challen once put it, "I love you, and I love Mommy; why can't you love each other?"

Indeed.

Logan, whom we've dubbed "the fairness police," articulated

the dilemma slightly differently: "It's not fair that I can't be with both my parents at the same time; it's not fair that I have to choose."

Amen.

I now live alone in a three-room cabin at 1,500 feet on the Cumberland Plateau, a broad forested plain, braided by rivers and creeks, that runs southwest to northeast and edges along the Cumberland Mountains of east Tennessee.

The cabin is a simple structure of cedar boards, pine floors, and light-filled windows, set at the back edge of sixty-eight acres of woods. Mature hemlocks, pines, and hardwoods interlace into a dense green canopy overhead, and sunlight dapples rich brown humus and dances on fronds of cinnamon and Christmas ferns.

Over past months, I have watched winter ebb, and I have witnessed the awakening of spring, an explosion of color from dormant ground ushered in by bloodroot and bluets and bird's-foot violets and trilliums—the first phalanx in a succession of blossoms that will continue until the first frost in October. Summer eased in on spring's coattails and established itself in an abundance of green that's closed in tight around the cabin. I've invested my hopes in the amazing regenerative powers of nature.

I have wandered through these woods in sunlight and starlight, basking in their wildness and marveling at their perfect order. I have encountered turkeys, deer, snakes, hawks, owls, hummingbirds, and pileated woodpeckers and felt, at times, like an intruder not yet pure enough to enter their world as an equal. The birds' voices have become as familiar to me as those of friends and family, and they mark passage through my day. The songbirds awaken me at dawn and shepherd me through the hours of daylight. The whippoorwills and barred owls commence after sundown and usher me to sleep.

Through my months in the cabin, I've learned many lessons on rustic living—lessons that my rural neighbors, who have been rooted here for generations, would regard as abundantly obvious. I've learned, for instance, not to underestimate the appetite of a woodstove in winter, and I've developed the aim and precision necessary to drop the splitting maul right into the tiny cracks that will explode a section of seasoned hardwood.

I've realized that chipmunks can make short work of a screen door if it's blocking their path to a single nugget of dog food. I've learned that shallow-rooted Virginia pines are no match for winter ice storms, and I've stood outside in the December dark, listening to the slow splintering of wood and the cascade of ice crystals that accompany the demise of sixty-year-old trees. I now understand that a chain saw is an indispensable tool that sometimes represents the only means of escape along a road strewn with toppled trees.

I've grasped that shedding one's clothes entirely is one way— perhaps the best way—to survive humid, ninety-nine-degree days in un–air-conditioned space in Tennessee, and that rayon shirts and cotton shorts will suffice when there's risk of being apprehended by unexpected visitors.

I've come to know the arc of the moon and the star-points of the constellations, chiefly those in the southwestern sky, which glimmer through my bedroom window on clear nights. And I have fathomed that sometimes, despite Western man's push to accomplish things and conquer worlds, there are times for inaction, for floating still on one's back in a pool of cool green water and watching clouds drift by overhead—the Zen of doing by not doing. All the while incubating things in a place buried deep, beneath the threshold of perception.

In my time at the cabin, I have learned to gaze inward. I have mourned and wept, played and planned, schemed and reflected. I have forged friendships. And I have built the foundation for a new life.

My cabin perches on a bluff one hundred feet above Clear Creek, part of a Wild and Scenic River system managed by the National Park Service, a worthy and respectful backyard neighbor. A small seasonal stream two hundred yards below my deck spills down over sloping mossy ledges, plunges into green pools, snakes through rhododendron tunnels, and falls into Clear Creek, which feeds into the Obed River, which feeds into the Emory, which feeds into the Tennessee. And I know that the water that passes behind my cabin is destined for the Gulf of Mexico.

I can hear Clear Creek through my open windows, and even from the distance of a quarter mile, I've learned to know its moods, fathom its depth, sense the urgency with which the water moves along its downward course, yielding to the tug of gravity. Sounds from the gorge become amplified, ricocheting off the bluff and gaining volume in passage from the river to my cabin, and I can hear kayakers talking as their boats bounce over the rapids far below me.

Their words are reduced to echoing murmurs, perceptible but unintelligible, and only the cadence of speech tells me that I'm hearing human voices. Often, for days, those are the only human voices I hear, and they remind me that my isolation is not complete, that a world shaped by politics, torn by conflict—a maddened and fast-paced world—lies beyond this fringe of forest. And knowing this—and remembering what it's like to live day to day in such a place—makes my retreat seem richer, its rewards more sublime.

I have eschewed newspapers and, except on rare occasions, radio—mainly because they offer nothing that has any pertinence to where and how I live. As for weather reports, I rely on the complexion of the sky and the dampness in the air to predict the arrival of storms. And I have come to cherish the flash of lightning through dark woods and the pummel of cold rain on the cabin's metal roof while I sit beside a blazing woodstove in a room lit by an oil lamp. An archetypal comfort—powerful and undeniable—derives from snug shelter in a storm, be it an onslaught of hailstones or heartache, and it equally rewards creatures that burrow into the ground, withdraw into caves, or build huts of branches or mud.

When I leave here to buy supplies, I scan headlines on newspaper racks about school shootings in Colorado or ethnic cleansing in Kosovo, and they strike me as events unfolding in a distant galaxy that have such little bearing on my constellation of trees and rock and water. I catch occasional glimpses of TV in the customer lounge at the Jeep dealer or when I go to buy birdseed at Wal-Mart, and commercials that once might have made me lustful for material things now seem inane, laughable, even evil.

There is a cut in the rock a few hundred yards behind the cabin, a rare passage to the river along a bluff that continues for miles unbroken and drops a sheer hundred feet to the creek. My daughters and friends and I have worn a path down to the water through the hemlocks and rhododendrons to a pool that extends 150 yards from mouth to mouth and spans 75 yards from bank to bank. In summer, when the channels at the head and base of the pool become dry creek beds and summer plants grow among boulders bleached white by the sun, the water in our swimming hole stays a constant twenty feet deep and always offers a cool respite.

A large gray mass of sandstone, the size and shape of a sperm whale, begins near the shore and tapers to a point at waterline. A ledge—the ersatz leviathan's tail—extends four feet beyond, lying fifteen inches below the water, and provides a perfect diving board. We've named the granite whale the "Rock of Contemplation," owing to the mood of reflection that seems to settle over anyone who sits on it, with knees gathered to chest, and peers out at the steep walls of forest or fixes the still green water with an open stare.

It is a profoundly private place, a place whose only port of access—the creek—is impassable during the dry months of summer. I have spent entire days alone on the rock, with thoughts drifting in a seamless stream through a mind as tranquil as the languid, limpid current of the summer creek. I say alone, but I am kept company by my golden retriever, Benton, and kingfishers and swallows and hawks and pileated woodpeckers and the smallmouth bass that duck in and out of submerged rock ledges in the deep green water.

My daughters, Challen and Logan, are creatures of light who entered my life on joyful days in February. When darkness crowds the secluded world of my cabin, images of sweet faces framed in blond hair, remembrances of voices brimming with love, the sensation of their small fingers gripping my hand and communicating absolute trust, remind me that life—despite the ache of loneliness—is an incredible gift. Unto all of us, each morning, the world awakens full of promise, offering a chance for starting over. And so I do start over, each morning, as I greet sun filtering through trees.

The girls spend weekends with me, exploring the surrounding woods; splashing in the creek; riding the tire swing; collecting rocks, toads, snakes, and bugs; singing camp songs by the fire after dark; and always, always, loving and affirming me despite my many failings as father.

I also have a job. I am communications director for a research center at the University of Tennessee, but I left that, too, for a time, with the blessing of my boss, a remarkable man who possesses the rare perspective that the hardness of science and softness of compassion were meant to be complements, not polar opposites.

When I asked for the six-month leave, he said, "Everyone in his life faces a time of change and difficult choices, and this is your time. Go, work things out, and come back to us in the fall."

And so, I moved west from our suburban home in Knoxville to Morgan County and the Cumberland Plateau, to a land of bluffs and rivers and mountains and simple country folk deeply rooted to this place. I settled into a cabin set far back in the forest where I could reduce the challenges shaping my life to essential terms.

My aim was simple. My marriage was ending, and I was in the throes of the most important transition of my life, short of the journey that will lead me from this life to whatever comes next. I didn't want to pass through this time of vital and profound change with blinders on, as many people do, reacting to, rather than shaping, circumstances; distracted by meaningless dissonance and clutter.

Perhaps Thoreau, whose retreat to Walden Pond has inspired generations of seekers like me, best explored the reasons for leaving the civilized world to enter nature.

"I went to the woods," he wrote in *Walden*, "because I wished to live deliberately, to front only the essential facts of life, and see if I could not learn what it had to teach, and not, when I came to die, discover that I had not lived."

While William Least Heat Moon, who found himself at a similar point of transition, packed his van, Ghost Dancing, and set out on the road, seeking motion along America's blue highways to soothe his aching nerve endings, I sought the permanence and stillness of a sheltered anchorage.

Such a quest required that I be present and focused, with time and space to reflect on options, to grieve the death of my marriage, to formulate strategy, to endeavor to be the best father, friend, and person I am capable of becoming. In short, I needed to depart the temporal world for a time to delve deep into the world of spirit, to plumb the depth of my faith, to become a pilgrim who had laid open his heart, who had learned to seek and listen and trust.

Much as the water has carved away the softer stone of these river gorges, leaving behind the hard, persistent rock, I hoped that my time in retreat would wear away artifact, vanity, fear, pettiness, and anger and reduce my life, my existence, to the things that were meant to endure. I realized that, in the process, through days spent in isolation, through evenings spent watching the sun dip below the bluff, through nights surrounded by forest lit only by stars and moon, I would witness fulfillment of some dreams, mourn the death of others, and come to discover that many things I believed to be true were figments of a troubled mind.

I realized, too, that leaving these soothing woods and reentering the world at the end of my leave would mark the beginning of a painful and disorienting process. But I also knew that the journey would be worthwhile and that I would carry a portion of stillness and peace back with me when I returned.

I had experienced those complications at the end of another journey into nature—albeit one predicated on motion—that led me on foot 2,100 miles along the Appalachian Trail, from Georgia to Maine, in 1979. It strikes me as fitting that my current journey into the wilderness began twenty years, almost to the day, after I started my trek through the Appalachians.

During my nearly six months on the trail, the rhythm of my life settled down. I had no deadlines, no commitments, no job awaiting my return, no schedule to keep beyond reaching Maine by summer's end. I ate when I was hungry, slept when I was tired, hiked alone when I felt crowded, or with friends when I felt lonely. I rejected mechanized timekeeping and yielded to the sense that the daylight hours provided more than ample time for fulfilling my obligations. I transitioned from a visitor to a resident of the wilderness. I achieved a level of peace that has abided through much—but not all—of the past twenty years.

That wilderness sojourn transformed me, toughened me in some ways and softened me in others, taught me lessons on the power of nature, the value of simplicity and self-reliance, the essence of friendship. Over the past twenty years, the voice of the wilderness had begun to grow faint to me, though still perceptible.

I'd welcomed the arrival of far too many seasons from the interior of climate-controlled containers, be they cars or buildings, where the temperature is a constant—and utterly artificial— seventy-two degrees. I'd begun to forget the smells of the wilderness: the aromatic bite of balsam spruce at six thousand feet; the dank scent of a rain-drenched forest; the sweet smell of flowering trees; and the shower of white blossoms carried on wind.

I longed to hear that wild voice again, full and rich, and to let it set my rhythm, establish the tenor of my life. And so I went to the woods.

This is a story of my search, my process—one leg of a lifelong journey. It represents one man's spiritual path, his efforts to define for himself the meaning of family, God, friendship, and faith. It is, ultimately, the path of a flawed, though earnest, pilgrim.

If there's anything of value contained here, it's rooted in the notion that hope abounds in this world. That families can survive being fragmented and re-form themselves into new loving wholes. It's rooted in the belief that time spent in reflection and retreat—retreat to mountaintops, to shorelines, to monasteries, to quiet rooms with soft chairs—is not time wasted. It's predicated on the belief that reflection brings clarity and insight that can ease the ache of lives tilted out of balance. It's based on the acceptance of nature as infallible guide; as pure, perfect articulation of the divine and that by entering nature, we return to the foundation upon which all life is built.

"Each separate being in the universe returns to the common source," says the *Tao Te Ching*. "Returning to the source is serenity."

Despite all the reasons—family, job, social commitments, financial concerns—not to disconnect from the world for a time, the reasons to do so are infinitely more compelling. I believe that those who leave, who go to a separate place, no matter how remote, no matter how long their stay, will return to the world enriched, healed, and empowered to lead more fulfilling lives. In short, if you hope to stay connected to the world, sometimes you have to leave it for a time.

I have chronicled my journey in the following chapters, some clipped and terse, some expansive, some full of doubt and sadness, some brimming with joy. They represent points along a path that, over the course of a year and a half, led me from a crisis of faith, of midlife, of family, to a place of wholeness and peace.

I

WINTER

ONE

A Suburban Sargasso

*Oh, Mama, can this really be the end? To be stuck
inside of Mobile with the Memphis blues again.*
—Bob Dylan, "Stuck inside of Mobile"

I had no notion of what happened behind the closed doors
of our neighbors' houses, but I knew all too well what took
place behind ours.

Tempers rubbed raw by ten-hour-plus workdays, disagreements over how best to parent, and squabbles that erupted from
nothing and seemed to lead nowhere had come to define my relationship with my wife, Susan, in our suburban Knoxville
home. The veneer of civility and respect we displayed toward
one another had grown thin over the previous few years, and the
slightest scratch revealed a core of anger that ran deep.

Susan and I married young—she was twenty-one; I was
twenty-six—and as she eased into her mid-thirties, she began to
gain a strong sense of self and a perspective from which to evaluate past choices. To her, my suitability as a partner had become
suspect, and I acknowledge truth in much of her criticism of me.

As a writer, I spent far too much time living in my head, formulating story lines and musing over detail and structure. I created a trail of clutter wherever I went and often seemed not to
notice the chaos I left in my wake. I was inclined toward unbridled candor, which frequently assumed a hurtful form. I admit to
an impetuous bent, and I was far too inclined to make unilateral
decisions, though I generally had the family's welfare at heart.

As Susan and I grew more distant from one another, I developed an adaptive knack for taking care of myself, and Susan came to interpret my care of self as selfishness. But the roots of our troubles likely traced further back, as most problems do. Susan's family was scarred by the divorce of her parents—the result of incompatible temperaments and interests.

Perhaps the cycling of divorce grows more from flawed choices in selecting life mates than from failure to invest emotion and energy in making viable relationships work. Meanwhile, though my family had never known divorce, we had experienced our share of marriages that perhaps lasted longer than they should have.

Whatever the reason, after eighteen years together, our lives had become increasingly divergent. We kept separate checking and savings accounts, we had few friends in common, and we pursued separate careers. Susan ran a home-based graphic-design business, and I worked as a freelance writer and communications director for a research center at the University of Tennessee. As the stressors in our daily lives increased, we became less intimate, less nurturing, less engaged in each other's pursuits, and as a result, we faced a widening interpersonal gulf that taught us all too well to tend to our own needs while neglecting care of the other. It saddens me to think that two people who lived in the same house, shared the same bed, and doted on the same children could evolve as strangers.

There was a time early in our relationship when we relied on each other for nearly everything, and the attraction we felt for one other was so powerful that I never imagined it would ebb.

We had met at a Halloween party in 1980 in a large house I shared with two other bachelors. The Marz Hotel, a bohemian outpost named in tribute to the Grateful Dead album, *From the Mars Hotel*, sidled next to modest homes of working-class people in a blue-collar neighborhood near a GM plant a few minutes north of Cincinnati. The twenty or so former high school buddies who lived there over the years were known collectively as Martians.

The Marz had become a party mecca of sorts, and for our All Hallow's Eve bash, revelers arrived by the dozens, some from out of state, including Susan, who had traveled with a group of fellow art directors from Chicago. The common link was my roommate's brother, who lived in Chicago and who had attended art school with Susan in Colorado.

I was, at the time, a happy bachelor and determined to stay that way, until that Halloween night, when I laid eyes on the Hershey's Kiss who entered through the front door with a gang of superheroes in elaborate costumes who'd assumed grandiose names. Among them was Chotar the Magnificent, whose papiermâché warrior's helmet boasted a hinged nose piece, which allowed him to drink beer without stepping out of character.

I recall standing in the entryway and peering down the hall and glimpsing the most profoundly beautiful creature I had ever seen, blond and lean and athletic, clad in a tapering aluminum foil wrapper. Brown hose-covered legs emerged from the bottom of the Kiss and seemed to extend endlessly to the floor. Meanwhile, I had assumed the guise of a green-faced Martian with wire antennas sprouting from a blue ball cap.

I remember thinking to myself, "Brill, you don't have a prayer," but I determined to see if charm and a little Martian juju could offset whatever I lacked in rugged good looks. We locked eyes, I approached, and we kindled a conversation that began sometime after nine o'clock and continued unbroken until four in the morning. For the seven hours we were together, my gaze never left Susan's beautiful face, and though we were awash in a sea of boisterous partyers, we might as well have been alone on a deserted island. A friend, who served as the official party photographer, snapped a couple of rolls of film of the two lovebirds, though neither of us noticed his presence or heard the clack of his shutter.

"I've never seen anything like it," he said, later. "It was like someone had shot you two with a tranquilizer gun or something. Neither of you moved all night."

Then it was time for Susan to leave, and as she piled into the car with Chotar and his band of superheroes, I felt a stab in my stomach, fearing that I'd never see her again. The next day, I was cranky and had no appetite, but not because I was hungover. The only thing I had overindulged in the night before was fantasy.

Later in the day, I tried to play tennis with my friend Grant, but my serves kept dropping into the net, and I stood staring blankly as his forehands blazed past me.

"Brill, focus!" he yelled, at one point. "You're losing it."

And I suppose I was. That evening, I visited my folks' house, and I told my mother that I had met the woman I was going to marry. This from a guy who valued his freedom over all else and had pledged to be a lifelong bachelor.

"She must really be special," Mom said. "Where does she live?"

"Chicago."

"How is that going to work?"

"Don't know, but I'll figure it out."

A couple of weeks passed, my appetite slowly returned, my tennis serves started dropping in, and I figured the vision in tinfoil was wowing Chicagoans infinitely more deserving of her than I. Then one afternoon, the phone rang at the Marz. It was my roommate's brother calling from Chicago. After a brief conversation, he said, "Hey, there's somebody here who wants to talk to you."

I tensed, my mouth got dry, and Susan's voice came on the phone.

"I had a great time with you at the party," she said, after a few pleasantries. "Any chance you'd want to come visit me?"

"Yes! When?" I struggled to control the quaver in my voice.

"How about next weekend?"

"Yeah, great!"

She gave me directions and her phone number.

"I'll see you Friday night."

At the time, I was the proud owner of an eight-year-old Chevy Vega with a broken heater and rust holes in both fenders large enough for a basketball to pass through. The radio didn't work, and the cassette player was marginal. I had only one tape in the car, which had Richard Nixon's resignation speech on one side and Jackson Browne on the other. The car was barely adequate for around-town trips and hardly roadworthy enough for a six-hour jaunt to Chicago in November. Besides, I was certain I didn't want my fantasy woman to cruise the streets of Chicago, freezing toes and fingers while listening to "Effective noon tomorrow, I will resign as your president. . . ."

As it turned out, my brother and a few of his friends were heading to Purdue University that weekend to hook up with some college buddies. Steve, who had just taken a job as an engineer at General Electric, had purchased a Toyota, and he offered to let me continue north to Chicago in his new Celica after I had dropped him and his friends in West Lafayette.

I arrived in the outskirts of Chicago at 2 A.M., and I remember that the airways were abuzz with people calling in to talk shows to discuss who had shot J. R. Ewing on the hit TV series *Dallas*. The assailant's identity had been revealed earlier that evening in the show's weekly episode. Though I'm proud to say I've not endured a single episode of *Dallas*, the show does help anchor that blissful period of my life.

Perhaps it was the heady experience of talking on the phone with the woman of my dreams, or my poor navigational skills, or the combination of the two, but the directions I had jotted down led me, not to Susan's apartment near the lake, but directly to a ghetto neighborhood on the south side of Chicago, a place where, I'd heard, deliverymen burned their headlights even during the day as a sign of respect to the street gangs, who might otherwise have taken potshots at them.

After meandering lost for more than an hour through alleys and side streets lit only by the glow of tavern signs and the occasional light post, I found a pay phone and called Susan. I described my location and read the names on the street sign above me.

"You *really* don't want to be there," she said, and offered me a hasty course correction. "Get back in your car right away and lock your doors."

A short time later I arrived, and we reconnected immediately and waded right back into the seven-hour conversation we had begun a few weeks earlier. The next day, we rode the el, visited the top of the Sears Tower, and ate French bread and drank red wine on the shoreline of Lake Michigan. Afterward, we hit the bars on Rush Street with my roommate's brother and few other expatriate Cincinnatians who had settled in the Windy City after college.

Though the setting was different, our time together was equally as blissful as our first meeting—and I suspect as revolting to our friends, who had to endure hours of dopey gazes and hand-holding. That night, Susan and I didn't sleep, but lay awake together till dawn.

Within a few weeks, Susan was flying into the Dayton airport every Friday evening, traveling free by virtue of her father's position as captain for TWA, and returning to Chicago, first on Sunday evenings, then Monday mornings. A couple of months later, she left her job in Chicago and moved into the Marz Hotel.

During the following summer, I set out with three other hikers on a four-month, 1,200-mile wilderness trek across the Pacific Northwest. It pained me to leave Susan, but the expedition had been planned long before the two of us had met. By that time, we had moved from the Marz into our own apartment, and my departure was tearful and frightening, largely because our relationship was still so new. I imagined that in my absence, Susan, beautiful and amiable as she was, would meet someone else, someone who wouldn't leave her behind to go climb mountains a few thousand miles away.

As it turned out, we were both poised to benefit once again from her father's position with TWA. A few weeks into my journey, I arrived in Orient, a tiny logging settlement in eastern Washington near the U.S.–Canadian border, just before noon on a Friday. I found a pay phone and called Susan at the ad agency where she worked as a graphic designer. After a month in the woods, sleeping in a tent with a hiking partner who smelled like a goat anointed with insect repellent, I was badly in need of a conjugal visit.

"I miss you," I said. "And Koegel's snoring is wearing thin. I know this is impossible, but is there any chance you can come out here?"

A pause.

"We'll it's two o'clock here, my boss is out, and I've got this project I should get done by the end of the day. But . . ."

Within an hour, she was packed and on the way to the airport to negotiate free passage on planes headed west, and I was standing out on the main road through Orient, with my thumb thrust in the air, hoping that some kindly stranger would shuttle my large orange expedition pack and me a hundred-plus miles into Spokane.

As it turned out, a guardian angel named Ed Calhoun, a forester who lived near Spokane and who had been cruising timber around Orient, stopped, offered me a ride, and drove me all the way to the airport Hilton. Before he left, he jotted down his phone number and told me to call him Sunday. He'd pick me up at the airport, let me crash at his house Sunday night, and then give me a ride back up to the trail in Orient the next morning.

Along the drive, Ed and I talked easily about a range of subjects, as hitchhikers and their chauffeurs often do, including love and marriage. He had just gone through a divorce and was still bruised and depressed. But rather than emerge from the experience cynical and resentful, Ed urged me to work hard, to make my relationship with Susan last. Over one hundred miles of pavement, we became good friends, and we corresponded with each other for several years after.

After Ed had dropped me off, I lugged my backpack into the lobby of the hotel, dug deep into my pocket to come up with thirty-five dollars for a room, and spent forty-five minutes in the shower, scrubbing off a month's worth of grit. Within two hours, I was at the airport, nearly trembling with excitement, waiting to spot Susan in the line of disembarking passengers.

We hadn't talked since that morning, and I was well aware that passengers traveling gratis are the first to get bounced. Until the moment I glimpsed her, wearing a yellow and turquoise polka-dotted white shirt and jeans, I feared that somewhere between Cincinnati and Spokane she had been grounded.

For two nights and two days, we stayed locked in the hotel room, making love and then dozing in each other's arms, aware that the clock hands were spinning and our time together was growing short. At one point, we decided we were hungry, and not wanting to waste precious time in a restaurant, I set out down the hallway, foraging for food and eventually found a picked-over hors d'oeuvre tray outside a banquet room. It sustained us through the weekend, along with the bottle of wine Susan had brought with her.

Sunday, Susan climbed on the plane home, and Ed picked me up in front of the airport and took me back to his apartment. I slept on his couch, and the next morning, he made me pancakes with fresh blueberries he had picked while up in the mountains. By Monday afternoon, I was reunited with my hiking buddies in Orient. They smelled just as rank as I had remembered, but the envious glares on their faces were new.

Susan's and my relationship survived my four-month expedition, and afterward we endured a period of lean earnings, during which, at one point, we were forced to eat leftover freeze-dried food from my trip. Despite our cash-flow problem, we seemed content just to have each other. I recall one Friday evening scraping together our pocket change and walking to a nearby store to buy a Scrabble game and a couple of steaks.

It was one of the best nights of my life, and I remember feasting on the steaks and then stripping down to play a game of au naturel Scrabble.

We were married the next fall, after I had entered graduate school, and we moved to Knoxville in 1985 and took jobs with a publishing company based here. We lived on a thirty-acre farm in a hundred-year-old farmhouse, and we spent much time, as most newlyweds do, planning our future, which, we agreed, would include children and dogs. As it turned out, the dog, a black Lab named Morpheus, came first and became our child through several frustrating years when a baby never came, which ended with the birth of our first daughter, Challen, in 1989.

Susan and I witnessed the births of our daughters, Challen, now ten, and Logan, who arrived two years later, with shared joy. But over the years, our connectedness gave way to separateness and aloof autonomy. I believed that we were still in love, but somewhere along the way, we had forgotten how to be loving.

I'm not sure the frantic tenor of our lives could have sustained the level of intimacy Susan and I seemed to have lost, even if we had been determined to regain it. There were many, many times I wished we could have stripped down, dusted off the Scrabble game, and resurrected the spontaneity and playful joy that attended our early years together.

My conversations with other suburban moms and dads revealed that they, too, felt scattered by obligations and had been left unfulfilled by careers that demanded so much but in the end offered little meaning or purpose. They, too, had lost the ability to play.

I couldn't recall the last conversation I had had with a friend who felt truly gratified by his work and whose enthusiasm in describing his job bore that out. In the end, most of us seemed to be working because it represented a means to an end, a way to meet the mortgage payment, the car payment, and to squirrel away a few dollars for our children's college educations.

Were we to ask our children which they would value more, increased access to their parents now or a free ride to college a decade or so hence, I think their choice would be clear.

But beyond the work world, even the pursuits that we term recreation seemed to be tinged with tension, and as I stood on the sidelines at Challen's soccer practices, I saw little of the joy I experienced as a Little Leaguer when I took to the baseball field with my buddies, surrounded as we were by dads who were completely present with us.

I recalled Mr. Emerick, Mr. Bashman, and my own dad, clad in shorts and T-shirts and wearing our team's official cap, showing us how to grip a baseball or swing a bat. They had left the office behind when they joined us on the field, and their focus on us communicated the importance they placed on spending time with us.

I confronted a different scene on the soccer field. In fact, pagers and cellular phones appeared to be part of the soccer parent's uniform, and I recall watching the father of one of Challen's teammates crimp his cellular phone between shoulder and ear for a twenty-minute business conversation while he worked the girls through various ball-handling drills. Though I'd never had occasion to phone out from the soccer field, I was as guilty as the next dad in terms of being emotionally sidelined by thoughts of the office during my time with Challen's team.

I could only imagine what effect that constant running and round-the-clock connection to work had on the other families, but there was no disputing the influence it was having on mine.

Frequently, I unlocked my office at the university at 7:30 A.M. feeling wrung out even before my workday began. And Susan's graphic-design business routinely kept her tethered to her computer long past midnight.

We and our daughters collapsed on Friday evenings with tired eyes, feeling perversely gratified that we had survived another week spent addressing other people's needs—or at least needs external to our family—while ignoring our own.

I spent far too many weekends working, and over the course of a year or so I noted a widening emotional gulf between my daughters and me. Evenings, they tailed me down the hallway, relating valuable experiences from their days at school. But I had become a passive listener.

"That's nice," I would say reflexively, barely registering the information they'd shared. I was preoccupied with tomorrow's obligations while I should have been focused on the all-important "now" with my family.

My halfhearted listening suggested to my girls that I valued my work over them, and I realized that someday they would turn away from me for good. I realized, too, that I was becoming the very person I loathed so much in my early days of parenting—the stereotypical workaholic father—and that I was damaging the most precious relationships I would ever know.

Then there was our morning routine, which I'd describe as falling somewhere between a masochistic scavenger hunt and a bruising game of human bumper cars.

I had bestowed watches on our children, hoping to teach them respect for time and encourage efficiency. Instead, I persuaded them to become slaves of timekeeping, and in my more cynical moments, I regarded our watches as shackles reflecting our indenture to the chronograph.

As it's turned out, the watches served more often to remind us that we were falling behind our time rather than to help us stay in front of it. And frantic mornings spent scrambling to find socks, shoes, and book bags "before the little hand was on the seven and the big hand was on the six" earned my daughters far too many tardy slips.

One fall morning, during a chaotic sprint to school, Logan

reached her breaking point. *"I'm so tired of rushing!"* she boomed, standing on the kitchen floor, tears streaming down her face. She had one sock on, its mate lost in a pile of laundry on the floor of her bedroom.

If I hadn't been so disturbed by the outburst and the level of distress it reflected, I might have found some humor in the cartoon-strip image of a howling seven-year-old clutching a white tennis shoe in her left hand, a half-eaten bagel dripping grape jelly in her right.

"We're *always* rushing!" she screamed.

Amen, I thought. At that moment, I was melting an ice cube in my coffee cup so I could chug down its contents without scalding my mouth as I mentally planned the agenda for an 8:30 A.M. meeting. Susan, edgy from a long night spent in front of her computer, dashed past me in search of her missing car keys.

"We've got to leave now!" she urged.

I noticed Challen, whom I'd hardly characterize as a morning person, standing zombielike in her bedroom, fully dressed but still in the grips of sleep, and I felt sad for all of us. In my younger, more idealistic days I never imagined that I would live that way.

Perhaps I would have been more resigned to the inevitability of an existence spent rushing if I hadn't experienced an entirely different way of living and being some years earlier while hiking the Appalachian Trail from Georgia to Maine. While on my journey, I spent nearly half a year living in the forests of the Eastern United States, and the experience exposed me to the beauty and power of the wilderness and imparted the value of surrendering to the gentle rhythm of nature. In my first book, *As Far as the Eye Can See*, a collection of essays based on my Appalachian Trail adventure, I wrote:

> Over my five months on the trail, the very rhythm of my life settled down. . . . I rose at dawn and covered my daily mileage with ample time to tarry at mountaintop vistas or soak my feet in streams and still make camp with enough daylight to roll out my bag, boil my noodles, write in my journal, and brew my evening cup of tea.

More recently, I wrote scripts for a national television series called *The Good Life*, which airs on Home and Garden TV. The show profiles men and women who fit one key criterion: They've dropped out of the career rat race to pursue their dreams. While researching and writing the scripts, I interviewed a former stockbroker who became an organic gardener, a once-harried ad-agency art director who had become a furniture maker, an executive who ducked out of the boardroom to create a museum for vintage wooden boats, a newspaper reporter who chucked the daily deadlines to operate a cooking school.

Though they followed different paths in achieving their goals, all had taken that critical first step in defining the lives they wanted for themselves and their families, and then they mustered their resources and planned their escapes. Ultimately, all realized their dreams, and I count them among the most self-contented people I've ever met.

Often, as I buckled into my car and sprinted off to the office, I switched off the radio and recalled the feeling of being clear-headed, focused on the moment, and embraced by the beauty of nature. Those feelings were central to my Appalachian Trail experience. And as the highway miles slid by, I would surrender to the fantasy of retreat that had stayed with me since I reached the pinnacle of Maine's Mount Katahdin at the end of my Appalachian Trail journey.

While the fantasy played out in my head, contractor Joe Sexton and a crew of carpenters were poised to begin work an hour away in Morgan County, Tennessee, constructing my fantasy board by board. Six months earlier, I had purchased a ten-acre parcel of undeveloped land situated on a wooded ridge overlooking Clear Creek at the edge of the Cumberland Mountains. There, Joe and his crew would soon begin fashioning a 630-square-foot cabin, and in the process, they'd play a pivotal role abetting the Brill family's escape.

But even before the cabin began to take shape, the property became a prime destination for frequent weekend trips. On our visits to the property through the winter, my family and I spent hours evaluating candidate trees for rope swings and hammocks. We watched deer and turkeys moving quietly through the forest.

We sat on the creek's shoreline, with snow swirling around us, imagining ourselves floating in cool water on hot summer afternoons. We stacked firewood, whittled walking sticks, collected bird feathers, and sat and listened to the wind move through the pines. We even began to experience the pang of regret that came when it was time to depart the woods and return to the suburbs.

In spring, the season my Appalachian Trail journey began twenty years earlier, the season I will forever associate with spiritual awakening, I realized that within a few months, my family and I would arrive at the property and see our dream cabin fully expressed and ready for habitation. And we would begin a new journey together. There, over weekends and vacations spent together at our cabin, I hoped we could strip away the distractions and stressors that had nudged us apart and, in Thoreau's words, "front only the essential facts of life," reach to the core of our commitment to one other, and mend damaged relationships.

Though I've never been one for grand gestures, the retreat cabin, at its heart, was just that. It represented my attempt to hold my family intact. The notion of divorce was completely at odds with my definition of family, and I never imagined I would arrive at that threshold. Somehow, I'd always considered marriage as a perpetual process of second chances and opportunities to atone for past mistakes. It was a naive vision and one that failed to recognize that any relationship can sustain only so much hurt and neglect before the damage is irreversible. But back then, I believed the cabin would play a central role in helping us get "unstuck" and move beyond the fear and inaction that had paralyzed us for the previous three years.

The coming months, I realized, would put my hopes for reconciliation to the test and launch a process that would shape—and perhaps redefine—the context of family for the four of us.

II

S PRING

TWO

Rhapsody in Blueprints

I will arise and go now, and go to Innisfree, and a small cabin build there, of clay and wattles made. . . .

—William Butler Yeats,
"The Lake Isle of Innisfree"

Bearded workers in flannel and denim, some wearing hard-hat liners, others toboggan caps or billed caps, sat in the cabs of their pickup trucks munching pork-steak sandwiches and sipping soda or coffee in front of Williams Market. Williams is a catchall country store in Morgan County that sells everything from nightcrawlers to kerosene to pipe wrenches to luncheon meats.

A boom truck from Plateau Electric Cooperative idled beside a flatbed loaded with lumber and tools. A Morgan County Sheriff's Department patrol car occupied the space next to the gas pumps. A hog captive in the back of a livestock trailer oinked plaintively from the back side of the parking lot.

Inside the market, Harry, clad in a ball cap and white T-shirt, stood at the cash register and punched keys while gabbing with his regular lunchtime customers. A line of patrons, dropping geometrically shaped mud clods from lug-soled work boots onto the floor, stretched halfway down the store's center aisle. Freta busied herself slicing lunch meat and preparing sandwiches at a table behind the counter.

I could smell chain-bar oil, gasoline, sweat, and wood smoke on Harry's patrons, and these essences struck me as infinitely more honest than the designer fragrances I might have detected at that very moment in the checkout line at the convenience stores in West Knoxville.

I was clad in Banana Republic khakis, a purple L.L. Bean Gore-Tex jacket, and Birkenstock clogs, and I felt conspicuously out of step with Morgan County chic. I stood surrounded by folks whose clothing labels could be traced to Sears, Wal-Mart, or the Family Dollar store in Wartburg. At best, I was dressed in a way that clearly identified me as "other."

At one point, I noticed a bearded workman nudge the man next to him and point at my shoes, hardly the "manly footwear" Merle Haggard sings about in "Okie from Muskogee." I had recently purchased a pair of Army surplus camo fatigue trousers, which Susan referred to as my "Morgan County pants," and I wished I had them on. In Morgan County, you can't go wrong in camouflage.

As I neared the counter, Harry looked up at me and smiled, apparently forgiving me my purple jacket. I suddenly felt validated and began to harbor hope that I could someday walk into the market as a Morgan County regular rather than a West Knoxville suburbanite.

"Hey, buddy, you built that cabin yet?" Harry asked, grinning from under the brim of the ball cap.

"No, but we're about to break ground," I said. I had arrived at the market to meet our builder, Joe Sexton.

"One of my kin is going to be working on Joe's crew," Harry said, reminding me of the weblike interconnectedness among the residents of Tennessee's small rural hamlets.

Just then, Joe walked in.

"Hey, you gotta watch this guy," said Harry, nodding toward Joe. All heads spun toward the door.

"How are ye', Harry?" Joe said, his mouth spreading into a grin.

Joe stands five-foot-six, sports a crew cut, and has forearms like Popeye's from years of twisting wrenches, hefting windows into place, and hanging Sheetrock.

Bright blue eyes peer through wire-framed glasses and communicate both honesty and a bit of shyness. And, as I'd come to find out, Joe doesn't like to waste things, whether they're two-by-fours or words. He crafts his sentences slowly and carefully, much the way he builds houses, and never utters a word he doesn't fully mean.

Joe spotted me in line. "Howdy, neighbor," he said, extending his hand.

I couldn't remember the last time anyone had called me "neighbor," and I liked the sound of it. Maybe there was hope that I could someday blend into the Morgan County populace.

It was a goal worth shooting for, and I determined to strive over the next year to reach a level of familiarity with Harry and Freta and the market's denizens that would allow me to sit at the kitchen table in the front of the store, sip coffee, and be simpatico with the locals. Being hailed as "buddy" and "neighbor" within five minutes of each other seemed to represent a good start, but I realized that the purple L.L. Bean jacket and the Birkenstocks might have to go.

Joe and I climbed into his red truck and drove the two miles to the property to inspect the house site. The week before, Dad and I had armed ourselves with surveyors' tape, hammers, and sharpened stakes and laid out the corners of the house, screened-in porch, and deck. We even taped off the interior walls of the bedroom and bathroom.

My father's unfailing penchant for precision has never stopped amazing me. I was stunned when he began ciphering using the Pythagorean theorem to get the angles right and jotting figures on a torn corner of a grocery bag. As we stretched out the measuring tape and drove in the posts, every angle was true and all lines fell within a quarter of an inch of being dead on, even though I realized we were merely roughing in the space. Joe and his crew would arrive with surveyor's scopes and treat our taped lines as rough reference points. But Dad wanted to see exactly how the house would sit in relation to the slope of the hill and the existing trees and the sun at various points through the day.

Neither he nor Mom was thoroughly convinced that building the cabin was a good idea—particularly in view of my marital struggles and the work-in-progress appearance of our house in the city—but I could sense Dad's enthusiasm for the project as we began to define the space. Every so often, he'd pause and survey the woods around us and say, "Dave, this really is a nice piece of property." It was one of the first of many times I would hear visitors utter those very same words.

Dad and I had been working side by side for ten years, since Susan and I had purchased our fixer-upper in West Knoxville. Together, we built decks, laid hardwood floors, knocked down some walls and erected others, and evolved as friends. Over time, I came to cherish my time with Dad, and I realized that our styles complemented each other perfectly. He's precise and meticulous, always measuring twice and cutting once. Meanwhile, I'm given to quick, on-the-fly problem solving. He intervenes before I cut a board two inches too short, and I nudge him into action when he burns too much daylight pursuing perfection on jobs that require only approximation. But in the end, I'd come to savor spending productive hours in his company and always delighted in pausing at day's end with a beer to survey the fruits of our labor.

So it was when we had finished taping off the cabin's lines in the forest. Once the lines were in place, I settled into the fanciful great room and peered down the hillside through an imaginary wall of windows. I projected myself months into the future and tried to visualize how it would feel to sit in the great room beside the woodstove and look through the windows at winter woods.

I found the fantasy both discouraging and exciting. On the one hand, I realized that months spent wrestling with building details and finances would ensue before studs, drywall, and paint replaced the taped lines. But on the other, with the orange tape in place, I could, for the first time, begin to visualize what the structure might look like.

At the moment, Challen and Logan had completely lost themselves in an engineering project of their own—one that spread across three hours and involved assembling a footbridge of logs and sticks over a shallow dip a few hundred feet from the cabin site. When they had completed their task, they sought the heaviest adult present to test the strength of their creation. The honor fell to me, and as I strode across the bridge, it performed perfectly.

Once on the other side, I asked the girls if they'd like to sit down in the great room of our cabin and scope out the view. Together, we sat on the ground in the rectangle defined by the orange tape.

"Okay, girls, imagine a door here, a woodstove here, and windows here," I said, maneuvering and gesturing inside the taped lines. I couldn't help but feel somewhat like the huckster in *The Music Man*, asking the girls to believe in something that, at the time, existed only in my mind. I could tell they were straining to make the leap from my words to mental images.

"And right up there is your room in the loft," I said pointing up toward open sky. Suddenly, they were engaged and realized that they, too, had a stake in the project.

"Hey, Challen, I have to go to the potty," Logan joked, walking into the tight square that defined our future bathroom. "Dad, where's the light switch?"

"Don't forget to flush!" Challen said.

When Joe and I arrived at the property, we walked back toward the cabin site along an old logging road I had hoped could be improved into a serviceable driveway. But Joe expressed some misgivings about the quality of the roadbed. He had witnessed firsthand the disastrous effect the repeated passage of heavy trucks can have on a soft-packed dirt road.

"David, this road is going to be rough going," he said. "The constant rains have saturated the soil; that's why these pines have popped their roots."

Pines had toppled all along the road after a late-February snowstorm and a few weeks of rain, some crisscrossing the path, others leaning against trees in the forest. The road itself was evolving into two deep, muddy ruts with a high ridge in the center. Clearly, the logging trucks that had used the road decades ago had a high clearance.

Beyond that, in the years since the logging operation had ceased, a number of trees had sprouted along the road itself, most of them fast-growing Virginia pines. Joe suggested that I cut them down level to the ground, which would allow his crew to drive over them and shuttle in building materials.

"Gettin' that block truck back in here ain't gonna be easy," Joe said, before explaining the challenge of getting the cinder block for the foundation back to the site. It's no small irony that the heaviest truck is among the first requiring access to a building site. If the block truck could make the passage, Joe assured me, all others could, too.

Though Jerry Walczak, the landowner who sold me the lot, had agreed to bring the road back to our building site, he clearly was in no hurry—largely because east Tennessee was in the grips of one of the wettest springs on record—and I knew we couldn't count on having the road in place when Joe and his crew started construction a few weeks later.

When Joe and I reached the cabin site, I noticed that deer had torn through some of the taped lines, but the basic shape remained intact. I had also taped three dozen towering pines that I thought might have to come down. Those that listed toward the house site or were long enough to reach the cabin if they fell were candidates for felling.

Joe cautioned me about cutting too many trees, and I began to appreciate the depth of his homespun knowledge, particularly regarding remote building sites.

"All them trees growed up here together, and they put down their roots in relation to the winds that hit 'em," he explained. Joe's dialect was pure country, but it was backed by the wisdom gained by living his whole life in once place and paying close attention to things. "If you cut a lot of 'em trees, you open new pathways for the wind, and you might cause a bunch of 'em other trees to topple."

I had to admit that Joe had touched on a fear of mine. The heavy snowfall in February had brought down dozens of pines, and it had taken me two hours to cut my way back to the cabin site with the chain saw. I could only imagine arriving at the cabin someday and seeing a seventy-foot Virginia pine creasing the metal roof.

Joe identified four or five trees that would have to come down to accommodate construction and advised me to leave the rest alone. He studied the building site for a few minutes and suggested that we shift it a few feet down the hill, which would allow us to spare a few large trees. So much for Dad's precise angles.

We walked back up the road to Joe's truck, and once inside, he handed me a contract. As he did, he apologized for what he seemed to consider an exorbitant price. It may have been steep by Morgan County standards, but from my perspective—quarter-acre lots were selling for as much as forty thousand dollars back in our suburban neighborhood—the bottom line seemed reasonable.

"David," he said, "just keep in mind that this ain't no rough cabin."

I had seen Joe's work on a house down the road a few miles, and as he walked me through the interior of the nearly finished dwelling before I hired him, I noticed that the edges of the molding were tight and clean and that the interior had gained warmth from his generous use of wood trim and solid-wood doors.

"This house started out as a drawing on one side of a piece of paper," he had told me. "The owner's sketch gave me an idea of what he wanted, and we took it from there." While many builders require elaborate blueprints, Joe was content to work from rough pencil strokes on a sheet of paper, a process that required both precision and creativity. In hiring Joe, I realized, I was hiring a craftsman, not just a builder.

He suggested that I take the contract home and call him with any modifications.

As I watched Joe drive away and held the contract in my hand, I realized I was about to reach the point of no return. As soon as I inked the contract, I'd set in motion a process that would, before it was complete, summon plumbers, electricians, septic system specialists, carpenters, floor installers, and stone masons to my patch of woods. All would begin making daily pilgrimages to the construction site, and soon a dwelling would emerge. Scott Burke, the loan officer at Farm Credit Services, had drawn up the papers, and he was ready to cut the check for the first draw.

Over the years, I had learned to trust my gut when it came to making decisions both large and small, and I decided to do the same regarding the cabin. Through the months of visiting the property and ambling through the woods, I hadn't, even for a moment, experienced a single pang of regret or misgiving. If there were warts, I hadn't seen them.

On the way home from the building site, I stopped by the Morgan County Board of Health to apply for a septic permit, a requisite to being hooked into Plateau Electric Cooperative's power grid.

As I filled out the form for the permit, I talked with a middle-aged woman behind a sliding glass window. I jotted down my address, and she handed me a large piece of paper.

"Addresses don't mean much out on those county roads," she said. "How about drawing us a map?"

I walked to my car and returned with a National Park Service map depicting Clear Creek and the Obed River and marked the cabin site with an X. It was the first time I had glimpsed the cabin site in relation to the natural features that surrounded it, and I realized I had only begun to explore the rivers, bluffs, and creeks that defined my new home.

THREE

Coming to Terms

Between the idea and the reality, between the motion and the act, falls the Shadow.
— T. S. Eliot, "Journey of the Magi"

The chainsaw, a Christmas present from Mom and Dad, bit into the trunk of a sixty-foot Virginia pine, and wood chips soon obscured the toes of my work boots.

"Arg! Arg! Arg!" I intoned, in reference to Tim Allen's character on *Home Improvement*. I was, at the moment, a suburbanite armed with only a vague grasp of the physics involved in felling very tall trees and a power tool capable of slicing through a forty-year-old trunk—or a human appendage—in mere seconds. It was a heady moment.

My aim was to drop the trees that had sprouted up along the road on my property in the decades since the area had been logged. Most were spindly pines, but a few exceeded sixty feet in height and more than twelve inches in girth. As a neophyte sawyer, I was a bit uneasy about felling big trees, particularly because they always seemed to fall precisely 180 degrees from the drop line I'd chosen for them.

As the saw bit deeper into the first tree, it began to topple down the road line, half of its trunk still intact, and it snagged in the branches of another pine. I now faced a spring-loaded tangle that was poised to recoil like a catapult or crimp down on the chain-saw blade and hold it fast until a more capable sawyer could come and rescue me from my predicament. On one of my trips to the property earlier in the year, I had driven by a farm-house with a large downed oak tree in the front yard. A stout branch had crimped down on the owner's chain saw midcut. The abandoned tool protruded at a right angle from limb and wore a blanket of snow.

I advanced to the second tree, and it, too, toppled down the road line without breaking clean through. I now faced two spring-loaded trees leaning against a third, and all three groaned and creaked under the strain.

When a friend of mine, J.J. Rochelle, an environmental health and safety officer for a local manufacturer, learned that I owned a chain saw, he reminded me that logging ranks as one of the most hazardous occupations in the country, somewhere behind deep-sea fishing and farming. Over the coming months at the cabin, J.J. would earn the nickname Mr. Health-and-Safety Man because of his preoccupation with the myriad hazards lurking out in the world. I took the information to heart as I studied the tangle of trees I had created.

I hooked Benton to the lead and secured him to a tree a safe distance away and completed the cut through the splintered trunk of the first tree. It tottered for a few seconds and then fell, taking the second tree with it, and I felt the ground shake from the impact and the rush of the wind blew my hat off.

I noticed my hands were shaking—in part from exercising new muscles, in part from raw fear. So I switched off the saw and sat down on the trunk of one of the pines. Suddenly, I was en-veloped in silence, and I fully registered how disturbing the sound of mechanized tools can be in a wild setting and how the saw, by necessity, shrank my perspective to the two or three feet directly in front of me.

The silence, by contrast, seemed to expand my awareness to encompass the entire forest. My ears still rang from the drone of the saw, but gradually I began to hear the breeze rustling the pine trees, and I decided that the chain saw had done enough work for one day.

I untied Benton, and we bushwhacked down to the creek past the rock ledges and bluff and through a thicket of rhododendron and mountain laurel, and it occurred to me that we had entered a tract of wilderness that, because of its remote location and steep slope, had never been disturbed by a chain saw or other mechanized tool. The massive hemlocks and white pines offered proof.

Earlier in the day, I had driven to Williams Market to meet Joe and work out the final terms of contract. Once we arrived at the property, we noticed that Walczak's truck was missing, so we took a seat on his cabin's front porch. To that point, Walczak had constructed two cabins on the sixty-eight-acre tract, and both sat near the entrance to the property off the main road. He lived in the first, and was trying to sell the second, a lofted cottage that had been roughed in and sat near the logging road on six acres.

I added the following modifications to Joe's original contract: I replaced the two-by-eights in the roof rafters with two-by-tens to allow for R-30 insulation (add $260); I added an extra course of cinder block on the foundation to boost the crawl space from sixteen to twenty-four inches (add $150); I opted for soft-copper water lines, which are less likely to freeze and crack than plastic (add $125); I extended the counter space and added a broom closet in the kitchen and a pine cabinet in the bathroom (add $631).

The total contract price came to $31,250, which didn't include drilling the well ($1,600), installing the septic system ($1,200 for installation and $600 for dynamiting the hole), the well pump ($1,422), installing the woodstove ($1,000), clearing the trees for the power lines ($300), or the cost of the ten acres ($18,000). Grand total: $55,372.

After I had calculated the final figure, it occurred to me just how far this project had evolved since the early days of the search when I had envisioned a roughed-in, single-room structure measuring eighteen-by-twenty feet, sans electricity or running water. I had gotten an estimate of $10,000 for the rough structure; the additional outlay of funds bought us a home rather than a hut.

When it came to negotiating the completion date, Joe cited unpredictable spring weather and the poor condition of the road and asked for 180 days. I pressed him for 90 days, and we agreed on 120, which meant that if construction started in April, the cabin would be completed by the end of July.

In many ways, I had waited nearly two decades for a cabin in the woods. Waiting a few more months wouldn't be such a big deal. Or so I thought at the time.

FOUR

Dreams Deferred

I went to the woods because I wished to live de-
liberately, to front only the essential facts of life,
and see if I could not learn what it had to teach,
and not, when I came to die, discover that I had
not lived.   —Henry David Thoreau, *Walden*

If you were to ask me why I decided to build a cabin in the woods, I'd tell you it was because I had to. The reasons were partly logistical, partly spiritual, partly practical. I'd dreamed about living in the wilderness—of being able to watch the trees sway through every window, every minute of every day—for twenty years, since my six months on the Appalachian Trail.

Many, if not most, of the hikers I've known who have completed the 2,100-mile trek emerge from the experience determined to remain connected to the natural world, and many make their homes in the woods and mountains. Some follow through immediately upon completion of the trail; others, like me, follow a more tangential route. My AT hiking partner, Dan Howe, for instance, returned to the mountains a couple of months after we finished the journey. It took me twenty years.

During my months on the AT, I nurtured a connection to the natural world that has become a fundamental part of who I am. Since my days on the trail, my forays into the wilderness, no matter how short or widely spaced, have always felt like a homecoming.

In the woods, I gain clarity in wrestling with worries that clutter my head in the city. The sounds of birds and crickets and

falling pine needles are my white noise. I'd trade the most soothing city-spawned experience for a mist-shrouded forest any time.
I would rather be ministered to by thunderstorms or sit and
watch irises and jack-in-the-pulpits stirred by early spring winds
than rely on any electrified gadget for amusement.

A friend of mine best characterized that connection a few
months earlier, midsummer, after we had bushwhacked down the
bluff behind the cabin site and made our way through the brush
to a rock perch a few hundred yards downstream. Briar bushes
had scarred our thighs, and mud caked our calves. Then the rain
started falling. In my eagerness to reach the rock perch, a favorite roost for watching the river move, I had forgotten, as I
often do, that not everyone shares my zeal for off-trail excursions, particularly those that involve physical discomfort and
sodden clothes and boots.

"The rest of us visit the wilderness," my friend said, once we
had stopped tearing through the forest. "You're connected to it;
the woods are in your cells."

Put another way, I had deferred my dream of a wilderness
home for twenty years. To varying degrees, I'd felt out of place
and out of sync for the better part of two decades, working a series of jobs that paid the bills but invariably separated me from
the woods. As a result, I'd caught only occasional glimpses of the
subtle cycling of the seasons through the year. While I was on the
trail, I watched the seasons change minute to minute.

The longing was most powerful in spring, the season I began
my journey on the Appalachian Trail. With every passing spring
and the attendant onset of what former Appalachian Trail hikers
refer to as "Springer Fever," named for the mountain that marks
the starting point for most AT sojourners, I suffered pangs of
separation from the wilderness. In April, if I closed my eyes, I
projected myself back to 1979 and Georgia's Chattahoochee
Mountains just as the wildflowers began to probe through winter's debris and the world was suddenly alive for me in a way it
had never been before.

But over time, the memories had become less keen. The sights,
sounds, and smells of awakening spring were less vivid. The
amazing sight of sunrises cresting over distant peaks and feeling

the first warm rays of sun on my back as I ascend to an open crest had begun to feel like experiences from a former life. They were becoming increasingly remote. Yes, I could have waited for my cabin in the woods, but waiting seemed more perilous to me than moving forward.

I've never been good at math, but I'm savvy enough to tabulate the figures on this one. I'd wanted a place in the woods for twenty years. Given average life expectancy, that means I'd harbored this dream for more than a quarter of my life. And while my more practical acquaintances offered perfectly good reasons to wait another decade or two, I took to heart an admonishment of one of my best friends, Jim McKairnes. Jimbuddy, as I call him, himself succumbed to the same longing for land and bought a ten-acre piece a half-mile up the gravel road from ours. Never mind the fact that he lives in Los Angeles.

"You're gonna be dead a long time," Jim is wont to say when he catches me enumerating reasons to hesitate and delay gratification. I regard Jim's favorite saw as the best modern-English equivalent to the Latin carpe diem I've yet heard. And though he's cited it frequently over the fourteen years I've known him, with my entry into my forties, I suddenly began to take it seriously. Unless I lived an extraordinarily long life—which is unlikely based on age of death of my elder blood relatives—I was well over halfway to being dead, and I was growing a little impatient.

For the first time in my life, I was making decent money—at least decent money by the standards of a midlevel university bureaucrat. And the previous year, Susan's income from her graphic-design business exceeded mine. Suddenly we were no longer eking; we were fluid, with sufficient disposable income to fritter away on countless small things.

I realized quickly that many small things can add up to one big thing, and I began to grasp the notion that if I stopped tithing ten percent of my salary to the CD store, the wholesale club, and the backpack shop, I would have saved enough for a monthly payment on a cabin. Put another way, I could make monthly payments on a new Toyota Camry or I could have a cabin in the woods. It was a remarkably easy choice.

Susan and the girls and I lived in a '60s-era ranchburger that Susan and I once described as the "ugliest house in West Knoxville" long before we ever imagined we'd live there. Eventually we grew tired of squandering rent money each month and realized that the landowner from whom we leased the one-hundred-year-old farmhouse set on thirty acres wasn't about to sell us a piece of his utopia. The ugliest house in town was a scant eighth mile from the sublimely picturesque farmhouse, and it happened to be for sale. At least we'd have an easy time moving.

We bid low on the house, which had been vacant for two years, outlasted an out-of-state seller who had no other offers on the table, and became the proud owners of a neglected house on an acre lot. We paid forty-five thousand dollars for the package in a part of the city where barren quarter-acre lots sell for that much and more. Over the next eight years, we knocked down walls, laid hardwood floors, built a deck, put in replacement windows, had duct work and central heat and air installed, gave the interior and exterior a few coats of good paint, and razed the cinder-block shed in the backyard that some neighbors told us used to be a chicken coop and others insisted was a chop shop where stolen cars were dismantled.

We tend to believe the latter. How else to explain the fifty-gallon drum of paint stripper and the windshields and car doors that littered the backyard when we moved in?

Eventually, we transformed the house from an embarrassment into a hospitable home and began to regard the dwelling's minor quirks—phantom light switches that activated nothing, bathroom windows that peered out into the garage, and an exterior covered in siding that more closely resembled dense cardboard than wood—as marks of character.

Meanwhile, the neighborhood around us transitioned from small family farms to subdivisions bristling with $300,000 houses—upscale by Knoxville's standards—and we realized that the house we had initially regarded merely as an ugly duckling had turned out to be a financial swan.

Though the value of our real-estate was tracking upward, my relationship with Susan was in a tailspin. Susan, who, at least in terms of relationships, seemed highly more proactive than I, had, on numerous occasions, suggested that I move out, though she'd stopped short of divorcing me outright. "This isn't working," is how she put it. "Don't you think it would be best for us to separate?"

I'd consistently answered with an unequivocal "no" and pointed out that I'd committed no divorceable offenses and didn't want to leave my family. But eventually my resolve began to erode.

On our anniversary, I picked up a card on the way home from work, and late in the evening, after Susan had gone to bed, I began to write a message. In it I effectively surrendered to what was beginning to seem inevitable. I told Susan that I imagined that this might be our last year together, and that I would try, henceforth, to dwell on the good times we had together and the two wonderful kids we produced.

In closing, I borrowed from a Bonnie Raitt song: "I can't make you love me if you don't. I can't make your heart feel what it won't." And crying, I walked back and put the card on her computer keyboard, knowing that she'd find it the next morning, after I had gone to work.

Soon after I arrived at the office the next day, she called.

"Have you forgotten our anniversary?" she asked.

"No," I said. "You'll find something from me in your office."

She called back a few minutes later.

"Thanks for the card," was the sum total of her response. I had secretly hoped she would protest the finality of the card's message, assure me that, with work, we could save our marriage. But she didn't. "Thanks for the card" was as far as it went.

Though I'd waffled numerous times after that, spun on my heels, determined again and again to stay put no matter what, particularly when my daughters squeezed me a little tighter than usual and seemed to sense that their world was about to be rocked by an event that would be one of the most profound and affecting of their lives.

As I did, I suspected that I was engaging in foolish exercises in denial, hoping that my steadfastness would somehow defeat Susan's resolve to call it quits. More and more, I began to recognize that Susan was right. It wasn't working. But the thought of loading up my car, leaving my home and my daily contact with my daughters, and taking up residence in a squalid apartment didn't strike me as a fair bargain.

I'd had enough divorced friends to be familiar with the drill: Mom stays home and keeps the kids; Dad gets the heave-ho, packs his boxes, and settles on someplace cheap, someplace temporary where he can sup on TV dinners and figure out how to get his life back together.

I realized that, should my marriage end, I could pay $385 a month for a place with mildewed carpet the color of a 1970s leisure suit—a place decorated in thrift-shop Mediterranean—or I could live in the woods. Given the crumbling foundation of my marriage, I wanted to settle into a place that would soothe me and afford me sufficient peace and space to figure out what came next in my life.

In the end, I built the cabin hoping that it would serve as a retreat for my family and friends and a technology-free zone where folks could scale down and slacken their pace. A place to build relationships, not dismantle them. But I also built it as an escape hatch should Susan prevail and terminate our marriage. If nothing else, I'd have someplace to go that would feel like my home, not borrowed space that involved a damage deposit and a six-month lease.

Not everyone shared my sense of urgency on the cabin. In fact, Susan regarded the decision to buy wooded land and build our cabin as, at best, premature and at worst, self-indulgent. I've never been quite clear on exactly where she expected me to go once she had cast me out.

Meanwhile, my mother, who upon every visit to our suburban home in Knoxville not-so-subtly reminded me of all the unfinished work on my primary residence, thought I should have waited until I had brought our house in the burbs up to acceptable yuppie standards.

But I'm not a yuppie. Not that I haven't given it an honest shot. I own two perfectly good suits—one summer, one year-round—and a half dozen ties, and I wear them when I'm bereft of other options.

I regard a wild tangle of forest as beautiful, while I consider

Bradford pears, monkey grass, and perfect, fertilizer-enhanced lawns as insults to nature. When people discuss with me landscaping schemes for the cabin—most of which involve importing trees and shrubs indigenous to God-knows-where—I can only laugh.

If there were a template—both structural and spiritual—for my Morgan County cabin, it was a place I visited in the early days of my Appalachian Trail hike.

I had set out on the trail as a complete neophyte, having backpacked only a couple of times before. The duration of my longest stay in the woods had been a few days—hardly enough time to impart even the most rudimentary backcountry skills.

The pristine condition of my gear at the start of my hike should have tipped off any observer to my lack of backwoods acumen, had my actions left any doubt. Band-Aids adorned fingers sliced by my new Swiss Army Knife. Knuckles and forearms bereft of hair testified to my frustrated early attempts at fire starting, which more often than not involved the not-so-judicious use of white gas. And all of my body's moving parts ached from a level of exertion and physical pounding that was totally new to me.

Then there was the rain—days of it on end—with temperatures that seemed to hover just above freezing. There's no describing the sensation of exiting a warm sleeping bag and climbing into wet shirt, shorts, and socks and setting out for twelve to fifteen miles in a downpour.

After a painful two-week initiation into the rigors of backpacking, I was beginning to speculate on the quickest route home. I didn't realize it at the time, but I was poised for my first encounter with what hikers term "trail magic." Simply put, just about the time circumstances have worn down your resolve and reduced you to a sniveling wimp, the trail extends a warm hand and inclines you to keep moving on.

In this case, my deliverance came in the form of a cabin in the shadow of the mountains just outside of Hot Springs, North Carolina, a no-frills town on the Appalachian Trail that, at the time, boasted the requisite amenities of small-town Americana:

a ma-and-pa market, a diner, a hardware store, a gas station, and one place unique to the entire AT route.

I had limped into Hot Springs after a marathon twenty-three-mile day and found my way to the Inn, a century-old manse set on a knob overlooking Main Street. In the late 1970s, and even today, the Inn's decor and architecture can best be described as a melding of late-Victorian and early Grateful Dead, owing largely to the collective of hippies who inhabited the place. The Inn had become a prized stopover for trail hikers in part because of the ambience and three amenities that top a long-distance hiker's wish list after a four- or five-day stint in the woods: food, music, and books.

At the Inn, now called Sunnybank Retreat, classical music filled the rooms, bookshelves occupied every available nook and corner, and the Inn's vintage cast-iron stove produced four- and five-course vegetarian meals built around fresh, organically grown herbs and vegetables.

After removing my boots and peeling Moleskin from blistered heels, I met the Inn's proprietor, Elmer, in the kitchen, where he ministered over several steaming pots containing the evening's feast. Within twenty minutes of my arrival, Elmer, who seemed to sense the mood I was in, had mixed me a mint julep and deposited me in a comfortable rocking chair on the Inn's second-story veranda.

Suddenly, life was good and about to get even better.

Later in the afternoon, I met Elmer's friend Randall, who lived in a Spartan two-room cabin on about sixty acres three miles outside of town. Randall had arrived with bags of fresh produce he had grown in his organic garden.

After dinner, Randall and Elmer asked Dan and me to go for a drive; there was something they wanted to show us. We piled into an ancient Rambler and coursed along a serpentine road through the darkness. Within ten minutes, we pulled off beside a sign that read SCENIC OVERLOOK.

It took my eyes a few minutes to adjust before the scene below emerged from the darkness: A small board-and-batten cabin with tin roof surrounded by open fields bristling with young sorghum plants. A small barn and a swinging footbridge crossing a creek that carried water from the mountains to the French Broad River, which ran along the edge of town. It was Randall's farm.

I had peered at such places, planted along blue highways, countless times but never really seen them. And I had visited such places on grade-school field trips to pioneer homesteads. We city kids all marveled at how primitive and, we assumed, how difficult, life must have been way back in the early days of this country. None of us imagined the bounty of gifts that derived from such a simple, uncluttered lifestyle.

But this was no museum; rather it was a home where a man of the modern ages passed his days and nights, living in isolation and tranquillity.

Despite the cabin's Spartan digs, or more likely because of them, I was, for the first time, beginning to grasp the countless options available to me in terms of how and where I wanted to live.

All that I had seen and experienced over the previous two weeks—the transition from someone who visited the wilderness but lived in the city to someone who lived in the woods, along with the spiritual awakening that was taking place in me—began to converge.

Later that evening, Elmer and Randall asked us if we'd like to stay with them for a few days. We would sleep in Randall's cabin and during the day help him hoe down the weeds in the sorghum fields. Evenings we would serve meals at the Inn.

Over the next ten days, Dan and I divided our days between the Inn and Randall's farm. Each morning, we supped on beans and cornbread cooked on Randall's woodstove. Evenings, we'd sit on an old car seat on the cabin's front porch and sip bourbon and spring water and listen to Randall play his fiddle, which, he insisted, encouraged his sorghum crop to grow. We stayed up late watching the stars and talking about God and spirit and the value of a simple lifestyle.

Nights, I'd lie on an old bed in the open-air loft reading haikus by an oil lamp or stand at the loft's open end and take in the smells of wet grass and spring flowers.

Through days of hoeing, we slaked our thirst with the spring water Randall piped down from the mountain just upstream from the pool where he bathed. Gravity alone caused the water to tumble down the mountain into the wooden barrel on the porch that collected water and served as refrigerator.

A hinged slice of the barrel opened and provided access to the cool jugs of milk—rich and yellow with colostrum—that Randall's cow Molly had given after the birth of her calf, which Randall had named Daisy. Dan and I had arrived in the barn early in the morning on Mother's Day, minutes after the birth, and we watched Molly lick her new calf clean.

Eventually, we realized that if we hoped to make Maine by the end of September, we needed to start covering miles, so, reluctantly, we bid farewell to Elmer and Randall, the Inn and the farm, and the wonderful town of Hot Springs.

Though it had been twenty years since our stay, memories of our time there burned bright. A watercolor painting of Randall's cabin hung in my office at home, just above my computer. During one of his visits, Dad sneaked a slide—a shot of Randall's cabin—from the tray of images from my AT trip, and presented the painting to me at Christmas, and whenever I peered up at it, it reminded me of why I was working and where I wanted to be.

I knew that the painting would hang in our cabin, once it was finished, marking completion of a twenty-year journey, a long loop in time that would bring me home.

FIVE

Hot Wheels

But at my back I always hear time's winged chariot hurrying near.
—Andrew Marvell, "To His Coy Mistress"

Do you realize that your cabin is fifteen miles from the nearest fire department?" my insurance agent asked, just before explaining why he didn't think he could issue me a homeowner's policy.

Apparently being removed from the noise and congestion of the city also meant being isolated from some utilitarian specialists, among them, professional-strength fire extinguishers. Should the cabin start to burn, I realized, we'd have to rely on a garden hose—or a bucket brigade stretching a quarter mile to the creek. By the time the fire crew arrived, there'd be little left to do but stamp out the last few flaming embers and offer condolences.

"And how do you plan to heat the house?" the agent asked.

"A woodstove."

"I was afraid you were going to say that."

"Yeah, but I take fire safety very, very seriously. So do my kids."

I remembered Logan coming home from school one afternoon singing the "Stop, Drop, and Roll" song before demonstrating the procedure on the family room floor.

"Dad, if you ever get caught on fire, *immediately* drop on the ground and roll," she said. "Or you'll die, and burning to death is *very* painful."

I opted not to share the story with our agent.

"I'll see what I can do," he said. "But if we do issue a policy, it's going to be pretty costly."

He said he planned to meet a colleague in Morgan County for breakfast, and both would travel to the property to assess the fire risk.

The issue of insurance coverage fed into a growing anxiety about money and about freedom. On the one hand, I envisioned the cabin as liberating my family, setting us free from the clutter of the city, allowing us to relax and ease into a pace governed by nature and the space surrounding the cabin.

But on the other, the cabin represented a number of added monthly expenses—chiefly electricity and mortgage. To that point, Susan and I had lived well within our means and not really wanted for anything. For more than a decade, we had ample income to pay our bills, support our hobbies, and provide plenty of mad money.

But in addition to the costs associated with the cabin, I had just bought a Jeep—the first car I've ever owned that wasn't both cheap and entirely practical. I could measure the years since I acquired my driver's license in terms of rusting Vegas, used Toyota station wagons, subcompact Nissans, rattling Subarus, rickety Honda Civics. And I surrendered each of them in turn only after their odometers had crossed one hundred thousand miles and their engines boasted weaker compression than a bicycle pump.

My Nissan Sentra had reached 130,000 miles and was beginning to burn oil, and I knew it was time to make a trade, but as I scanned the used-car lot for Milquetoast subcompacts, a bright red Jeep caught my eye.

I'm convinced that, had the Jeep been green or blue, I wouldn't have given it a second glance. But it was red, fire-engine red, with WRANGLER stenciled in silver letters across the hood.

As for practicality, I realized that four-wheel drive would come in handy when snows blanket the road or long spring and fall rains turn it into a Class VI river. The car salesman made me a respectable offer on the Nissan and accepted my terms on the Jeep, and I drove off the lot two hours later in what would soon be described by a male friend as a "midlife-crisis" car and by a feminist acquaintance as a "Freudian extension of my feelings of sexual inadequacy."

I wholeheartedly embrace the validity of the former and am still mulling over the latter, but the Jeep was also a fun car. I made the purchase on a sunny springlike Saturday in February, and within twenty minutes of arriving home, I had peeled the top off and loaded in both kids, the dog, and Susan, and together we took off for a drive. The wind blew my hair, the sun warmed my face, the girls giggled in the backseat, and for the first time in my life I realized that driving had a purely pleasurable—as well as practical—side.

Mom and Dad arrived for a visit later in the day, and as I returned home from a run, I saw them circling the Jeep and kicking the tires. As I approached, Dad turned to me, smiling.

"You could have bought a Miata, but you're not the sports car type," he said. "This Jeep is definitely you."

Dad and I spent the next morning attending to a few chores around the house before heading to the cabin site. We spent the afternoon taking turns with the chain saw, felling the few remaining trees along the road. Late in the afternoon, we drank beer and sat on a downed pine tree talking. He asked me how things were going with Susan. Though I was disinclined to draw him into my marital nightmare, I leveled with him. It was time he knew the truth.

"It's the pits, Dad," I said. "To be honest, I'm not sure we're going to make it."

"Dave, just be sure you're giving it all you can. Those little girls deserve that much."

"I am, but it's hell being married to someone who doesn't seem to want to be with me. Susan seems to regard me as an irritant, and that feels like shit, all day, every day. I don't know how much more of this I can take."

"Dave, the best family is one that has a mother and a father, and those girls need you." This was Ward Cleaver, the seminal 1950s TV dad, talking, and he was loath to acknowledge divorce as an option, even in the most dire circumstances. If someone in our extended family was going to stoop to divorce, Ward was determined to see that it didn't happen on his watch, to one of his kids.

"I'm not going anywhere, at least at the moment," I said. "Maybe once this cabin is finished, Susan will be able to relax here and ease up on me a little."

"Just think about what's best for your girls."

"Dad, if I believed that my own suffering would somehow ease theirs, I'd sacrifice myself and bleed slowly for the rest of my life," I said, and I could feel tears coming. "Their welfare is much, much more important than mine, but I'm just not sure the best way for me to protect them is by staying. Right now they're seeing two parents who don't treat each other with much love or respect. Susan seems pissed off at me all the time. I may be harming them by staying, and if I'm ever persuaded that that's true, I'll have to leave and hope that I can be a better father away from Susan."

"Dave, you're in a bad place, Mom and I realize that, and if you're in this much pain, maybe it's best to end things."

Ward Cleaver had just uttered words that I didn't think were part of his vocabulary. For the first time, Dad was acknowledging that the fragmentation of a family unit might be justified, even preferable to perpetuating a horribly flawed union.

"This is bound to be damaging you," he said. "Dealing with this day after day has to be taking a toll."

"The worst part is that I can tell it's hardening my heart. The rejection doesn't really hurt anymore; it feels familiar, almost normal. Sometimes I feel like a laboratory animal on an electrified grid. For a while, I struggled to escape; now I've come to accept that the pain is part of my life, and I'm not fighting anymore."

"Maybe there is a time to end things," he repeated.

I looked over at Dad, who looked older and more frail than I had ever seen him, and I recognized how painful this had been for him, too. I was poised to be the first person in my family to get divorced, and I knew Dad well enough to know that he was taking some of the responsibility on himself. I knew that he wondered during his idle moments where his parenting had gone wrong, what lessons he hadn't properly imparted, how his lapses had set me up to fail in my marriage.

At that moment, I recognized on an emotional level, that the casualties of divorce start with two and ripple steadily outward and even forward through generations. Just as my father wrestled with his role in my failure, I would take on myself responsibility for my daughters' future struggles, wondering always what I might have said or done differently, how I might have saved them from torment. And I realized how imperfect I am as a father and how little tolerance for error there truly is in parenting.

Over the previous few months, I had watched my father vacillate between someone whose value system didn't acknowledge the option of divorce and someone who, first and foremost, was a protective father, wanting more than anything to shelter his son from harm. But while the protective father persona had begun to assert itself, the marital purist seemed to remain dominant.

"Dave, don't regard this as my stamp of approval, because I haven't given up hope for you two," he said. "I pray every night that you and Susan will come to your senses."

Though my marriage had begun to appear moribund, there were some real corpses that needed burying, and the cabin's environs seemed the perfect place to stage a funeral.

SIX

Interring the Arctic Fox

Merry-go-rounds and burial grounds are all the same to me: horses on posts and kids and ghosts are spirits we ought to set free.
—Michael Martin Murphy, "Cosmic Cowboy"

D on't know exactly how to ask this, but next time I visit your property, I'd like to bury something," said Jeff Duncan, a graduate student who worked with me at the university. Jeff, a former Californian, wears his long blond hair gathered in a ponytail and sports a tattoo of a white-tailed kite on his shoulder.

"Are you talking about a corpse of some kind?"

"Yeah, it's a dead fox. It's been cluttering up my freezer."

"Okay, Mr. Dahmer, any other body parts you want to tell me about?"

"No. Just the fox. I ate everything else."

Three years earlier, Jeff had been speeding along the highway and watched a gray fox get hit by a car. Recognizing that the animal's pelt might be worth salvaging, he picked up the fox, put it in the back of his car, and drove home.

At the time, his scholastic duties were such that he had little time for skinning and tanning, so he slipped the dead fox into a clear plastic bag and stored it in his freezer. Over time, Jeff became accustomed to the cartoonesque sight of the dead fox, its red tongue lolling out between clenched teeth, wedged on the shelf beside frozen pizzas. His new girlfriend, Laura, a vegetarian and animal-rights activist, had different feelings on the matter.

"Sure, bring the dearly departed over next weekend," I said. "I'll grab a hymnal and a few folding chairs for the graveside service."

In the interim, I scanned our freezer at home and spotted a frozen trout curled into the shape of a *U* and sealed into a plastic bag. Two years earlier, Logan's kindergarten class had made a field trip to the Cross-eyed Cricket trout farm, and though Logan was emotionally okay with hooking the fish, she had lost her appetite for trout after watching the farm owner open the fish and remove its guts. Thus, Logan arrived home with a dead trout in a plastic bag filled with ice, and Susan deposited it in the freezer.

If we were going to be interring dead wildlife, I figured, we might as well make it a mass burial.

We stowed the dead animals, along with a shovel, in the Jeep. Jeff sat in the front seat, the girls climbed in back, and Benton endured the hour-long drive seated on one of the wheel wells, leaning against the Jeep's plastic window. He remained relatively placid until, en route to the property, the frozen creatures began to thaw. Benton, his interest piqued by the irresistible smell of decomposition, began to probe the gear in the back with his nose.

We arrived late in the morning. I drove the Jeep as far back along the road as I could and drew within 150 yards of the cabin. I started the chain saw and trimmed the last few trees down to the dirt.

In the middle of one of the cuts, I stood to stretch my legs and relaxed my grip on the saw, dropping the bar onto my pants at the thigh. Though the chain wasn't moving very fast, it shredded my jeans and came within a half-inch of flaying open my leg. I was relieved that I had been wearing loose-fitting jeans.

Jeff had been clearing brush from the road and happened to be watching. He shook a reproving finger at me. I was just happy that J.J., Mr. Health-and-Safety Man, hadn't witnessed the lapse. If J.J. had been there, he would have regaled me for an hour with a description of death by severed femoral artery.

As I gazed down at my torn jeans, I wondered how many amateur sawyers had wound up in nearby emergency rooms after severing digits or slicing open legs or arms.

Within two hours, I had cut two dozen stumps down to the ground and could drive the Jeep all the way back to the building site. As I walked back up the road to the car, four does bounded across the field toward the cover of the woods.

"Challen, look, it's Bambi," Logan shrieked, pointing toward the fleeing deer.

"Dad, look, it's dinner," Jeff joked.

Once our chores were complete, Jeff, the girls, and I walked back to the bluff to conduct a burial. Jeff and I took turns digging, while Logan and Challen, on hands and knees, studied the dead animals nearby on the ground.

"Look, Logan, he's biting his tongue," Challen said, sticking her tongue out of the side of her mouth and rolling her eyes back in her head.

"He looks like a cartoon animal," said Logan. "Like Wile E. Coyote after he's been run over by a truck."

After we had finished digging, we shook the carcasses out of their plastic shrouds and into the hole and were about to cover them with dirt when Logan suddenly yielded to morbid curiosity.

"*Wait,*" she said, sticking her head down into the hole and reaching out to touch the fox with her finger. I suddenly felt a surge of parental panic.

"Good God, Logan, don't touch that thing!" I shouted, imagining that deadly disease organisms were at that moment leaping onto Logan's finger. "You'll, you'll get cholera or something!"

Jeff bent double laughing and dropped the shovel. "Cholera! Go easy, Dad, she won't get cholera."

"Just the same," I said, "Logan, get out of that hole, and don't touch the dead fox!"

Within a few minutes, Jeff and I had filled in the hole, and the girls grabbed a flat rock to use as a headstone.

"I feel like we ought to say something, some special words," I said.

"Yeah," said Challen. "Like a real funeral."

"Jeff," I said, "you knew the fox better than any of us. After all he did spend three years in your freezer. Anything come to mind?"

"To my friend, the frozen fox," Jeff began. "He will be missed."

"Logan, this is your trout," I said. "How about saying something special about him."

"From the pond at the Cross-eyed Cricket to our property," Logan said. "Good-bye, Mr. U-shaped Trout."

We loaded our gear back into the Jeep and started for home. We stopped at the Jett Bridge river access and found the parking lot filled with trucks and cars, all with boat racks, from as far away as West Virginia, and a half dozen kayakers were climbing into their boats and easing into the current. Early spring rains had brought the river up, and what had been a tranquil pool during the previous summer was now raging whitewater.

Benton decided to go for a swim, and despite his frantic efforts to swim back to shore, he shot downriver like a piece of driftwood in the strong current. I ran along the shore after him and saw him heading toward a roiling stretch of rapids. A kayaker in the water paddled over to him, grabbed him by his collar, and pulled him back to shore.

"He was in trouble," the kayaker said. "He's young, isn't he?"

"Yeah, about a year old," I said.

"He'll have more sense when he gets older," he said.

"Maybe."

Benton may have been the first to underestimate the swift currents coursing around the cabin. But in the days and weeks that followed, I, too, would begin to feel the tug.

SEVEN

Mind Games

The dream is the theater where the dreamer is at once scene, actor, prompter, stage manager, author, audience, and critic.
— Carl Jung,
General Aspects of Dream Psychology

I found it increasingly difficult to focus on my job. My heart and mind remained fixed on the cabin as I approached an intense stretch of work: writing workshops to teach, speeches to make, articles to write, in addition to my day job. I kept telling myself that once I pushed through the work grind, I could rest at the cabin. Besides, I reminded myself, the freelance articles would help finance the construction. In fact, when article assignments came my way, I tended to regard them in terms of what they'd pay for. A $3,000 article would pay for the septic system and well. A $1,200 article would pay for the woodstove and cover the cost of lighting fixtures.

As if the wakeful preoccupation with the cabin weren't bad enough, my cabin anxiety finally punched through to my dream world. In the dream, I was sitting on my porch enjoying the breeze when I heard the rumble of big trucks approaching. As I watched, a caravan of sixteen-wheelers, motorcycles, tractors, and other mechanized vehicles passed directly by the porch en route to an overnight parking area in plain view of our cabin.

As disturbing as the dream was, it was less unsettling than reality at home with Susan. She seemed to be riding me about everything, pointing out my inadequacies, usually without uttering a single word. Susan was never particularly capable of verbally communicating the position of her emotional barometer—something that she confessed bothered her immensely and left her feeling "emotionally inadequate"—though her nonverbal signals were impossible to misinterpret.

A loaf of bread left on the countertop, a swig directly out of the gallon jug of orange juice, an empty glass abandoned in the family room, a tool left on the garage floor, consumption of a peach that was meant for the girls all elicited what I began to refer to as the "sigh borne of long-suffering"—spirited expulsions of air that, combined with the eye-roll, communicated total disdain.

Over time, I began to feel like the proverbial bull in a china shop but, in my case, I was maneuvering through a shop whose cups, plates, and bowls remained invisible until I sent them crashing to the floor. I began to feel like I couldn't move without breaking something.

One evening the four of us gathered around the dinner table, straining to be civil. The girls started talking about pets, and Logan said that she hoped that her hamster, Meagan, would die so she could get another pet.

The comment stung me. Even though it referenced a tiny rodent with a brain the size of a BB, Logan had articulated a sentiment that seemed to be on Susan's mind. You travel to the pet store full of joy at acquiring a new companion, and you bring it home and play with it nonstop for a week or two. The novelty wears off, new things capture your attention, and all you notice about the hamster is that it requires feeding and that its cage stinks.

In my jaundiced mind, there were obvious parallels with marriage: first comes the anticipation, the joy of sharing your life with someone else, and then reality intrudes. Irritating habits and disappointingly human qualities begin to emerge, and they supplant the idealized image you once had of your spouse. Soon, all you see is someone who sips directly out of the gallon jug of juice. The cage starts to stink, and rather than clean it, you continue to neglect it until you can't bear it anymore, and then you haul it into the backyard and try to forget about it.

The girls hoped their hamster would die and clear the way for new furry acquisitions—the notion of disposable pets. And I was beginning to feel like a disposable husband. I had done my bit in providing sperm cells, but my presence was becoming an irritant; I was in the way.

"Girls, getting a pet involves taking responsibility and seeing that the animal is well cared for," I said. The notion that I was talking in parables was, I'm certain, apparent only to me. I was passionate on this point, in part, because Susan had been asking me to find a new home for Benton.

By then, Benton, a thoroughly loving and uncomplicated creature, had become a valuable companion and unwavering ally to me, though to Susan, he was an eighty-pound shedding and slobbering nuisance.

Just then, Logan and Challen started playing footsie under the table and laughing, and I told them that I didn't feel that they were being very respectful. They continued to laugh, so I sent them to their rooms. As I did, I realized I was guilty of overreacting. My response grew in part from the sense that Susan's attitudes about me, about Benton, and about the cabin were beginning to infect the girls, that somehow what I thought didn't matter much anymore.

As I sat at the table, and as my concept of family began to erode, I realized it was time to turn over a spade of new earth. It was time for us to begin building new lives, or at least to build a new structure—and context—for containing them. But a shelf of pink sandstone and a disintegrating roadbed would stand in our way.

EIGHT

Breaking Ground

Look with favor on a bold beginning.
—Virgil, *Georgics*

"Don't look good," said Jerry, the septic system installer, lighting a Winston and adjusting his NASCAR ball cap. "You've got a solid slab of rock down about three feet, and we're probably going to have to do some blasting."

When a Morgan County workman tells you that you've got problems, you'd be well advised to value his assessment. The county's tradesmen are nothing if not resourceful, and there aren't many challenges they can't surmount with a roll of duct tape, a hank of bailing wire, and a generous spritz of elbow grease. Consider, for instance, the fleet of vehicles on the roads dating back to Nixon's first term of office. But clogged carburetors are one thing; rock layers are yet another.

"Nope, don't look good a-tall," Jerry repeated. "We'll likely have to call in the powder men."

"Is blasting expensive?" I asked.

"Can be—'pends on how much powder you have to use. You're probably looking at five hundred to six hundred dollars, maybe more, to drill 'em holes for the charges and blast out that rock."

The only previous experience I'd had with explosives involved bottle rockets and firecrackers, so I was at Jerry's mercy. He could have been contriving the whole thing, but I trusted Joe, and Joe had hired Jerry, so by extension, I trusted Jerry as well. He seemed earnest enough, and five hundred dollars didn't seem exorbitant for blasting a ten-by-ten-foot hole in solid rock. In fact, I suspected that it might provide at least a couple of hundred dollars' worth of entertainment. It isn't every day you get to hear dynamite detonate in your backyard and see shards of pink sandstone hurtling fifty feet into the air.

Jerry had assured me that installation of the septic system would happen quickly, in advance of construction on the cabin, but months of delays—owing in part to difficulties in finding a bonded and insured blasting crew—intervened, and the powder boys wouldn't show up until July, after the cabin had been completed.

Joe Jr. stopped at Walczak's cabin on the way out to ask about the road, which continued to deteriorate, and Walczak repeated what had become a mantra: "You tell me when it's going to stop raining, and I'll tell you when I'll finish the road." In Walczak's defense, I recognized that he had no reason to share our sense of urgency. He had merely sold me a piece of land; he hadn't committed to taking part in our rush to break ground.

In the interim, I assured Joe Jr. that I'd pay to have gravel dumped on the worst sections of the road in an effort to keep it passable while Walczak waited out the rain.

Within two weeks, the footers and floor joists were in, and Joe's crew began to frame the walls. I imagined that at that pace we'd be happily ensconced in the cabin in a month or so, but I tried to take to heart Joe's assessment that roughing in a structure goes quickly; the finished carpentry and trim work take weeks.

"David, don't get to thinkin' that everything's gonna move this quick," Joe cautioned. "On every job I've ever worked, there's always something slows things down, gets you a little *flustrated*."

As usual, Joe was spouting the truth, and the road-cum-mudslide and cuts for the power lines would stall us dead by midsummer.

It became impossible to contain my excitement, and I spent

far too much time at work daydreaming and at home jabbering about the cabin. It was wearing thin with Susan.

"This is your cabin, not mine," she said at one point. "So don't tell me you're building it for us."

I hoped the girls would share my enthusiasm, even if Susan didn't.

NINE

The Girls' First Glimpse

No house should ever be on any hill or on any-thing. It should be of the hill, belonging to it, so hill and house could live together each the happier for the other.
— Frank Lloyd Wright, *An Autobiography*

On the first weekend in April, Benton and I drove to the property through a light spring rain and had to use four-wheel drive to navigate the muddy road back toward the cabin site. As soon as we exited the car, the clouds cleared, and I peered through the trees to see particle-board walls rising up from the foundation. Joe's crew had framed in the doors and window openings and laid the plywood floor.

We would head to Florida the next week for spring break, and I was reluctant to leave. In part, I was concerned that Joe, in my absence, might misinterpret the plans. At Joe's current pace, any miscues might, by week's end, be irreversible, part of the permanent design. But then, Joe didn't get things wrong. In fact, at a couple of key junctures in the building process, he hauled materials all the way back to Sunbright just because they didn't seem to look right.

We had originally decided to use brown vinyl, for instance, instead of cedar fascia boards to edge the eaves as a cost-cutting measure. Joe called me one day midafternoon at work to let me know that he was concerned about the aesthetics.

"David, just don't look good," he said. "Cedar boards will cost you a few dollars more, but that cabin'll look a whole lot nicer. You'll hate yourself if you stick with that vinyl, but I'll go with whatever you decide."

Friends at work had warned me about the unavoidably adversarial relationship that evolves between contractor and client.

"You have to constantly check their work," one woman said. "If you don't, before you know it, they'll start cutting corners, and their lapses will become permanent parts of your house."

Not so with Joe. Through the planning and construction, I got the sense that he was building the cabin for himself first, and us second. The name of his company, Quality Home Builders, seemed to be more an expression of principles than a catchy slogan.

I called Joe once Benton and I had returned home and pointed out that he had neglected to frame in one of the windows in the bedroom. He told me he knew that already but just hadn't gotten to it yet and asked me if I had thought about a color for our fixtures in the bathroom.

"Let's keep it simple," I said, hoping that Joe would offer a suggestion. I had never built a house before; Joe had built dozens and seemed to have sense of what looked best. His tastes always tended toward the simple over the ornate, perfect for a cabin in the woods.

"Can't go wrong with white," he said. "Off-white or beige would look 'spicious in that little house."

"White it is."

"We also need to talk about the road. My trucks are starting to bottom out; the road's just giving way under them. I should a knowed this would happen. It happens ever' time with an old logging road." The edge of *flustration* was back in his voice.

'What do you suggest, Joe?"

"We can bring in some gravel and fill in the worst places while we wait for Walczak to put in the road."

"How much we talking about?"

"I 'spect it'll run about three hundred dollars for the dozer and three hundred dollars for gravel."

"Any other options?"

"Nope. If we can't fix the road, we may have to pull off the job till things dry out."

We arrived back from Florida a week later, and the girls, Benton, and I made a beeline to the cabin site on Sunday morning.

It was a picture-perfect day—temps in the sixties, sunshine, clear skies—and for the first time, the hour-long drive seemed like an exercise in emotional endurance rather than a welcome decompression period. This marked the girls' first glimpse of the evolving structure since we had broken ground a few weeks earlier, and as they spotted the cabin through the trees, they started giggling. From their perspective, the cabin had sprouted up out of the hillside in one piece, as if by magic.

Joe's crew had applied the roof felt and completed the decking for the porch. The workers had also built the floor for the loft.

"Look, Challen, it's our bedroom!" Logan shouted, pointing to the loft. Whatever image had lodged in their mind after my description some weeks earlier from within the taped lines had been supplanted by a structure of two-by-fours and particle board.

I found a ladder in the crawl space under the cabin, and let the girls ascend to their room. The loft had been Joe's brainstorm, and the gently sloping shed roof provided ample headroom for adults and plenty of space for slumber parties.

Logan inched up the ladder tentatively as the floor dropped away eight feet below her. Her descent was a bit more spirited. She had come face-to-face with a cicada killer—a two-inch-long wasp with a bulbous rust-and-black-striped abdomen—up in the loft, and she bounded, shrieking, down the ladder in three quick strides.

Logan had a serious bug issue that we were going to have to work on if she planned to spend time at the cabin. I would see it fully expressed while she and I were on a father-daughter hike to the White Mountains of New Hampshire later in the fall. We were perched on the open summit of Mount Monroe in the shadow of 6,288-foot Mount Washington, when a swarm of tiny, nonbiting insects made her lose her cool. After a few seconds of grunting and waving her arms frantically in the air, she snapped. She tipped her head back, thrust her arms forward, palms up, and cried, *"What was God thinking when He created bugs!?"*

Laughter erupted from the hikers tucked in the mountain's

folds around us, and Logan suddenly gained composure when she realized that she had an audience.

I knew that we'd share our home in the woods with countless wriggling creatures, and I was bracing for some ugly interactions. I had neglected to share with Logan an account of my encounter a few weeks earlier with a Spielbergesque arachnid on the floor in what would become the bathroom. It was after dark, and I was navigating by the beam of a headlamp. At one point, I directed the beam toward the floor, and two red eyes, spaced a half-inch apart, glowed back at me. The spider, its furry legs spanning four inches, and I both froze in place. Eventually, it scurried off and disappeared into the crack between walls and floor. For all I knew, it was still resident in the cabin and was rearing a brood of eight-legged titans somewhere behind the walls. I could only imagine the emotional eruption that would result when Logan pulled open her sleeping bag and found a startled spider nestled in the nylon folds.

The cicada killer forgotten, we sat on the porch decking and ate a picnic lunch while we basked in the sunshine. Disinclined ever to sit still for long, Logan rose and began circling the deck, tap dancing, gripping her sandwich, and sprinkling shredded lettuce and bread crumbs as she went. Challen, in repose, dangled her feet over the edge and peered quietly out into the greening forest. I watched them both, as they celebrated a beautiful spring day in their own ways, and rejoiced in my remarkable good fortune in being their father.

Would they love this place as much as I did? Perhaps not, but I was certain their affection for the piece of ground would build over the coming months and beyond, into their lives as adults and parents. Would they, decades hence, gather on this same tongue-in-groove floor and tell stories about their dad and his dog, Benton, who loved these woods so completely?

TEN

Benton's Mud Hole and the Hammocks from Hell

There are some who can live without wild things,
and some who cannot.
　　　　—Aldo Leopold, *A Sand County Almanac*

Benton jumped out of the Jeep and dashed toward a quagmire ten feet wide and seventy-five yards long that I hoped would eventually become my driveway.

"Benton, don't *even* think about it!" I said, wagging a finger at him.

My relationship with my golden retriever had evolved to the point that I addressed him in complete—often declarative—sentences, not that he had the slightest notion of what I was saying. He paused, looked at the mud hole, and glanced at me with an expression that said, "Alpha Dog, I know you're gonna be pissed off, but you'll get over it."

Before I could stop him, he had immersed himself up to his shoulders in sun-warmed muck. The blissful expression on his face suggested that he was yielding to some perverse archetypal longing. Eons ago, Benton's behavior might have masked his scent for the hunt or provided an escape from the heat; in the waning years of the twentieth century, a mud-caked golden retriever was *caninus non grata.*

Benton eventually emerged from the muck and immediately executed "the shake," which spackled my sunglasses and coated jacket and pants with a fine spray of brown grit.

Before I could chide him, I found myself laughing. He may

have been descended from a noble breed, but he was still just a dog. Besides, I was eager to scope out progress on the cabin, so I forgave him his transgression.

It was the first weekend in May, and the cedar siding was on and the doors and windows were mounted. Construction was proceeding apace, and my only concern was the roadway. The muck was the consistency of brown Jell-O and reached three feet deep. Joe's crew had to resort to hand-carrying supplies—including sixteen-foot cedar boards—back to the site through the trees, and despite his even disposition, Joe had reached the limit of his patience and told me that he might have to pull off the job until Walczak put the road in.

In terms of building the road, we encountered a sort of catch-22. The road at the edge of our property would require several loads of gravel, but the road leading in was too muddy to accommodate the large truck that would haul in the stone. In short, we needed a road if we hoped to bring in gravel, but if we had a passable road, we wouldn't have needed gravel.

Joe devised a reasonable short-term solution. He would bring the gravel truck as far back as possible, dump its load, then shuttle the gravel to our "mud hole," as Walczak had begun calling our road, in the bucket of the Bobcat.

The mud hole grew deeper and wider with each passing week. Because it sat below the level of the woods, it wouldn't drain.

I determined to let Benton's coat dry while I swung in a hammock strung between two hemlocks. As I watched the tall Virginia pines bend gently in the breeze, a scarlet tanager landed in the branches above me, the first I had seen since I was on the Appalachian Trail, and I watched him flit from branch to branch until I dozed.

I awakened a few minutes later when a white-tailed doe walked within ten yards of the hammock. My heart pounded as I watched her move slowly past me, hoping she would linger for a few moments before moving on. Benton, under the influence of yet another primordial yen, was determined to keep that from happening. As soon as he spotted the deer, his predatory instincts took over, and in an instant, he became a wild dog in pursuit of dinner, and there was no stopping him.

My frantic calls didn't even register, and he chased the terrified deer off into the woods. I watched the two of them sprint off toward the bluff, and I wondered if a dog on the hunt or a deer in flight would acknowledge the edge of the bluff and the hundred-foot drop beyond, or would they plunge off into the void pawing the air and following the steps of some age-old dance?

I knew I was powerless to intervene, so I settled back into the hammock and waited. Twenty minutes later, I heard Benton crashing through the trees toward me, and he soon settled onto the ground beside me, panting and looking somewhat bewildered by the undeniable arousal he had just experienced.

As I swung in the hammock, knowing it was time to return to the city, I kept finding reasons to stay, and I let my mind wander where it would. I began to hatch a strategy for gaining permission from my boss to work at the cabin one day per week. Since I had taken on the job of communications director for the research center, my time for creative tasks had dwindled. Perhaps if I had one day per week at the cabin, away from constant interruption of coworkers and phone calls, I could devote more time to the writing tasks I enjoyed so much but had been forced to surrender to subordinates while I assumed a more supervisory role.

Through the afternoon, I alternated between dozing and planning, and soon the sun began to fade. At dusk, I mustered the will to swing my legs over the edge of the hammock and begin the walk back to the Jeep. Benton followed along beside me, and I noticed that the dried mud hung from his coat in matted pleats—like canine dreadlocks.

"Rasta dog, you need a dunk in the creek," I said. On the way back home, we stopped at the Jett Bridge river access.

"Benton, go get clean," I said, and he plunged into the water. I noticed a cloud of muddy water spreading away from his coat as he swam. Yet another advantage to living on the creek, I thought, as Benton climbed up the bank restored to his natural color.

The next weekend, we drove to the cabin after Challen's 8:30 soccer match, and Susan had the chance to inspect the progress.

As soon as we reached the edge of the field, we noticed that the road had been graded and graveled. A short way down the road, we met Donny-the-Backhoe-Driver, brother of Tubby-the-Road-Builder, the proprietor of a vast fleet of trucks.

Donny climbed off his machine and immediately peered at his watch, declaring that he had been on the job since dawn at 6 A.M. It occurred to me as a somewhat abrupt introduction, until I recalled that I was paying for the job by the hour.

He explained that he had probed our mud hole and found it virtually bottomless. Rather than watch load after load of gravel—at $250 per load—vanish into the muck, he had decided to clear a new roadbed that ran parallel to the old one. He had spread two truckloads of large stone before topping it off with a load of lighter rock. I found myself less interested in the process than the finished product, and I was delighted to see a firm roadbed stretching from the field back to the cabin. For the first time, we were able to drive the minivan to our doorstep.

While Donny tended to be taciturn, much more comfortable at the controls of his backhoe than interacting with clients, his beaming, portly brother Tubby was the consummate man of the people. Tubby, clad in a T-shirt and ball cap and wearing an irrepressible grin, arrived a few hours later to inspect the job, and he shared with us stories about our neighbors and various hotly contested political seats. At that point, every fence post in the county boasted a veritable wall of political posters promoting candidates for sheriff, judge, clerk, school board, and various lesser offices.

"We need to get after these ped-o-philes, drunks, and dope smokers," Tubby told us at one point, articulating his political platform. He was contemplating a run for county sheriff. As it turned out, his business dealings would prevent him from tossing his hat into the ring, and over the coming months, I'd frequently pass vehicles that were part of his fleet and hear radio ads on the country station for "Tubby's Construction."

When Susan, the girls, and I stepped inside the cabin, I noted that the deck rails were in, the drywall was up, and the ceiling had been textured. Susan scoped out the emerging structure with apparent detachment. She kept saying, "*you* ought to do this" or "*you* ought to do that" in making suggestions for decoration and embellishments.

"Susan, tell me what *we* should do. This is *our* cabin."

She adopted the more inclusive language and suggested that *we* leave the small, shallow closet space next to the loft ladder open and install bookshelves instead of a door. A solid idea. I had been mulling where to place shelves to contain the nature guides and adventure books I hoped to keep at the cabin.

Then her artistic sensibilities kicked in, and she suggested that we paint the wall rising to the cathedral ceiling bright red or paint a tree sprouting from the floor with branches spreading out across the steep-pitched ceiling. She had been urging me to avoid building a cookie-cutter cabin that was predictable and lacked character. A mural of a spreading oak tree would surely help us escape building a cliché.

"Sure, why not?" I said. "We could even paint a few birds in the branches."

While Susan and I explored the cabin's interior, the girls were off in the woods looking for items for their "nature boxes," which contained butterfly wings, unusual rocks, cocoons, bird feathers, and other artifacts of the natural world that had caught their eye during our many trips to the woods. When Susan and I joined them outside, they showed us a handful of wild turkey plumes they had found behind the cabin. The volume of feathers heaped in one place suggested that a hawk had taken a young gobbler or hen.

I had first encountered turkeys on the property some months earlier, when I visited the site with my parents. I had neglected to wear my glasses, which left me somewhat nearsighted, and as we reached the cabin site, I had peered off into the woods and spotted what appeared to be heads of five men in formation, walking quickly away from me. Thinking that I had spooked a group of trespassing hunters, I ran after them. When I reached within a hundred feet, the human heads sprouted five-foot wings and lifted into the air, navigating with amazing grace and precision through the dense forest.

I returned to my parents with my heart pounding, in part because I had been primed to confront trespassers, in part because of the thrill of an up-close glimpse of the huge American icons.

After the girls had deposited the turkey feathers in their nature boxes, they asked if I would string up their hammocks. I obliged, and while I was at it, put up all four. Logan was the first to attempt the gymnastic feat of climbing onto a hammock featuring a spreader bar at either end. She sat on the edge, flipped her feet up, and as she did, the hammock spun like a revolving door and deposited her on the ground with a thud. She lay facedown in the dirt for a second or two before stirring, and I braved for one of two responses: anger or tears.

I was relieved to see that she had chosen the former.

"This hammock is defective!" she shrieked, kicking the dirt with her sneaker.

"No, it's not defective, Logan," I said. "It just takes a bit of skill to climb into a hammock. Here, watch me."

I eased my butt into the center of the braided cotton bucket, scooted to the precise center, and flipped up my legs. Just as the word "See" issued from my lips, the hammock seemed to come to life and deposited me right where it had dumped Logan.

"Damn!" I said, knowing I was about to be apprehended by the potty-mouth patrol.

"Ah, ah, ah!" Challen said. "Daddy used a bad word!"

It wasn't the first time I had been busted. My very proper mother-in-law, Sis, was visiting one weekend when Logan picked a particularly public opportunity to reveal my occasional verbal transgressions. As we walked from our car to the soccer field to watch Challen's game, we headed down a narrow gravel path, merging with dozens of other parents and kids. At the precise moment we reached the center of the crowd, Logan, who was five at the time, decided to make an announcement to Sis and everyone else within earshot.

"My daddy says *shit* sometimes," she said. There was no apparent context; the thought had entered Logan's mind, God knows why, and she had spontaneously given it voice.

Sis laughed. I cringed. And the other parents quickly hustled their kids away before Logan shared other forbidden utterances that had issued from her father's mouth.

As I dusted off my trousers and approached the hammock for a second try, I was relieved that the expletive I had used was a relatively minor one. No telling when or under what circumstances Logan might report on the incident.

Over the next ten minutes, Susan, the girls, and I endured the necessary learning curve for hammock use, and eventually all four of us swung gently under the hemlocks. As it turned out, most of our guests would face the same challenge over the following months. And the hammock mounted to a metal stand on the screened porch became the closest thing we had to an initiation rite for first-time visitors, who, with rare exception, were summarily dispatched facedown onto the tongue-in-groove floor.

For a while, I was conscientious in warning people about the hazard, but eventually I decided to let them learn for themselves. I secretly delighted in seeing the comedic sketch repeat itself over and over. I even worked up a brief scripted response for victims who looked somewhat bewildered as they dusted themselves off.

"You have been duly initiated," I began saying. "You are now a member in good standing of the hammock club."

Early in the afternoon, my good friend Sam, an engineer for a manufacturing company based in Vonore, Tennessee, arrived to check out the progress. As an engineer, and as a home-improvement specialist who owned—and maintained—an apartment building, Sam lent a fresh perspective to various construction challenges. He advised me on the proper height for ceiling fans in the great room and on the screened-in porch to maximize air flow and instructed me on how to thin polyurethane to create a glasslike finish on the pine floors. Though I had purchased several gallons of paint—a light sage color—for the interior walls, Sam advised me that the drywallers hadn't applied the final coat of "mud" to the seams and that I should wait. He joined us on the deck for a picnic lunch and shared with us some of the frustrations he had been experiencing on the singles scene.

He had been involved with a woman who vacillated between being red hot and tepid, between being fully committed to their relationship and thoroughly disinterested. Sam, like most of my close friends, was up to speed on my marital problems, and he knew that Susan was tentative about the cabin—and about her marriage to me—but for some reason, he was inclined to idealize my life. Sam was thirty-seven, and perhaps the bezel of his biological clock was indicating that he'd entered the red zone. For whatever reason, from his perspective, I seemed to have it all.

After seeing Susan doze off in one of the hammocks, he said, "She's gonna love this place, Dave. She'd be crazy not to. In fact, everybody's gonna love this place. If you weren't so ugly, I'd envy you all that you have."

Sam went on to tell me that, from his perspective, I had the perfect life. A beautiful wife, great kids, a decent job, a cabin in the woods, a portable career that would allow me to work anywhere I could find a wall outlet to plug in a laptop computer.

"If you weren't married and if you had hooters, I'd be all over you," he said.

"Sam, my life is far from perfect," I said. "In fact, it's a mess right now. Susan may be acting the part of a contented partner, but she's miserable in this relationship. She's looking for an escape hatch, and this cabin may provide her with one."

"What do you mean?"

"Once this cabin is built, she knows I'll have a place to go, and it might pave the way for her to press me to move out. And to be honest with you, once this place is finished, it's going to exert some powerful gravity on me. It already pains me to leave this place, and it's not even nearly finished."

"Nah, Dave, Susan's gonna love this place as much as you do. It just might take some time."

"Sam, I'm hoping you're right."

Sam and I began toying with the idea of returning to the city to gather a few supplies and then camping out at the cabin that night. It was a beautiful spring evening, and I had yet to spend an entire night there. The girls overheard us talking.

"Dad, can Challen and I sleep here tonight with you and Sam?" Logan asked. "We don't want to leave."

ELEVEN

The Buddy System

Each friend represents a world in us, a world possibly not born until they arrive.
       —Anaïs Nin, The Diary of Anaïs Nin

Through my life, I have been blessed with many friends who have shared in my moments of discovery, counseled me through nights of fear and doubt, accompanied me on footloose romps through wilderness, and reminded me often of what Whitman termed the "manly love of comrades."

Though I didn't realize it at the time, as the rough structure of the cabin evolved into a finished dwelling, two acquaintances, J.J. Rochelle and Sam Jones, were about to evolve into dear friends who would play a central role in shepherding me through the painful journey that lay ahead.

I picked up Sam at a bagel shop in West Knoxville and drove to Oak Ridge, where we met J.J. in his Land Cruiser. He had Jasper, his long-legged hound, and Maggie, a black Labrador, in the back, and we caravanned to the property. It was J.J.'s first visit, and I had hoped that the land and structure would elicit some affirming comments from a guy given to understatement.

I had met J.J. a decade earlier when I taught writing at a community college in Oak Ridge. He was one of a steady stream of students who scheduled consultations with me in the Writing Center.

After I left the college in 1992, I didn't see J.J. until he arrived at my office door at the university in 1996. He had become an environmental health and safety officer for a manufacturer and was attending a conference on the floor above me.

Before I even turned to see who had knocked on my door, I heard, "Watcha doing, guy?" and I knew immediately it was J.J.

J.J. stands six-foot-one and has the lean body of a former competitive swimmer. He sports a close-trimmed beard and wears his thinning blond hair cropped short. J.J.'s most notable characteristic, though, is a devilish grin that lights up his whole face when he smiles, which is almost always. It's as if he's perpetually contemplating some act that's both mildly improper and totally pleasurable. By all rights, his likeness should be featured in the dictionary beside the entry for *shit-eating grin*.

We went for a run at lunch the next day and started getting together for occasional beers after work at a gathering that became known as Wednesday Night Prayer Meeting. The meeting, an assembly of friends—writers, musicians, environmental activists, businessmen, and various others—convened at the Great Southern Brewing Company in Knoxville every Wednesday night, and it had been an inviolate tradition for most of us since 1994.

We had chosen the name for the gathering based on the notion that just about everyone else in the Bible Belt was praying on Wednesday nights, so why shouldn't we? Never mind the fact that the gathering was purely secular; our only sacrament involved equal measures of beer and conversation. Sam and J.J. were both regulars at our Wednesday night revivals, and over our nights together at the bar, we moved beyond the palavering that links acquaintances and entered the realm of close friends.

J.J., like Sam, had, for a time, been operating under the faulty belief that I somehow had my life together and boasted the perfect family. By the time J.J. arrived at the cabin for his first visit, I had made him privy to the truth, and he was beginning to grasp the important role the cabin would play in my life, regardless of where my relationship with Susan led. Over the coming months, J.J. would be a regular fixture on my deck on Friday nights, in part to see that I was doing okay, in part to relax and unwind from stressful workweeks that involved endeavoring to see that his company didn't poison the environment or its workers as a consequence of its preoccupation with the bottom line.

J.J. emerged from the cruiser sporting a ball cap and Ray-Bans and, assuming the persona of Mr. Health-and-Safety-Man, mentioned that I had maintained just the right speed through the twisting turns to the cabin. He launched his sentence with "you know," which I had come to regard as the signal that I was about to receive a lecture from the manual on safe conduct.

Through the workweek, J.J.'s fax machine spit out reams of health and safety advisories, and as a result he displayed a troubling affinity for pointing out the hazards hidden behind what the rest of us regarded as innocent activities and pursuits.

"You know, those Jeeps have a short wheel base, and they'll roll on you if you take a turn too fast," he said.

"Thanks, Dad."

"You know, it would be a shame for those two little girls to grow up without a father."

"It would be a shame for their father to grow up without his Jeep."

J.J. started to circle the cabin on his first site inspection. Meanwhile, Sam acted as a somewhat effusive tour guide.

"Isn't this incredible? I don't know about you, but you can color me green with envy. It's perfect, don't you think?"

J.J. reserved comment until he had scoped out the structure from every angle and had explored the interior. He cracked open a beer and sat on the bumper of his vehicle.

"Nice," he said. "Real nice."

For J.J., such muted praise was as good as it got, and I could tell he was quietly mulling over my current circumstances and considering that, when it came to a place to live, a guy could do a lot worse.

"You guys want to shoot?" he said after a pause.

I knew that J.J. didn't travel far from home without his pistol. He knew that I had been wrestling with the decision to buy a defensive weapon for the cabin and had promised to let me shoot it in hopes that I'd grow more comfortable around guns.

We propped a piece of drywall against a tree, and J.J. dumped a pile of bullets from a fresh box onto the hood of the cruiser. As he loaded the clip, he ran through *all* the particulars of handgun safety and provided Sam and me with earplugs and safety glasses. The lesson, which even explored the toxic effects of lead bullets in soil, took twenty minutes.

J.J. fired first, blasting an expanding hole in the center of the target. The explosion of gunpowder echoed through the trees, and I flinched with each report. I realized that a fraction of a second of poor judgment could end a life—either someone else's or one's own. No take-backs. No do-overs.

As J.J. reloaded the clip, we could hear another target shooter discharging his weapon on the other side of the bluff.

"Hear that?" J.J. said. "Happens all the time. You shoot, then you hear them shoot. They're saying 'I'm here, and I have guns; don't mess with me.' It's a good idea that your neighbors are hearing us shoot. They'll think you're armed, too."

It struck me as the rough equivalent to Benton pissing on trees around the cabin, marking his turf. Dogs piss, men shoot.

The smell of gunpowder hovered around us as J.J. finished filling a clip for Sam, who, as an engineer, had an abiding appreciation for well-designed machines, even lethal ones. Sam gripped the gun and emptied the clip into the drywall. Next it was my turn.

The gun felt heavy in my shaking hands, and I fired through the clip quickly. Though I tried to sight down the barrel, the bullets missed the target and kicked up dirt.

"I can't do this," I said. "I can't own one of these things."

"You just need to shoot more often," J.J. countered. "You'll get used to it."

"No, I don't have the psychological makeup to be a gun owner. I'm a ballistic wimp."

It occurred to me that, more than anything else, I was worried about my own absentmindedness or impulsiveness and the potential consequences.

J.J. packed up the gun and picked up the casings from the spent rounds, and we loaded a daypack for a trip down to the creek. When we arrived at the swimming hole, J.J and I stripped down and plunged in. Sam lingered on the bank in his boxer shorts with his hands gripping the waistband.

"Get naked!" J.J. called.

"Sam, why get your shorts wet?" I shouted. "There's nobody out here but us."

In all my trips down to the creek, I had only once seen other people. Four kayakers had paddled by in the early spring when the water was up. Now, late in the boating season, spring rains had ended and the water level had dropped. Any floaters who attempted to run the stretch from Barnett Bridge to Jett Bridge would have to drag their boats through long stretches of dry streambed, essentially "hiking with their boats," as one of the National Park Service rangers put it. Besides, skinny-dipping is one of life's undervalued pleasures, and there are scant few places left where people can swim in the buff without risk of offending prudish onlookers or being arrested for indecent exposure.

Sam was unpersuaded and remained clothed and waded into the creek in his shorts. J.J., clad only in ball cap and sunglasses and that devilish grin, swam toward the Rock of Contemplation gripping three Heinekens in his left hand.

We gathered on top of the Rock, which had been splattered with the droppings of great northern herons, and it gave the appearance that some sloppy painters had dripped whitewash while painting clouds into the sky.

We swam through the afternoon, and eventually Sam shed his shorts and the three of us sat naked on the rock, our skin drying in the warm sun.

Joe called the next day to tell me that the Sheetrockers were finished and the walls were ready for paint, a job I had agreed to take on as a way to cut costs. Joe asked that we complete the painting before he laid the floor because any drips or spills would fall harmlessly on plywood rather than pine planks. Though the work of Sheetrockers and electricians and plumbers and carpenters represented skills well beyond my grasp, I had worked on and off through my college years as a painter, and rolling on latex, particularly in circumstances that didn't require me to be overly neat and tidy, provided a way of contributing to the cabin's evolution without risk of damaging anything.

Jeff Duncan, who had buried his fox in our backyard, offered his assistance. We rolled on the sage-colored paint through the day, pausing frequently to duck outside and savor the warm sunshine. When we had applied the final coat, we stowed a couple of beers in a daypack and headed down to the creek. Within ten minutes, we were naked and perched on the Rock, dripping from a quick swim.

We returned to the cabin just before dark and settled onto the deck railing, sipping our second beers. Whenever the breeze died down, we discerned a subtle, almost imperceptible tapping sound and eventually realized we were listening to pine needles fall. Such was the depth of the silence at dusk.

Eventually, the daylight waned then vanished, and we sat in the darkness, and I remember mentioning to Jeff that the place felt much more secure in the darkness than I had imagined. Suddenly all my concerns about safety and shotguns seemed unfounded. The cabin felt like a safe haven, and the forest encircled us like a powerful buffer between the cabin and anyone with evil intentions.

We were both expected back in Knoxville that evening, and we made halfhearted efforts to rise and walk to the Jeep for the trip home, but it became apparent that neither of us really wanted to leave.

"Let's sit just ten more minutes," Jeff said at one point.

"Yeah, ten more minutes," I repeated.

When the time had elapsed, neither of us stirred.

"Ten more minutes, then we *really* need to go," Jeff said.

"Yeah, okay."

And so it went, until our dalliances had consumed more than an hour. It had been a long time since I had sat without hearing so much as the drone of a distant car engine.

"This is *yours*?" Jim asked, incredulous, as he exited his rental car. "You built *this*?"

"Yeah, it's much easier than you think. You scope out land, go to the bank, borrow money, and then these guys with hammers show up. In a couple of months you have a cabin."

Jim McKairnes and I met at a Knoxville publishing company, where we both worked in the mid-'80s. He had traveled from Los Angeles for a weekend visit. Though we had no power or water, the cabin was nearly finished.

In the early years of our friendship, Jim and I had often discussed the feeling that, though we were well past the age of majority, we still didn't quite feel like adults.

"You mean I could do this?"

"Sure, as a TV executive, you could add a pool house, tennis courts, and servants quarters."

"You have no idea how this place feels to me right now."

Jim, a vice president at CBS responsible for prime-time scheduling, had spent the previous week in New York enduring back-to-back meetings with network bigwigs and high-strung producers jockeying for the most desirable time slots.

"Sounds awful," I said.

"You can't even imagine," he said, climbing into a hammock.

"Careful!"

It was too late.

"Sweet Jesus!" he shouted, as the hammock flipped him face-down in the dirt. "Is this a trick?"

"More of an initiation rite, really," I said. "You passed."

Jim dozed in the hammock as I fixed a pasta dinner on a camp stove, and I could almost feel the stress draining from him as he snored softly, a paperback book laying open on his chest.

It had been a day of firsts. Jim and I had hiked down to the creek, and he confessed that it was the first time he had swum in a mountain stream. It seems that his options in that regard were somewhat limited through his boyhood in Philadelphia. He had also begun for the first time to grasp that he, too, could have a cabin in the woods.

After dinner, I walked him down the road to the last ten-acre parcel yet for sale. We walked along the taped boundary lines, gazed up at mature white pines, and located a cabin site.

"I think I'm going to buy this," he said, "unless there's a good reason not to."

"Only that it might make life back in L.A. seem even more torturous."

"Yeah, but knowing this place was waiting for me would make it all more bearable."

"We'd love to have you in the neighborhood."

After dark, we rolled out sleeping bags on the deck and soon dozed, but sometime after midnight, I was awakened by Jim's snoring.

I grabbed my sleeping bag and walked out to recline in the hammock. I should have anticipated what would result from the combined effects of drowsiness, slippery nylon fabric, and a hammock with spreader bars.

I lay awake, watching the sun come up and studying the cabin structure, which was nearly complete. As I did, it occurred to me that we had neglected one vital task.

TWELVE

Benton's Run

*I think I could turn and live with animals, they are
so placid and self-contained, I stand and look at
them long and long. They do not sweat and whine
about their condition, they do not lie awake in the
dark and weep for their sins. . . .*
—Walt Whitman, *Leaves of Grass*

Few of the discussions we labored over in finding property
or designing our cabin caused as much angst as fixing on
a name for the retreat. My suggestions—primarily cryptic Latin
phrases and lofty mythological allusions—were quickly dissed by
the girls, who pointed out, sensibly, that no one would want to
visit a place he couldn't pronounce.

Susan suggested that we postpone naming the cabin until we
had spent some time there and its real character began to emerge,
and I regarded her thoughtfulness on this issue as encouraging.
She could have said, "Name it whatever you want; it's of no consequence to me."

I seconded the motion. The next weekend, as we rounded the
last bend in the gravel road and the cabin came into view, Benton awakened from his nap and pressed his nose to the car window. His wagging tail became a blur of energy. Once I opened
the door, he dived past me and trotted off into the woods—his
woods, as far as he was concerned—and it occurred to me that,
among the four of us, Benton would have to make the fewest ad-
justments in settling into our wilderness home.

"Hey, Dad," Challen said, watching the dog gambol through
the trees. "Why don't we just call this place 'Benton's Run'?"

Before I could even construct the Latin translation in my

head, Susan and Logan voiced their approval. Susan may have disdained having a shedding eighty-pound dog in her house in the city, but she found his charismatic demeanor and slobbery kisses as endearing as the rest of us once we reached the woods.

" 'Benton's Run' it is," I said.

Though Benton had been fully integrated into our family unit, he was a relative newcomer and a replacement for our fourteen-year-old black Labrador who had died a year earlier in the spring.

The death of Morpheus, a.k.a. "The Black Dog" (she had a charming wackiness about her), marked an important rite of passage for the girls. Previously, they had dealt with death only in the abstract, notwithstanding the demise of numerous goldfish and a tiny frog that had leaped out of the aquarium and expired on the countertop while we were away on vacation. The remains of Mr. Frog, as the girls called him, appeared as little more than an elongated raisin when we arrived home, and it inspired more curiosity than grief.

But Morpheus, who had been an integral part of the family since before either of them was born, was different. As I dug the grave and then laid a dear old friend in the ground, the girls were inconsolable, and their tears necessitated laying aside my own grief to help them work through the experience. But what began as trauma soon evolved into a meaningful ritual for the three of us, and I regretted that Susan was out that evening and couldn't take part.

Though I didn't share it with the girls, I realized I might face a potentially gruesome logistical challenge in interring Morpheus. She had died sometime early in the day in the recesses of her Dogloo, a plastic igloo-shaped doghouse that was supposed to shelter her from heat in the summer and keep her warm in winter.

I've no doubt the Dogloo fulfilled it promise of protection from the elements, but it was also equipped with a remarkably tiny door. Morpheus had been dead long enough that rigor mortis had set in, and she lay on her side with stiff legs fully extended. As I dragged the Dogloo down the hillside to the grave site, I was hoping that I wouldn't have to resort to undignified prying to dislodge Morph from her plastic tomb. Accommodating to the very end, Morpheus tumbled out of the Dogloo's door and dropped on her side in the hole.

Before I covered the body, the girls ran inside and returned with markers and paper and a few of Morpheus's favorite toys, including her tennis ball and Frisbee. They penned sweet heartfelt odes to the dog and laid them in the grave with the toys. As I shoveled in the dirt and the sun went down, I struggled to explain the unexplainable: the cycle of death and life, endings and beginnings. Then, leaning on the shovel, I suggested that we stage a wake and share our favorite funny stories involving Morph.

I recalled the day I had released her from the leash as we walked along the high-school classroom building behind my parents' house on a Saturday morning. She ran ahead, and as soon as she reached the end of the building, she broke into a sprint. I had forgotten all about the Little League baseball games played every Saturday morning on the field just around the corner.

I ran after Morpheus, and as I turned the corner at the end of the building, the batter tagged a line drive past the third baseman. As the ball rolled out toward the left fielder, Morpheus, the consummate retriever, dashed to intercept it. Gripping the ball in her mouth, she insouciantly pranced around the ball field, maneuvering past the enraged players, who were now throwing their gloves at her. Both stands were full of spectators, who were now on their feet. Half of them booing, half of them laughing and cheering on the black dog.

I sprinted out onto the field, ran past the pitcher, and just as Morpheus dashed past me, I dived on top of her and wrenched the ball from her mouth. I handed the slobbery orb to the pitcher, and the stands erupted into cheers as I led Morpheus away on the leash. When I had finished the story, the girls asked me to tell the one about Morpheus, the Easter Bunny Bandit, and I was happy to oblige.

When Susan and I lived in the farmhouse, Morph was an outdoor dog with thirty acres of turf to explore, but over time, her curiosity led her beyond the fences and into the upscale neighborhoods that surrounded the farm. Susan and I used to joke that when we left for work in the morning, Morph would punch the time clock and begin her daily rounds. Often, we'd arrive home in the evening to find various offerings—things she had pilfered from our neighbors' yards—waiting for us on the front porch. She had a thing for Frisbees, which she brought home by the dozens. On one occasion she somehow managed to retrieve a bedpan.

On our first Easter Sunday in the farmhouse, I arose at eight in the morning, poured myself a cup of coffee, and opened the front door. I was momentarily stunned by the sight that awaited me. The porch boasted a heap of no fewer than ten stuffed rabbits and ducks and a few woven baskets. Morph sat in the middle of the sidewalk, wagging her tail and wearing an expression that said: "Quite a take for one night, eh?"

Parents had lovingly deposited the baskets and stuffed animals on their front porches when they had gone to bed the night before so their children would awaken to treats from the Easter Bunny. Apparently Morpheus had found the booty too tempting to resist, and through the night she had run at least ten sorties into the surrounding neighborhoods. The story became known as "How Morpheus Stole Easter."

The girls smiled at a story they had heard many times before and shared their own stories about life with Morpheus. Then, after a period of silence, Logan, crying, looked upward. "Dad, I see Morpheus's face in the clouds," she said, pointing toward the dimming sky.

And as Challen and I looked up, right on cue, a flock of Canada geese flew overhead in perfect formation—an elegant footnote to my feeble efforts to explain the process of life springing from death.

As we walked back to the house, I braced for a long night of crying. Instead, I got my first indication that childhood mourning is self-limiting. The girls stopped and peered at me through tear-soaked eyes. Suddenly, their faces brightened.

"Does this mean we can get a new puppy?" they asked in unison.

"I don't know," I said, reflecting on at least three months of soiled carpets and chair legs gouged by canine milk teeth. "We'll have to think about it for a while."

As it turned out, the mulling process lasted exactly one month. The tiny ball of fluff I brought home from the breeder quickly metamorphosed into an eighty-pound free spirit named Benton. And Susan, by virtue of her in-home office, became the one who chased him from the flower beds, dabbed at muddy paw prints on the carpet, and cleaned up his occasional indoor indiscretions through the day.

Benton didn't seem to have much use for the suburbs, but at the cabin, he settled into the wild ancestral landscape as naturally as a barred owl might roost in a Virginia pine or as perfectly as snowflakes might fall on the arched boughs of a hemlock. And when he slithered into a mud hole or presented us with a dead thing he found in the woods, he reminded us that clean shoes and careworn faces are artifacts of the city.

III

SUMMER

THIRTEEN

Imperfect Union

Medicine, to produce health, has to examine disease; and music, to create harmony, must investigate discord.

—Plutarch, *Lives*

D. B., you're a *very* lucky man," said Kit Howes, exiting his SUV and uncapping a well-deserved beer after a twelve-hour trip up from south Florida.

"Oh, it's *soooo* peaceful here," said his wife, Candy, letting go a long sigh before gripping me in a hug.

I had met the Howeses years earlier on the Appalachian Trail, and they had arrived to spend the weekend at the cabin.

"D. B., I hope you built a guest bedroom," Kit joked. " 'Cause you're gonna have a hell of a time getting rid of us."

He and Candy were unaware of where things stood with Susan, who was home in West Knoxville with the girls. The Howeses had been dear friends to both Susan and me for more than a decade, had stayed at our house many times on their way north to visit Kit's family in Maine, and had spent dozens of days and nights with us on the trail. I was reluctant to expose two dear friends to the awkward revelation that two people they loved and had always regarded as a matched set were drifting apart.

Kit and I spent Saturday evening on the deck of the cabin, drinking bourbon and smoking a couple of Cuban cigars he had smuggled up from Florida. We were serenaded by whippoorwills, bobwhites, and hoot owls, and just after we had climbed into our sleeping bags on the deck, a pack of coyotes down on the bluff started baying.

Theirs is the eeriest of night sounds, and the intermingling of voices—some piercing, sustained yowls, others staccato yips—echoed through the trees for several minutes. Through such calls, I knew, coyotes alert their packmates to their positions. The baying also helps reunite them after they've scattered during a hunt.

Kit grabbed Benton's collar to prevent him from charging off to hang with the wild dogs. Though Benton would have arrived wagging his tail, eager to join in the fun, the coyotes would likely have surrounded and killed him because he had intruded on their turf or because, at eighty pounds, he represented an irresistible food source. Coyotes are masterful predators who work in well choreographed packs capable of bringing down prey as large as calves and deer, often through ambush. Our neighbors, Bob and Willow Reed, had found fresh coyote scat containing deer fur near their property.

When Kit and Candy returned to our house in the city Sunday evening, they saw Susan and me together, and though we were civil toward one another, the iciness was palpable.

"What's going on?" Kit asked me after dinner, as we sat on the back porch. "You guys don't seem too cozy."

"The Brill family as you know it may undergo some modifications."

"No. Not you guys."

" 'Fraid so. Susan is just so unhappy. I think she's outgrown me."

"Is there anything we can do to help?"

"Too late for intervention. It's all up to Susan and me, and we haven't quite figured things out yet."

"Keep us posted, and let me know if our visit is getting in the way."

"Not at all. It's great having you guys stay with us; you're like part of our family. And when you're around, I can't help but reflect on happier times, times spent in the woods. Susan used to love being out on the trail as much as I did. But now she says she won't be upset if she never spends another night sleeping on the ground. And that's just one example of how our interests have diverged. Lately, there aren't many things we enjoy doing together, except maybe doting on our kids."

"How are they doing?"

"Who knows? They're not talking much, except to plead with Susan and me to stop arguing. And we pretty much have, but we've also stopped communicating. We may as well be living in separate universes."

"Damn."

"Yeah, damn."

"David, I'm gettin' real *flustrated* with that road," Joe said when I called early the next week. "I'm 'fraid we're gonna have to pull off the job for a while."

Until the power had been switched on, he explained, he couldn't finish the floors, so we were left to languish, waiting for Walczak to fell the final few trees and clear the way for the power lines. Walczak and the crew from Galloway Construction, which we'd hired to do the cutting on our property to accommodate the power lines, had been responsive to Plateau Electric's requests for more cuts, even though they never seemed to be enough.

Walczak's business partner, Norman, who was overseeing the cutting, joked that even if we clear-cut the property, Plateau Electric would continue to call to tell us "you still lack a few trees."

Despite the delays, the property continued to provide peace and contentment, and it was evolving into a home. There was always an abiding sense of peace that surrounded the cabin, and watching the hemlock branches rise and fall in the breeze always soothed me. But over the previous few weeks, I'd felt unsettled there and suffered pangs of guilt over not being more deeply anchored at home.

There was an element of fear, too, in feeling myself becoming increasingly disconnected from Susan. Not that Susan very often protested my leaving. It occurred to me sometimes, that, if I left, we would be creating the family dynamic she grew up with: Mom and the kids, with Dad off somewhere else.

But a connected family seemed to be what she longed for most. While on vacation in Florida five years earlier, the four of us had spent the entire day together, beginning with breakfast and ending with a stop at an ice-cream stand and a walk along the beach at dusk.

As the four of us walked on the sand, dodging the waves and looking to the rest of the vacationing world like a poster family, Susan turned to me.

"This is one of the happiest days of my life," she said. "We've been together all day. We never did this when I was a kid. We never had a day like this."

At that moment, it occurred to me that we had come from different worlds. Each summer through my childhood, my parents would pile my brother and me into the car and head to the beach for two or three weeks. We were together every day, and beach walks and ice-cream cones were part of every trip.

I had no emotional context for understanding the feeling of loss or separation Susan must have felt. I also realized that she really didn't have a context for a functioning family of Mom, Dad, and the kids. As a pilot, her dad was gone most of the time.

To some extent, Logan seemed to be taking her emotional cue from Susan. She seemed little bothered by my frequent trips to the cabin through the spring and summer. Not so with Challen. Often, as I prepared to leave, she was never more than a step away from me, shadowing me from room to room and finally to the car, chattering all the while as I gathered my things.

There was an urgency to her chatter, and I realized that it had much less to do with sharing information with me than it did with seeking affirmation. It occurred to me that she wanted me to validate her, to reassure her that I wasn't leaving for good, or that if her mom and I split and I did leave, that I wouldn't forget her.

Though I'd told both the girls often that they were, and always would be, the very center of my universe, they were savvy enough to understand that the problems between Susan and me ran deep.

One day, Challen asked me, "Dad, are you and Mom going to get divorced?"

In the past, I might have dismissed that notion quickly: "No way, your mom and I will go on forever. . . ."

But this time, I had to be honest. "Challen, I really hope not," I said, after lifting her onto the countertop in the kitchen and looking into her pained face. "But Mom and I aren't getting along very well."

"I know," she said. "I hate it when you fight, but I don't want you to get divorced."

Just then, Logan entered the kitchen and told us that one of her friend's parents had separated, as if to suggest that the breakup of Susan's and my marriage wasn't totally out of the question.

"Her dad moved out for a while," Logan said. "And she's sad."

"Yeah, I bet she is," I said. "But maybe they'll work things through. Sometimes people just need to be apart for a while."

To that point, Susan and I had managed to protect our children from most emotional shocks, but we'd also failed to display much in the way of tenderness toward each other.

In those rare moments when Susan and I did display affection toward one another, Challen and Logan rushed toward us and physically pulled us together, wrapping us in their own embrace.

Though I still derived comfort from holding my whole family close, it was clear that some deep fissures had formed between Susan and me. And I was about to learn a key lesson on the difficulties—and risks—involved in breaking apart things that time had fused together.

FOURTEEN

The Powder Men

*Come one, come all! This rock shall fly from its
firm base as soon as I.*
   —Sir Walter Scott, "The Lady of the Lake"

Burly tattooed men with big shoulders and tanned backs settled into the hole Jerry-the-Septic-System-Installer had scraped clear with his backhoe fifteen yards behind the cabin. Working in shifts, they stood three feet down on a floor of pink sandstone and leaned into their pneumatic impact drill, a thundering contraption that bounced and spun, biting in tiny increments deeper into the rock. A dense cloud of rock dust hovered about the workers and clung to their sweat-soaked torsos. Indigo tattoos disappeared beneath a coating of grit.

After three hours of boring, sixteen holes organized in a grid reached four feet into the rock, each awaiting a stick-and-a-half of dynamite. Once the charges were set, colored wires issued from the holes and snaked across the ground to the battery-powered detonator, and Jerry covered the blast site with dirt to prevent rocks from raining down on the cabin roof. He dropped the blade of his backhoe on top of the dirt mound as an additional measure of safety.

As we stood ready to shatter a huge slab of rock into tiny pieces, I couldn't escape the parallel with my marriage. The slab, as long as it remained intact, represented a barrier to the building process and suggested that *de*struction was sometimes a necessary prelude to *con*struction.

Likewise, my family in its present form represented an obdurate slab, a chunk of stone that was blocking our paths to happiness. Powder charges would be necessary to alter the stone slab into a form that could be moved and manipulated and ultimately cleared away. Would similarly drastic measures be necessary to free the four of us to move on?

The foreman, a squat bearded man wearing a railroad conductor's hat, twisted the wires around the contacts on the detonator and cautioned us that the pyrotechnics were about to begin. I witnessed the procedure with mixed emotions. On the one hand, I knew the ensuing explosions would clear a pit in the rock and open the way for flush toilets—a requirement, as far as Susan and the girls were concerned. And the excitement of hearing the detonation of explosives held a certain appeal for a guy who, as a kid, kept a ready supply of bottle rockets hidden away from Mom and Dad in a dresser drawer.

But on the other hand, the blasting should have occurred at the earliest stages of the construction process. Delays kept nudging it back. Because the blasting had been postponed, it now posed a significant threat to my 210-foot-deep well and the cabin's cinder-block foundation. Collapsed wells and dismantled foundations were the occasional result of tardy blasting, though Jerry, as per my request, had hired a crew that was bonded and insured. At least if I had to endure the torture of rebuilding the cabin, I wouldn't have to bankroll it.

The foreman pulled up the plunger on the detonator, shouted "Fire in the hole!" and all onlookers braced and squinted and cowered behind the edge of the cabin, awaiting the blast. The plunger went down, and as it did, we tensed and waited.

Nothing.

About that time, the Laurel and Hardy skit began.

The foreman studied the detonation unit with a quizzical expression. After a time, he determined the problem.

"Damned battery's dead," he said, pulling open the battery chamber. "You got a spare nine-volt?"

Fact was, I had nothing but the shell of a cabin complete with empty drawers.

"No, 'fraid I don't," I said.

"Hey, let's try the other detonator," called the assistant, opening the truck door and rummaging around on the cluttered floor for the spare.

"Here, try this one," he said, handing the device to the foreman.

Wires were transferred to the new device. Again, we cowered, squinting, around the side of the cabin.

"Fire in the hole!"

Nothing.

"Son of a bitch," the foreman said. "That battery's dead, too."

A long pause.

"Hey, we got another battery!" said the assistant. "There's one in the truck!"

I was picturing a tiny spare nine-volt, but the assistant had something else in mind. In a few minutes, he walked to the foreman carrying the car battery from under the hood of the truck.

"Yup, that otter work," said the foreman. "Fire in the hole!"

The warning had lost its urgency. I halfheartedly ducked behind the side of the cabin and peered at the hole with open eyes.

The foreman touched bare wires to the terminals on the car battery.

A series of fifteen *kabooms* followed, spaced a few seconds apart. The ground shook with each explosion.

A geyser of dirt clods arched high in the air and thudded to the ground and peppered the metal roof, and I found myself facedown on the ground with my arms covering my head, a knee-jerk reaction caused, no doubt, by having watched too many World War II movies as a kid. In the movies, invariably, some sergeant shouts "Hit the dirt!" as an incoming round whistles toward his position, and his men dutifully drop facedown.

"Wow!" I said. "That was amazing!"

My professional associates offered a more learned assessment.

"That sounded like a good blast, a real good blast," said the foreman. "Broke that big rock up into little pieces. But we got a problem. One charge didn't blow."

Down somewhere in the hole, a stick-and-a-half of dynamite was live and perhaps at that moment smoldering toward detonation.

We waited. And waited some more. Finally, when we determined we were dealing with a dud, Jerry climbed up on his backhoe and scraped away the dirt, revealing the rock. The foreman checked the wires, and as he leaned directly over the open hole, he asked the assistant to touch the wires to the terminal.

Nothing.

After another go at the wiring, the charge blew, and again, the powder men assured me that the blast had been a success.

"What you got in there now is gravel-sized rock," said the foreman. I found his confidence inspiring.

But then Jerry went to work with his backhoe, shoveling out the dirt and dropping the blade down onto the rock. He hooked the blade edge on a rough section of stone, and as he tried to lift it out, the backhoe groaned and its back end came off the ground. Instead of gravel, he encountered a ten-by-ten-foot stone slab, a pink sarcophagus lid worthy of an Egyptian king.

"Damn," said the foreman.

"What's wrong?" I asked.

"Done hit a soft layer about three feet down while we was drilling," he said. "Charges blew out that seam and just lifted up that top slab a few inches before setting it back down. We're pretty much right back where we started."

I cringed as I realized I had just paid four hundred dollars for the pleasure of watching a huge slab of salmon-colored rock leap up three inches and drop back securely in place.

"I'm running short on time today," he said. "But we'll be back on Monday to do the job right. We just have to pack more powder in those holes."

I was picturing a cabin foundation that looked like something from war-torn Bosnia.

Within fifteen minutes, the dust had settled and the powder crew had lit out for home. Jerry and I stood at the edge of the hole and peered at the pink rock. As the evening settled around us, he shared with me bits from his life spent in Morgan County.

Like many Morgan county residents, Jerry had pieced together a number of related trades into an occupation. He installed new septic systems and cleaned out old ones. He built roads and hauled dirt and gravel. He trenched out indentations for swimming pools. He and his backhoe traveled the county from corner to corner moving earth.

Jerry had persevered through a welter of complications in setting in my septic system, and in the end, he made good on his word. The crew returned the following Monday, drilled more holes, increased the power of the dynamite charges, and pulverized King Tut's sarcophagus lid. Jerry dropped the septic tank in place by the end of the week. When I traveled to the cabin the next weekend, I noted the scar marking the tank and the one hundred feet of field line snaking down through the forest. The cabin still stood soundly on its foundation.

By the first week in July, we had a fully functioning septic system, but the ceiling fans were still motionless. According to Plateau Electric Cooperative, we still "lacked more trees."

As we reached the end of the construction process, I found myself increasingly absorbed in the details. Joe's crew of carpenters, plumbers, and electricians were nearly finished, and I wanted to be present when the power first surged through the lines and the cabin became a living creature.

I tried to escape to the property with Logan on a Sunday afternoon, but Susan had other ideas. I had the car packed and was ready to pull out when she approached the car and reminded me of all the things that needed doing around the house.

"Dave, you can't run out on your responsibilities here just to be at the cabin," she said. "We need your help, and the cabin can survive a couple of weeks without your presence."

Though both Logan and I were disappointed, Susan was right. I *was* escaping to the cabin, and each time I did, my contribution to our suburban household dwindled further. I was becoming an absentee father and husband.

As I reflected on where I wanted to be, how I wanted to live, and what I wanted to be doing, I realized how far afield I had wandered from the distant point of land I had scoped out for myself before I met Susan.

Twenty years ago, I imagined a life of adventure. I pictured myself and my family surrounded by mountains and streams. I imagined a life spent with one leg in wilderness and one in civilization. I pictured my children shouldering packs and smiling as we crested ridges and ambled along mountain streams. Now I realize I was envisioning life at the cabin.

Over the intervening years, I had lost my bearings; I was bumbling along an errant path, like a man lost, rather than moving free and fast and pushing hard and true toward a clear destination. I was straying dangerously close to the life that Thoreau cautioned against, one of "quiet desperation," and was certain that I didn't want to die with my song still in me.

The next weekend I spent my first night alone at the cabin, though still without power. It was a beautiful, clear evening, and as I lay on a cot on the porch, I was serenaded by cicadas and crickets. Their music seemed to be guided by an unseen conductor. Individual chirps were joined by other voices, and soon the woods throbbed and oscillated to a crescendo before dropping away to measures of silence. Owls filled the rests with their own doleful calls. Then the movement started all over again. Benton lay by my side and lifted his head as new voices joined the nocturnal chorus. Moonlight fell on maple and oak leaves and hemlock boughs, motionless in dank summer air, giving a subtle iridescence to the surrounding woods. The nearest artificial light was almost a mile away.

As I drifted off to sleep in the still air of a Tennessee summer night, my mind hovered over the snowy slopes of a 14,400-foot mountain thousands of miles, and months, away.

FIFTEEN

Testing Middle-Aged Legs

These are times in which a genius would wish to live. It is not in the still calm of life, or in the repose of a pacific station, that great challenges are formed. . . .
—Abigail Adams, letter to John Quincy Adams

Okay, don't bullshit me, do you think I can actually make it to the top of Mount Rainier?" my brother, Steve, asked between gulps of air. A mixture of rain and sweat cascaded down his face and plastered his shirt to his chest as he eased himself down onto a boulder at six thousand feet in the Smokies.

After forty-some years of learning how to motivate my brother, the overachiever, I was inclined to push a few familiar buttons and play on his fears: "The only way a fatass like you is getting to the top is via an airlift. . . ." But instead, I opted to offer him a food pellet rather than an electric shock.

"Sure, probably, but don't cut back on training, and don't settle back onto your sofa," I said.

Steve and I were bound for the summit of Mount Rainier in August, in part to thumb our noses at middle age, in part to bond. For me, the trip was also a chance to surmount a real mountain in hopes that gaining a literal summit would help me scale the more metaphoric peaks I faced back home. Mountaintops are renowned for offering perspective and insight.

Several years earlier, in an article for a national magazine, I had profiled a man named Dick Bass, who became the first man to climb the highest peak on each of the seven continents and the oldest man to reach the summit of Mount Everest. The trip up

Everest, his third attempt, almost killed him. Bass told me that, prior to his ascent of Everest, he suffered anguish and self-doubt while his personal life hit the skids and his business enterprises threatened to avalanche. His first wife divorced him and rising interest rates nudged his business toward bankruptcy.

"For about two years after I went through my divorce, I felt gutted," he said. "I rolled and tossed in agony at night. I'd get up in the morning, and I'd be aching all over with fatigue and be mentally just shot."

The perspective from 29,028 feet shifted his thinking. On his return, he said, the problems that beset him at sea level had dwindled into molehills.

"That mountain gave me peace, not a superficial sense of well-being, but the peace that comes from going through the fiery furnace, by God, hanging in there, and coming out alive," he told me. "And as long as there's life, there's hope."

I wanted some of the peace and hope and whatever else Bass discovered on the snowy slopes of Everest, though I wasn't inclined to climb quite as high as he had to achieve it. Though the Rainier summit was a mere 14,400 feet, I knew it would test me and force me to delve deep into my mental, physical, and emotional resources. I regarded Mount Rainier as a test: If I could kick steps all the way to its summit, exposing myself to the risks of avalanche and rock fall, surely I could muster the courage to surmount the problems with my marriage.

Though Steve's designs on the summit were less philosophical than mine, they were no less passionate. Over the months since Christmas, he had transformed himself from a middle-aged couch potato into a well-conditioned athlete, and during our shakedown hike in the Smokies, he had burned up the trail ten yards in front of me all the way to the summit.

The physical challenge of the ascent didn't provide for much conversation, but when we reached the top, we sat in the rain and I opened up my life to him. Over the years, Steve and I had remained close, but we shared few interests and pursued vastly different lifestyles. His was a world of big houses and nice cars and impeccably dressed friends with high incomes and respectable jobs. While he was going upscale, I was "going country."

But despite our differences, we had always shared a solid connection, and though our contact with each other was sporadic, it was always brotherly and loving. Over the previous few months, we had spoken every couple of weeks to compare training regimens or discuss equipment needs.

To that point, he knew that Susan and I were struggling, but he didn't know the particulars about our relationship, our waning affection for each other, my growing sense of hopelessness regarding my marriage, my thoughts of giving up.

"I had no idea," he said, when I had finished. "There was a time when I would have asked you if you were giving enough, if you were trying hard enough. But maybe it's too late for those questions. It sounds like things are pretty bad."

As we descended the trail back to the car and dropped down out of the clouds, we talked in a way we hadn't for years, maybe ever. We talked about, among other things, Dad's prostate cancer, which had been diagnosed and treated six years earlier. We knew enough to realize that the radiation treatment had delayed the spread of the disease, not cured it, and that eventually we'd get a call from Dad saying that the cancer had come back. As it turns out, the call was a scant five months away.

"Brother, even though Dad seems pretty healthy right now, every time he and Mom call, I wonder if it's *the* call," I said. "It's got to be worrying the hell out of him."

"Yeah, maybe so," Steve said. "But we'd never know. He'd endure a lot just to keep us from worrying."

"That's a damn shame. He's helped us through a lifetime of scrapes and struggles, and it's only right that he should lean on us a little from time to time."

"Dad has always kept his suffering private. Maybe that's the way he wants it."

I recall only once seeing Dad fully give way to grief. One night when I was sixteen, I heard the phone ring at 3 A.M. It was my Grandpa Brill, crying inconsolably, telling Dad that Grandma was dead. She had died of a heart attack during the night.

My Grandma Brill was the closest my family has ever come to

producing a saint. She had been a doting mother to Dad and an indulgent grandmother to Steve and me. She was never too tired or too sick or too busy to drop whatever she was doing to lead us off into the woods up the street from her house or fire up her sewing machine to make us Superman capes or rise early to fix us our favorite breakfasts. The "candy drawer" in her kitchen was always stocked with our favorite treats. And whenever she'd put us to bed, she'd snuggle between the two of us on the double bed and tell us stories about her brothers and sisters, aunts and uncles, parents and grandparents—long-dead characters who were a part of us, sculptors of our DNA, key pieces of the family's collective lore.

In many ways, I trace my pilgrimages into nature, both on the Appalachian Trail and through the cabin, to my first exposure to the natural world as a child at the hand of Grandma. On our frequent trips "up on the hill," as she called the woods near her house, she showed Steve and me how to nip the ends off honeysuckle blossoms and taste the sweet drop of nectar that clings to the tip, a practice I've since passed on to my girls. She showed us how to join small green twigs into crosses and squares by peeling back some of the bark and using it as twine.

The night she died, Dad entered my room, told me Grandma was dead, gripped me in a hug, and cried for less than a minute before moving on to Steve's room. That was the only time I saw Dad let go long enough to display his grief, though his eyes frequently well with tears when he sits in his chair in his family room and gazes out on a room full of grandchildren or when he reads something I've written that touches him or when some sappy Hallmark commercial plays on the TV in the days before Christmas.

The bounty of goodness in Grandma had been passed along to Dad, our own Ward Cleaver, but with infinitely more depth than the quintessential TV dad.

"Dad's one of the greatest guys I know," Steve said. "And there aren't many men who can say that about their fathers."

"A real-life hero."

"When he checks out, the world's gonna seem a lot more empty."

"Yeah, a lot more."

SIXTEEN

Bound for the Top

I think that maybe we do not climb a mountain because it is there. We climb it because we are here.
                                        —Jon Carroll

For anyone who's spent time scaling mountains, summits thrust up from the plain of metaphor just as surely as they rise from the surrounding topography. They represent a struggle—against gravity or adversity—that leads to emergence onto high ground and the promise of a new perspective.

Perhaps the most compelling reason to grunt your way to a mountaintop involves the grand vistas from open summits that have a way of shrinking woes that, down at sea level, can loom so large that they block your line of sight. To see past them, you have to rise above them, and that involves ascending. Ascension: the metaphor of the optimist, the glass of water that's half full, rather than half empty.

I decided to ascend Mount Rainier not so much "because it's there," as George Mallory might have quipped, but because I was "here," stumbling lost in the lowlands of a dying marriage without a clear exit route. I sought an experience that would challenge me physically, emotionally, and mentally and force me to tap resources I hadn't called on for a very, very long time. I wasn't convinced they were still there, but I'd hoped I'd find them waiting in reserve.

At just under 14,500 feet, Rainier ranks as the tallest peak in Washington State. The dramatic vertical gain from sea level to the summit is perhaps best appreciated from the perspective of Seattle. On a clear day, it dominates the landscape, hovering like a massive, inverted Sno-Cone on the southeastern horizon. The mountain is cloaked in snow from about six thousand feet up; above ten thousand feet, the snow assumes the form of glacial ice and comprises the largest system of glaciers in the contiguous United States.

As we approached the mountain from Seattle, Steve sat beside me at the wheel of the rental car. Two years my junior, Steve had spent the better part of the past decade going soft, creating a deepening indentation in his couch.

After watching the *Everest* film at an IMAX theater the previous Christmas—and after turning forty a month before—Steve had experienced the first rumblings of his "Oh-my-God-I'm-halfway-to-being-dead" crisis and decided he wanted to be a mountaineer, notwithstanding the fact that he had never really climbed a mountain. Though Everest was out of the question, he set his sights on Rainier—challenging but accessible to neophytes. Well-conditioned neophytes, that is.

Not one to face danger alone, he had extended an invitation to me. If Steve was halfway to being dead, I figured, I had a two-year jump on him, so I accepted his invitation.

Though over the ensuing eight months Steve had dropped twenty pounds and spent evenings and weekends running stadium steps while shouldering a full backpack, it wasn't until the volcanic profile of Mount Rainier filled the windshield of the car that he seemed to fully grasp the magnitude of what we were about to do.

The hulking volcano had an equally sobering effect on me. Though I had climbed the mountain once before some nine years earlier, I had never glimpsed its full profile. On my 1989 climb, in fact, from the time I had left Seattle to the last few steps to the summit, the mountain remained shrouded in clouds.

Though I regard myself as passably articulate, at the moment I first saw the mountain, I found myself stunned. The only words I could form were "Holy shit!"

Steve reacted the way he often does in moments of extreme excitement and reached for his cellular phone to call his wife, Linda.

"Oh, my God, Linda, it's huge! Massive!" Steve said, cradling the cell phone between shoulder and ear and framing the mountain with his point-and-shoot camera—all while driving.

If you were to ask me at which point on the journey I faced the greatest objective danger, I would have to say it was while we were speeding down the interstate at seventy miles an hour while my brother, in the grips of a heady emotional moment, engaged in a little high-tech multitasking.

To this day, Linda describes that cell-phone conversation as one of the most alarming of her life: Two guys with graduate degrees babbling in expletive-laced Bubba-speak.

Fortunately, our journey to the summit of Rainier would start slowly, as the culmination of a three-day process that began the day after our arrival at the mountain's base at a place aptly dubbed Paradise, elevation five thousand feet. We arose at dawn and participated in a snow-and-ice-climbing class offered by Rainier Mountaineering Inc., the guide service that would lead our expedition.

The course instructs neophyte climbers like Steve and me in basic mountaineering technique. We learned how to walk in crampons (the steel spikes that we strapped to the bottoms of our plastic mountaineering boots), how to use our ice axes for self-arrest should we take a spill during the climb, and how to maneuver on a rope team.

The instructors impart technique while evaluating the strength and skill of their clients. Weak or poorly coordinated aspirants who pose a danger to themselves and others on their rope teams get benched. Rainier ranks as the longest endurance climb in the lower forty-eight states and involves a cumulative gain and loss of nearly twenty thousand vertical feet in two days. (On my previous climb of Rainier, twelve of the twenty-four climbers who started for the summit bailed out along the route.)

The following day, at the guide hut, Steve and I met the other twenty-two climbers on our team. At ten A.M. we started the five-hour climb to Camp Muir, a compound of three huts perched at the edge of the Cowlitz Glacier at ten thousand feet. Muir would serve as base camp where we would be assigned to one of six rope teams, be issued hard-shell climbing helmets, and spend a sleepless night listening to the hut door squeak open every ten minutes as one overhydrated mountaineer after another exited to off-load excess fluids.

I can't speak for the others, but I know I was relieved when, at midnight, Jason, the expedition leader, entered the hut, and his headlamp pierced the darkness.

"Everybody up!" he said. "It's perfect weather for climbing a mountain."

The weather forecast was for cold and windy conditions, but clear. As long as winds near the summit didn't surpass thirty miles per hour, the expedition was a go.

At 1:30 A.M. Jason checked the security of our sit-harnesses and used locking carabiners to clip us on to the 165-foot ropes. As he did, I felt groggy and very cold and was beginning to question my sanity. Then I scanned the scene around me. Meteors streaked across a star-studded sky, the cloud layer below us at seven thousand feet shimmered under a crescent moon, and the volcanic peaks of Mount Saint Helens, Mount Adams, and Mount Baker probed above the clouds and glowed in the ambient light. Ahead of us sprawled the white expanse of the Cowlitz Glacier, sliced randomly by gaping crevasses.

At that moment, I felt abundantly blessed and remarkably puny in a land of mammoth mountains. Definitely worth the price of admission, I thought, as Jason clipped himself into the rope, gave it a firm tug, and we started up the mountain.

We switched on our headlamps and started kicking the twelve-points of our crampons into the ice, angling upward across the Cowlitz and up and over Cathedral Rocks. Beyond, we slabbed across the Ingraham Glacier and approached a vertical pitch of rock and ice named Disappointment Cleaver.

The Cleaver, composed primarily of loose rock—or scree—marks the most dangerous stretch along the route. A shelf of rock and ice the size of a ten-story apartment building looms above, and the loose scree of the Cleaver itself is prone to rock slides. In 1981, a massive ice-fall buried an entire climbing party under thousands of tons of debris, killing eleven people. It provided little comfort to learn that their bodies are still up there—human flotsam in the glacier's slow, fluid course down the mountain. The previous spring, the Cleaver claimed another victim after an avalanche swept a climbing team down the slope.

Danger aside, Disappointment Cleaver also represents the longest and steepest pitch on the route, where we gained more than 2,500 feet. Once at the top, the combined effects of altitude, fatigue, and cold began to take their toll.

Mercifully, the guides allowed us a short "maintenance break" at the top of the Cleaver to take in fluids and munch energy bars. Even though I was clad in two layers of polypropylene, two layers of fleece, a Gore-Tex jacket, and a down parka, the ten-degree temperature and stiff wind cut right through to my sweat-soaked skin. I had been miserable at this point on the climb the first time around, and I was miserable now. As I shook uncontrollably, I glanced around me to find Steve among the huddled figures crouching in the starlight. I saw him, his head bowed, his back to the wind, about ten feet away.

"You doin' okay, brother?" I asked.

The feeble tone of his response told me he was struggling. Having been there before, I realized that at that moment the romantic notion of scaling a big cold mountain, which had filled his days before the climb, was giving way to the reality of actually *being* on a big cold mountain. He was poised to make the transition from armchair mountaineer to bona fide adventurer—if he didn't decide to quit.

"Hang on," I said. "This is as bad as it gets."

Within ten minutes, we were back in formation, crunching steps in the ice, and soon I felt the first rays of the sun on my back. We switched off our headlamps and peeled off clothing layers for the final push to the summit.

At 8:30 A.M., seven hours after departing Muir, we reached the southeastern rim of Rainier's volcanic summit. I turned to watch Steve take the final few steps. Below us, beyond the snow-cloaked shoulders of Rainier, the peaks of the Cascades and Olympic mountains of the Pacific Northwest trailed off to the horizon.

I had learned from my first climb of Rainier that, at the southeast rim, we were in fact a hundred feet below and a quarter-mile short of the true summit on the northwest rim. Most of the rest of the climbing party seemed content enough to end their uphill trek at the lower summit.

Call me a "peak-bagger," but I wasn't about to trudge all that way and be denied the opportunity to stand on the highest point of ground. I clipped out of the rope and started down through the snow-filled crater. I peered back and noticed that Steve was following me. Within twenty minutes, we stood on the true summit and encountered a Norwegian team that had ascended to the summit via the more technical route on the mountain's northern side.

I welcomed Steve with a hug. His voice quavered, and tears spilled from under his glacier glasses. For the moment, I reflected on what this peak must have meant to him.

I had spent a portion of the past twenty years moving among mountains. All had taught me key lessons on mental and physical toughness; many had rewarded me with beautiful vistas. Steve's climb from his sofa to the summit of Mount Rainier had begun a scant eight months earlier. This was his first real peak.

"Steve," I said. "You are a steely-eyed mountain man."

"Brother," he said, "for the first time, I understand why you love this so much."

It was bonding at its finest, and I can envision the two of us relating the details of the climb to our grandchildren, though I suspect that the degree of danger and difficulty will grow with each telling.

I had made a commitment to myself that if and when I reached the summit, I would, to the extent the weather and my energy level allowed, savor the moment and reflect on where my life was going. I had believed that the crisp mountain air and unobstructed panorama might impart clarity and perspective, and I couldn't imagine a more suitable place for making resolutions.

If, through raw determination, I reasoned, I could scale this ice-clad behemoth, I could also surmount some of the emotional mountains looming in my path back in Tennessee. More daunting summits, to be sure, but attainable nonetheless.

With the spikes of my crampons firmly set in ice, and with the world spreading away below me, I resolved to muster the courage to split from Susan if it became obvious that our paths to fulfillment were necessarily divergent. I resolved to accept circumstances that I could not change and to become more proactive in shaping those I could. I resolved to be happy—not merely content—even if that meant dramatically altering the course of my life.

I lingered on the summit for ten or fifteen minutes, snapping pictures and marveling at the view and didn't notice that Steve had begun his descent. I spied him down the slope one hundred feet away, seated on the snow, his head grasped between his gloved hands. I assumed he was still fighting to get a handle on his emotions.

Then I remembered that he had schlepped his cell phone to the summit. He was calling Linda.

I sat down beside him and listened to him relate the events of the morning to his wife, trying to find words to describe what we had experienced. I've realized after years of trying that it just can't be done. Even if no one else could fully appreciate our day on the mountain, for Steve and me, the images would endure through a lifetime.

That struck me as more than sufficient as we started the long, ten-thousand-foot descent back to Paradise, then back to sea level, and, for me, back to Tennessee, where a new home waited.

SEVENTEEN

Moving In

Houston, Tranquillity Base here. The Eagle has landed.
—Neil Armstrong, on reaching the moon

I got a call from Joe: The power was on, and the floors had been sanded, stained, and sealed. It was time to move in. I went on a shopping spree behind the wheel of a diesel-powered U-Haul truck and picked up a refrigerator, futon, and fold-out couch. I loaded in a few cast-off lamps, tables, and chairs from the garage, and started the slow slog to the cabin at a maximum speed of forty-five.

I wanted to have the cabin fully appointed with furnishings for Susan's and the girls' next visit. Paul, an Oak Ridge friend, and his dog, Quasar, arrived just before sundown, and after Paul and I had unloaded the furnishings and plugged in appliances, we cooked steaks on a makeshift grill and sat on the deck and ate by lamplight.

My first few hours at the cabin were awkward and tentative. The structure was now a living beast—animated and fully powered up. But I found myself treating it as if it were still the primitive outpost I had visited through months of construction. When I needed to empty my bladder, I instinctively walked outside. As I entered the cabin after dinner, I noted the glowing red eye on the stove I'd neglected to turn off after boiling corn on the cob.

The new stereo sounded eerie and loud and incongruent, and I couldn't quite decide on the "right" music. I shifted from rock to reggae, from ethereal New Age to classical, and finally settled on country. Despite his aching twang, even Jerry Jeff Walker sounded overproduced.

Then I experienced a yen to remain indoors in the space I had spent thousands of dollars creating. I wanted to hole up, to be catered to by appliances and cooled by fan blades, to lie on the couch with a book, to serve myself a drink chilled by ice cubes from my new refrigerator.

I paced, I tinkered, I opened faucets, and water drawn from 210 feet down splashed into my sinks, but I wasn't sure if I should drink it; absent the tang of chlorine, it tasted *strange*. The ceiling fan in the great room, left on the highest setting, created a cyclone of loose paper and dust. Then there were the lights.

Though I had waited for months for the power to be turned on, later, as I sat by a campfire and saw light shining out into the woods through the cabin's windows—woods that had never, through eons, been exposed to artificial light—I felt a pang of sadness. The structure had lost its innocence, and to some extent, its purity. It was now powered up and tethered to the outside world through the sagging wires that began miles away at the power station, snaked along rural roads, trailed across the field, and cut through the woods to my meter box. There was a bit of loss in the gain. I was reminded of camping out in the backyard as a kid and feeling that the experience was compromised by proximity to a house and all the comforts it contained.

After a few uncomfortable minutes by the fire, I went inside and turned off the lights. I switched off the stereo, too. Even though I knew it was inevitable that incandescent bulbs and digitalized melodies would eventually flood the forest, I wanted to enjoy one final evening of primitive unadorned existence in the woods.

That night, I slept fitfully on the new futon, feeling the disorientation of a traveler who, in the groggy grips of somnolence, awakens, wondering for a moment where he is. But a glance through the window revealed stars, familiar, though dimmed, through glass.

Over the coming months, I would often turn and gaze at those stars, steadfast and placid, as my marriage and my future became more uncertain.

EIGHTEEN

Land of the Toads

The forms of things unknown, the poet's pen turns them to shapes, and gives to airy nothing a local habitation and a name.
—William Shakespeare, *A Midsummer-Night's Dream*

What are we going to do about our relationship?" Susan asked abruptly as I walked out the front door en route to a conference in Chattanooga. Though I didn't realize it at the moment, the perspective I'd gained on the summit of Mount Rainier was about to be tested.

"I think we should return to counseling," I said.

She had a different plan. "Why don't you move out so we can give separation a try?"

As always, I countered by saying I hadn't done anything wrong and shouldn't have to leave my home and family.

She got angry. "You don't expect *me* to move out, do you?" she asked.

After some thought, I said, "You're the one who wants to separate; maybe you should be the one to move out."

"Like you could handle this house and these kids?"

"I might not be as capable as you, but we'd manage."

"You're not willing to take any responsibility for our problems," she said. "You're dumping this all on me."

She was right. While her approach was proactive, even if that meant nudging me out the door, mine tended toward withdrawal and inaction. Though I had refused to leave, I had also stopped giving, stopped caring, stopped nurturing. It was a quiet protest, and perhaps even more hurtful than Susan's expressed anger.

Our house had come to reflect my inaction. Backyard gardens begun on hopeful spring days had been left to languish, edged halfway round then neglected and given over to weeds. Two years earlier, we had started painting our bedroom walls a light blue. We had covered two of the four walls, then we just gave up, like suburban Miss Havishams from Dickens's *Great Expectations*. In the story, the aging recluse's existence had ended at the hour, decades earlier, when she was jilted, and she lived the remainder of her life clad in her graying, threadbare wedding dress, one shoe on, one shoe off, the clock hands stopped at the precise moment her fiancé had forsaken her.

For two years, the two-toned walls in the bedroom seemed to represent our impasse: two adjoining ivory walls standing defiantly against two tinted powder blue.

Susan trailed me down the hall and slammed the door behind me as I left the house, and over the two-hour drive to Chattanooga, I felt my spirit ebb toward hopelessness. I was being rejected, and I could no longer pretend that, if I waited patiently, Susan's attitude about me would change.

While in Chattanooga, I visited the IMAX theater and watched the film *Everest* for the second time. Seeing the mountaineers stand triumphant on the summit reminded me of my day atop Mount Rainier and the resolutions I had made.

The next weekend, we departed for the cabin early Saturday morning. It would be Susan's and the girls' first visit to the now-completed home, though after Susan's invitation that I move out, my hopes were fading that she would ever regard the cabin as her home as well as mine. Not so with Logan and Challen, who erupted into shrieks of delight at seeing the ceiling fans turn. They twisted the on-off knob on a table lamp, regarding the glowing bulb as a thing of magic. Then they skittered up the ladder to their loft room and opened and shut the windows and flicked the light switch.

They eventually found their way outside and into the woods behind the cabin, scurrying about as diminutive, frenetic Magellans destined to discover new worlds. In about fifteen minutes, they had sighted land, an imaginary world they dubbed *Loco-Cheria,* the Land of the Toads, owing to the profusion of toads bounding through the forest.

"Look, Dad, we have an elevator," said Challen, standing on a splintered maple that had been toppled by the backhoe. The split trunk angled up from its roots, and she bounced on it as if it were a diving board.

"And over here," said Logan, sitting on a large chunk of pink rock, "is the potty. And notice the special handle for disabled people!"

Challen then demonstrated the log bridge that led from one stone—or toad house—to another.

A while later, Logan entered the cabin, rummaged through her overnight bag, and withdrew what would become the first exotic pest species to be introduced to the woods around Benton's Run, a green Giga Pet.

Any parent who has been assigned the care and feeding of these devices while his children are away at a slumber party or at school surely shares my disdain for these virtual pets. The small plastic medallion houses a tiny, electronic soul that requires constant attention. A series of buttons provides food, medicine, rest, exercise, and water.

That evening, after dinner, the four of us sat in overstuffed chairs and on couches, reading. Susan was halfway through *The Day Diana Died,* and Logan and Challen flipped the pages of *Nancy Drew* mysteries. I read Thoreau's *Walden* for the third time, and it spoke to me in a whole new way in the austere surrounding of the cabin.

Saturday night may have been serene, but Sunday morning began far too early, with Logan in a complete panic.

"*Aaaahhhhhh!!! My Giga Pet has a comma!*" she screamed, clad in pajamas and clutching the green plastic medallion. "*It's dead, dead, dead!*"

"Logan, that's *coma;* a comma is a punctuation mark," Challen instructed, sleepily, from the fold-out bed.

Logan's Giga Pet had expired sometime during the previous night when no one had responded to its electronic beeps. What with the coyotes baying and the crickets chirping, no one had heard the critter's plaintive cries for food or medical intervention. Logan, who didn't realize that the reset button on the device would result in complete resurrection, was inconsolable.

Challen rubbed her eyes, yawned, climbed from bed, and grabbed the device from Logan. "Logan, get a grip!" she said, pushing the reset button. "Giga Pets never die."

"Pity," I muttered.

"It's alive!" Logan shouted, and planted a big kiss on the clear plastic screen. "Mmmm."

After breakfast, the girls returned to Loco-Cheria, rode the elevator, sat on the handicap-accessible potty, and started collecting toads in an old coffee tin.

Susan started cleaning, something she does when she gets edgy. I had hoped to make the cabin a labor-free zone for her, where I would cook, clean, and tend to chores while she relaxed.

When I suggested that she hand me the broom and go outside and enjoy the woods, she balked.

"No, I feel like cleaning right now," she said, and I could sense her tension.

"Okay," I said. "If that's what you want."

The girls entered the cabin, Logan clutching a large brown toad. She approached Susan just as Susan emptied the dustpan into a large plastic bag filled with garbage. At that moment, the toad made an ill-timed leap for freedom and tumbled down through eggshells, remnants from the previous night's pasta, and a bunch of stale crackers and disappeared in the folds of the garbage bag.

Logan looked on, stunned, then shouted, *"Aaaahhhhh! You've killed Mr. Toad!"*

"Logan, Mr. Toad is fine," Susan said, rummaging around in the moist trash. "Here," she said, handing the wriggling amphibian to Logan, its legs splayed between her fingers. A piece of eggshell clung to its head like a tiny helmet. "Take him outside!"

Logan greeted the resurrected toad much as she had her restored Giga Pet. She planted a kiss on its slimy mug. *"Mmm!"*

"That's disgusting," said Challen.

"My prince!" said Logan, kissing the toad again.

*   *   *

The next morning, I awoke at 5 A.M. and couldn't get back to sleep. I couldn't shake the disappointment I felt over Susan's indifference toward the cabin. Her silence and apparent misery with me were becoming unbearable, and I felt as though I were reaching my limits, that I was approaching the point a divorced friend advised me of a couple of years earlier.

"When it's time to leave, you'll know it," he said over dinner one night. After the first time Susan had asked me to move out, I had called him. "It will be more painful to stay than to go."

At that point, I still harbored hope that we could make things work, but when I asked Joel, based on his experience, what the likely outcome would be for Susan and me, he offered a sobering assessment.

"I can't say for sure," he said, "but I suspect you'll split."

As I lay awake in bed, an hour before the sun came up, I reflected on Susan's amazing toughness. I felt a tenderness toward her welling in me as I gazed on her beautiful face, relaxed and placid in sleep. And I wished we could both find a peace that would attend our wakeful hours each day and usher us gently into a world of happy dreams.

IV

FALL

NINETEEN

Goings and Comings

If I can just get off of this L.A. freeway without
getting killed or caught, I'll be down the road in a
cloud of smoke to some land that I ain't bought.
— Guy Clark, "L.A. Freeway"

As I approached the cabin, I noticed that *all* the lights had been switched on and was sure that Jim, in town for a weekend visit, had been nervously peering out the window, down toward the bluff, watchful for the errant zombies I had convinced him combed the woods looking for hapless victims. He emerged from the cabin, clearly relieved to see me.

"This cabin is perfect!" he said, gripping me in a hug. "Perfect!"

Jim hadn't seen the cabin since his visit in May, when the structure was more of a shell than a finished dwelling.

For some reason, he held a tape measure in his hand.

"Well, how did you measure up?" I said, gesturing toward the tape.

"I was measuring your *cabin*."

"*Sure* you were. Why?"

"Just wanted to see how my cabin's dimensions relate to yours."

"Cabin envy?"

"Sort of."

Once inside, I stowed a few groceries while Jim maniacally calculated dimensions of rooms, walls, couches, tables, sinks, tubs, lamps, cabinets, electrical cords, closets, countertops, wall outlets, windows, stoves, refrigerators, rugs, chairs, pillows, and shelves. He compared his readings from the tape measure against the blueprint he had laid out on the old chest that serves as a coffee table.

"Yours is bigger," he said, scribing figures on a piece of paper.

"What?"

"Your great room is bigger than mine. By four feet."

"Oh."

"Do you think your couch would fit in my cabin?"

"I don't know, but you can't have my couch."

"If you're going to try to be funny, you need to warn me in advance."

"Don't forget to figure that your exterior doors are going to open into the great room. That will chew up a few feet."

"Yeah, right. I wonder if I should call Walczak and have him make the room bigger."

"Now's the time if you're going to make changes."

Walczak, the landowner, was poised to begin construction on Jim's cabin and had promised a turn-key dwelling when Jim returned for Thanksgiving.

Later, as we sat on the deck, eating a steak and pasta dinner, I realized that Jim was about to enter the period of vigilant waiting, and it occurred to me that he faced the greater challenge in that regard. While my family had been able to visit the cabin site each weekend and assess the progress, Jim would be forced to bide his time in L.A. and rely on the snapshots I would send him to chart the evolution of his cabin.

The next morning, I had the chance to witness what had to be a Morgan County first: Jim, the CBS executive, clad in T-shirt and shorts, engaged in manual labor—unpaid, at that—with no cellular phone in sight. Consider it pro bono work.

Over the previous few months, my family, friends, and I had been slipping and sliding down to the creek along a tangled path that shot, rather than meandered, down the steep hillside to the water. As a consequence, we had created a chute that, in heavy rains, would create an erosion problem and carry silt into Clear Creek. My presence in Morgan County, and the work of the backhoe, had already resulted in a conspicuous hole in the forest; I didn't want to increase my environmental footprint to include damage to a Wild and Scenic River.

I determined to construct a trail—a series of steps and switchbacks—that would afford us access to the river but limit the impacts of our passage. The problem was, the trail would fall inside the boundaries of the National Park Service.

A couple of weeks earlier, I had encountered a National Park Service ranger for Clear Creek and the Obed River. I explained our dilemma and asked if he had any thoughts on how we might provide for access to the river while minimizing our impacts. My hopes were that he would dispatch a crew of National Park Service professionals to construct the trail. Instead, he gave me his blessing but left the heavy lifting to me.

"Go ahead and build a *minimalist* trail," he said. It was up to me to define the term.

Though I had hiked thousands of miles on mountain trails and had developed a healthy respect for those who had constructed the footway, I had little appreciation for the art—and difficulty—of trail building. In my naivete, I had imagined that Jim and I would construct a tidy continuum of steps in the morning, break for a quick lunch, then head down for a swim in the afternoon.

I could blame our slow progress on temperatures in the high nineties and a television executive who had spent a decade overtaxing his brain while ignoring his body, but it was more a matter of pure physics.

After four hours of groaning and straining, of prying and leveraging rocks that felt like small Hondas, we were finished for the day.

"I can't do this anymore," said Jim, sweat-soaked and curled into a fetal position in the brush. "My body craves beer."

We had constructed exactly seven steps that extended less than ten yards. As I gazed down the hillside to the river and realized that I faced months of work building trail, I began to identify with the Egyptian slaves who built the pyramids.

Jim and I stowed the work tools at the cabin and headed down to the creek for a swim. We sat on the Rock of Contemplation and talked through much of the afternoon.

Jim related details from his job in L.A. and the constant stress that filled his days, beginning and ending with gridlock on a congested L.A. freeway; the seventeen miles to work consumed thirty-five minutes. Despite the headache, he loved television and had, from the time he was a kid, dreamed of entering the industry.

Though his temperament seemed completely out of step with the ego-centered prima donnas who dominate his profession, Jim possesses a rare gift that suits him perfectly for a career in TV: He is a walking, talking encyclopedia of television facts.

Cite any program, tracing back to the 1940s, when America's cathode ray tubes first flickered to life, and Jim can give you all the particulars.

"When did the *Dick Van Dyke* show first air?"

"October 1961. Produced by Danny Thomas and Carl Reiner."

"*The Cosby Show*?"

"September 1984."

"*Texaco Star Theater*?"

"That would be 1949, starring Milton Berle."

"Which episode of *Cheers* drew the highest ratings?"

"Duh! The finale. Drew about sixty-one market share."

His gift both amazed and occasionally irritated his colleagues at CBS. Jim related an experience of facing down a boardroom full of suits who were poised to assign a new program a name that involved use of a gerund, a verb form that ends in "ing" and acts as a noun in a sentence (e.g., *Watching* TV is good for you).

"I'm not sure you want to do that," Jim interjected.

"Why the hell not?"

"Just about every program whose title used a gerund died in one season."

Grumbling.

Jim responded by citing an exhaustive list: *Going Places, Having Babies, Going to Extremes, Breaking Away, Living in Captivity.*

"How in the hell do you know this stuff?"

"Should I go on?"

"Okay, smart-ass, what about *Growing Pains*?" someone challenged.

"Adjective, not a gerund."

"What the hell! You are a goddamned savant!"

Before he launched his career in TV, while he was working as a magazine journalist, Jim had been assigned to write a profile of Norman Lear, who had created a number of hit series, most notably *All in the Family*. Jim's knowledge of the industry so impressed Lear that he offered to call the network bigwigs and put in a good word, which didn't hurt when Jim arrived at CBS's offices in L.A. looking for work. Jim credits Lear with his position at the network. In less than ten years, Jim had advanced from an assistant to vice president in a competitive and notoriously unforgiving industry.

Though Jim's professional success inspired awe—and to some extent envy—among our former coworkers at the publishing company, to me he was still Jim, the recovering Catholic from Philadelphia given to occasional outbursts of neurotic angst worthy of Woody Allen.

Over the years, Jim had proved to be a wise and insightful counselor who helped talk me through crises ranging from depression to infertility. He had known Susan and me since we arrived in Knoxville in 1985 and spent so much time with us that one of our mutual friends jokingly referred to him as "the Brill Child." To Challen and Logan, he was "Uncle Jim." Like a family member, Jim understood Susan's and my relationship about as well as anyone.

Jim and Susan joked often about their tendency to be frenetic and high-strung, and they used to chide me for being far too laid-back. At times, when I was with the two of them, I felt like Stan Laurel in the presence of Jerry Lewis and Pee Wee Herman, as they chattered away under the influence of way too many cups of coffee.

As we sat on the Rock in the afternoon sun, I described the state of my marriage and shared with Jim details that, to that point, I had kept mostly to myself. Among my friends, he alone had the context necessary to grasp how Susan and I had arrived at the impasse.

I explained to him how Susan had told me that she was miserable, that she had confessed that she felt like she was slowly dying in our relationship, and that she had begun to insist that I leave.

"Dave, Susan is full of anger and unhappiness right now. A big part of it is because of you, but some of it probably has nothing to do with you," he said. "She's in her mid-thirties, about her mom's age when she got divorced, and she has two kids and a career piling all sorts of demands on her. She's struggling, and you can't help her; only Susan can do that. Maybe the best thing you can do is get out of the way."

"But if I leave, what about the girls?"

"It doesn't sound like the two of you are making much of a home for them right now," he said. "The best thing you can do for them is be happy."

"The notion of being happy while Susan is miserable smacks of betrayal."

"Your suffering isn't going to make any difference; it will just increase the casualty count."

My grasp of Susan's suffering grew in part from my own bout with depression in 1986, when my tendency toward optimism had succumbed to an achingly bleak worldview, and I began to loathe myself for flaws and weaknesses that seemed to overshadow any redeeming qualities I had to offer to the world.

The year before, we had moved from Indianapolis to Knoxville so I could take a new job as editor of a magazine, which meant that Susan had to abandon her job as a graphic designer with an advertising firm in Indiana.

A few months after we arrived in Knoxville, I started hating my job and endured a level of stress I had never experienced before. I longed to be off pursuing the assignments I was doling out to other writers. Instead, I was bankrolling their adventures and then massaging their copy into shape once they had returned home and sent in their expenses.

As it became clear to me that I was never cut out for the job I had taken, I began to feel guilty for asking Susan to abandon her own post so I could report for a job that was making me miserable.

At about the same time, Susan and I had tried unsuccessfully for three years to conceive, and medical diagnostics indicated that the problem lay with my plumbing, not hers. She desperately wanted children, and I was standing in the way. Never mind the fact that I had become a withdrawn, despondent housemate, and she was forced to live with an emotional invalid during the years of her life that were supposed to be full of child-rearing and happiness.

Eventually, under the capable guidance of a therapist and a year's worth of antidepressant medication, I started to emerge from the darkness. I quit my job to pursue my dream of being a freelance writer, and eventually I succeeded. By the late 1980s, I was hopping on a plane every few weeks bound for adventures as far away as Japan and Brazil. I scaled mountains, rode in bicycling races, and scuba-dived with treasure hunters. I profiled actors, businesspeople, and adventurers. And I was writing my stories in the den of a one-hundred-year-old farmhouse, peering through the window onto thirty acres of pastureland.

Meanwhile, once the stress eased and my depression lifted, my fertility miraculously improved, and by spring of 1988, Susan was pregnant with Challen. Like most guys, I fell victim to the dangerous tendency to equate worthiness with virility, and Susan's pregnancy buoyed my spirit like nothing else could. My career was kicking butt, my beautiful wife was pregnant; life was sweet, and I was back among the living. I foolishly assumed that it would all last.

Shortly after Logan was born in 1991, the pressure of two young children began to take a toll on us. And by 1994, Susan's job as art director with the same Knoxville-based publisher I had once worked for was about to end. The company, which had drawn so many talented editors and art directors to Knoxville, was turning belly-up, and Susan was about to lose salary and benefits.

At about the same time, the University of Tennessee, for which I had been working ten hours a week, offered me a full-time salaried position with benefits. It would mean that I would have to abandon my office at home and reenter the workaday world. Susan and I talked it over, and we decided that we'd engage in a little tag-team careering. I'd don the suitable work attire and punch the clock, and she could stay home and freelance. When the workaday world had begun to wear me down, we'd slap hands, and she would reenter the ring, while I'd settle back into shorts and Tevas and work at home.

The transition worked out well for both of us: I eventually was appointed director of communications for the research center at the university, and for the first time in my life earned a decent income, and Susan's earnings from her freelance work soon exceeded her salary at the publishing company. But while our financial futures brightened, things began to come unraveled at home.

Susan was juggling her freelance work while shouldering other responsibilities that cut into her limited free time. She became the troop leader for the girls' Brownie and Girl Scout troops, she volunteered as a teacher's helper at the girls' schools, and she drove the girls to school and picked them up every afternoon at 2:45. Her work responsibilities often kept her up past midnight.

And while I logged ten-hour days at the office, my contribution to running the household, which had never been equitable to begin with, began to decline. When we returned from Christmas holiday at my folks' house in 1997, Susan confessed that she felt like she was falling apart.

"I thought I was going to lose it at your parents' house," she said. "I feel like I'm dying, like I'm slowly dying."

After that, I began to withdraw, too. It hurt too much to stay engaged emotionally. And by the time I began the search for property and contemplated building a cabin, I hoped that the retreat would create some neutral ground where we could reestablish our relationship and distance ourselves—if only temporarily—from the turmoil that shaped our life back in the city.

I still held hope that the cabin would play that role in my life and in the lives of my children—that it would become our Eden—even if it failed to work its magic on Susan. But I realized, too, that developing a deep connection to a place can take time.

To that point I had regarded the cabin as perfect, but I still waited for the rapture to come; I awaited the peace and reflection I had hoped the place would inspire. Both arrived in measured amounts, but I always had the sense that I was experiencing the cabin's gifts in titration while I craved a full therapeutic dose. Dropping in on weekends wasn't sufficient; I longed for complete immersion. But that would require me to redefine my responsibilities at the university. To some extent, I was already living at the cabin—in the emotional sense. My thoughts dwelt there even while I was at home in Knoxville or positioned at my desk at work.

A few months earlier, one of my colleagues, who had arranged to work from her cabin in the Appalachian Mountains just outside of Hot Springs, North Carolina, cautioned me about the tug the cabin would exert on my life.

"You'll count the hours until Friday afternoon and your departure for the cabin," she said. "And you'll cry every Sunday night when you have to come back."

Though my Sunday afternoons weren't tearful, they were difficult, and I found myself lingering longer and longer at the cabin on Sunday evenings before mustering the will to close up and return home. And often, once I had arrived back home and reentered the silent struggle with Susan, I often wished I had remained in Morgan County awhile longer.

TWENTY

Counseled by the Gentle Giant

The best mirror is an old friend.
—George Herbert, Jacula Prudentum

"P*lbst plg nph lug glrg flurg plmnym blmp!*" Russ said,
breaking the surface of the creek. It struck me as shoddy
elocution, particularly for an English professor at the University
of Tennessee, then I realized he still had the snorkel gripped in
his teeth.

"What? I'm afraid I didn't get that."

"The pool is more than twenty feet deep!" he repeated, after removing the snorkel's mouthpiece. "Straight off the edge of the rock,
it's wide open all the way to the bottom. No problem diving."

I had lectured the girls about the dangers of diving into creek
water. ("You'll wind up breaking your neck on some submerged
object and will be paralyzed from the neck down. They'll put a
tube in your throat to help you breathe—that is, if you live.")
Logan's look of abject horror suggested that I might have been a
bit too strident in articulating the dangers, which J.J., Mr.
Health-and-Safety-Man, had enumerated on an earlier visit.

Russ's explorations assured me that the ledge at the waterline—the "whale's tail," as I called it—could be used as a diving
board.

Russ disappeared again and soon resurfaced.

"*Phlgs! Mnlph phlgs!*" he shouted as he broke the surface.

"Russ, the snorkel."

"Fish, big fish, mostly bass, but a few bluegills, too!"

"Yeah, I know, I've hooked a few of them. How big?"

He held up hands about eighteen inches apart.

"That would be Walter-the-Son-of-a-Bitch Bass," I said, borrowing the moniker from the movie *On Golden Pond.* "Every time I cast out from the Rock, he emerges from under that ledge and shows himself. I think he's taunting me."

"I'm going to explore upstream," Russ said.

He stroked across the surface, his fins churning the water to froth, heading upstream toward the head of the pool. Benton, delighted to have an aquatic playmate, trailed behind.

Through the afternoon, I sat on the Rock, casting out into the open pool, angling for Walter. Meanwhile, Russ and Benton explored the creek.

At six-foot-eight and with a voice booming enough to reverberate his listeners' dental work—that is, when he's not gripping a snorkel—Russ Hirst is about as unobtrusive as Liberace standing amid a gathering of Jesuits. Add in his trademark Australian bush hat, which spreads away from his bespectacled head like a large brown awning, and he's impossible to ignore.

At a rally on campus, I scanned the crowd of a couple hundred students, faculty, and staff and immediately spotted a lone oak towering above the throng. If there were any question as to his identity, viewing him as I was from the rear, the outsize hat resolved all doubt.

Russ and I had met five years earlier at a reception, where both of us were uncomfortably clad in coats and ties. As soon as we were able to steer the conversation away from inane cocktail-party banter—"So what do you do at the university?"—we discovered a shared love for guy things, principally, scratching, spitting, fishing, and hanging out in the woods.

Russ is among a group of friends I affectionately refer to as "the Christian Brotherhood," a collection of guys—some of whom I've known since high school in Cincinnati; others more recent acquaintances—who are devout Christians. The Brotherhood and I hook up twice a year for backpacking trips to the nearby Appalachians or Cumberland Mountains. I had invited Russ to join the group a couple of years earlier.

Brought up as a Mormon, Russ—and his family—eventually departed Brigham Young's flock and took up with the Presbyterians. I realized that his religious tenets, which tend toward the conservative, would align nicely with those of the rest of the group.

Our semiannual outings inevitably segue into fireside discussions in which I singlehandedly represent the liberal worldview. Meanwhile my friends do their best to convince me that Al Gore is the Antichrist, that gay love is a sin against God, that the Bible is to be interpreted literally, and that artists—like photographer Robert Mapplethorpe—whose works depict mature themes, should be muzzled, if not shot.

Though neither side has ever claimed any converts, and though the discussions are often impassioned, the Brotherhood and I share a few key beliefs in common, particularly belief in a benevolent God and that the love and fellowship of good friends is a powerful gift.

Over the past couple of years, the Brotherhood and I have stood together under canopies of stars on open snowcapped mountaintops; we have camped by rivers and spent long sunny afternoons swimming and rock-hopping; we have ambled through open meadows fringed in rime frost. And invariably, our conversations lead to discussions of God and spirit, precisely what, I contend, humans were meant to contemplate in wilderness settings.

Over our weekends together, we have opened our lives—and hearts—to each other, and though our spiritual beliefs are occasionally at odds, we have forged enduring friendships. The Brotherhood has often prayed for me and with me, asking God to find a way to touch Susan's and my hearts, to lead us back together, to heal our family.

I shared my marital problems with Russ soon after we met, and he consistently urged me to turn to God for help and to remain steadfast, to refuse to leave, regardless of how unbearable conditions at home became. As far as Russ was concerned, divorce was not an option, except in the most extreme cases of abuse, and staying the course, regardless of how difficult conditions became, was the only just path.

"God has the power to redeem even the most hopeless sinner," he said one afternoon while we lunched together under the trees on the edge of campus. "And God can touch even the most hardened heart. I pray often that he'll help mend your relationship."

Russ, like many of my friends, had remained available and attentive through the years of marital crisis; he also, on occasion, used my current circumstance to our mutual advantage, as have other friends. He had frequently effected a pained countenance and plied the phrase "Dave's in crisis" to negotiate a "hall pass" from his wife, Rebecca, to come spend the weekend with me. As a result, he had become a regular at Benton's Run and always found a way of repaying me for my hospitality, often through a few hours of free labor.

Russ had arrived on Friday afternoon, immediately donned his sombrero, cracked open a beer, and welcomed the weekend. Before departing Knoxville, he had loaded his station wagon with guy toys, including mask, fins, and snorkel (to confirm that there were, in fact, fish in the creek); fishing rod and tackle (to hook the now-confirmed fish in the creek); a seven-foot-long walking stick worthy of Moses (doubles as a weapon for thrashing aggressive dogs and bad guys); a sleeping bag and seven-foot-long, three-inch-thick foam pad (to soothe a bad back); a hatchet and Bowie knife (ancillary weapons for dogs and bad guys); a saw, hammer, nails, and tool belt (in case we wanted to build something); a garden rake (for tidying up the forest); a cooler full of steaks and a quantity of beer sufficient for a postmatch rugby party ("I'm bigger than you, so I need to drink twice as much beer to get the same buzz"); various headlamps and flashlights (for when we went exploring after dark); and camp chairs (for those rare moments when Russ was in repose).

"Damn, Russ, the Lewis and Clark expedition didn't have this much stuff," I said, as we unloaded his car.

"Didn't know if I'd need everything, but I brought it just in case."

He emptied his first beer in one gulp and opened his second.

"This place is *great*, Dave ol' buddy; the perfect place to live and write," he said. "I'll have to remember to stop feeling sorry for you."

"If feeling sorry for me helps you earn weekend passes from Rebecca, I fully endorse your having pity on me."

He ambled off into the woods to relieve his bladder and released the long sigh of a stressed-out city dweller who's secured a furlough. The afternoon sun filtered through trees, and the first dry, cool bite of fall hung in the air. With head tipped back and arms stretched wide, as if to hug the forest, Russ basked for a moment in the wonder of God's creation and a house set in the woods. Then his thoughts turned to productivity while our heads were still clear enough to wield chain saws and hammers.

"Any construction projects need doing?" he asked. "I feel like building something."

"As a matter of fact, I was thinking of using some of these downed pine trees to construct an amphitheater of sorts around the fire ring."

"Let's have at it," he said, clipping on his tool belt.

Within an hour, we had rolled four eight-foot pine logs—casualties of the construction process—into place around the fire pit, propped them up on short sections of hardwood, and nailed them in place.

The next morning, we cooked up leftover steaks and ate them with eggs before loading up day packs and heading for the creek. After Russ tired of swimming, he joined me on the Rock for a tepid beer.

"Dave ol' buddy, you have somehow managed to achieve the most fortunate circumstances imaginable for passing through an unfortunate experience. I don't know whether to envy you or feel sorry for you."

"Russ, in my time here at the cabin, I feel as though I am right where I'm supposed to be, right where God wants me to be," I said. "That feeling offers me a lot of comfort, particularly in view of what's happening with my marriage."

"Dave, it strikes me that the New Age attitude that if you feel okay inside, then you're necessarily right with God is flawed," he said.

"I believe that we need to move beyond feeling okay and open ourselves to the guidance and influences God has in mind for us," he continued. "We need to let him shape us into the people he wants us to be and prepare us for his service."

"Russ, I pray every night for God to guide me," I said. "My antennas are fully extended, and I'm ready to receive the signal."

"I believe your heart is pure and that your prayers are sincere. Maybe over the next few months, things will become more clear."

"In many ways, I feel that God has been subtly guiding me since the wake-up call I got seventeen years ago."

"Oh, you mean the dream?"

"Yes, the dream."

In my second year of graduate school, during a period of my life when everything seemed to be rolling my way—beautiful wife, perfect grades, solid job prospects—I had begun to believe that I alone was responsible for my destiny, that by plying my brains and will, I could achieve anything.

And on some level, the outward trappings of my life supported that belief. But inside, I was experiencing a gnawing spiritual emptiness that drew me increasingly to Christians who had given their lives over to God. Among them was a man named Joe who worked with me on the student newspaper. Over the next several months, I experienced a couple of events, both under Joe's guidance, that culminated with a dream that was, at once, terrifying and enlightening and that cranked up a level of dissonance that I couldn't manage to quell.

Unlike some other Christians I'd met who relied on chastisement to win converts, Joe was savvy enough to realize that if he got in my face and started proselytizing and wagging a reproving finger at me for my arrogant, sinful ways, I'd shut him out.

Instead, he shared with me the details of his own spiritual journey and the profound peace that filled his heart. Joe also knew that, as a columnist for the campus daily newspaper, I was always looking for story angles, and he invited me to visit a maximum security prison where he ministered twice a month to the inmates.

"You'll be sitting right next to murderers and other violent offenders who have confessed their sins and reached out to Christ," he said. "I guarantee you a powerful experience."

I accepted his invitation, more out of curiosity than any yen to witness firsthand the power of redemption, and on a hot summer evening, Joe picked me up and we headed down the road to the jail. As we approached the huge brown fortress, I played the consummate journalist: hungry for a good story but emotionally detached and invulnerable.

We passed through several guard stations and checkpoints, where I was pat searched and stripped of my pencil, writing tablet, and tape recorder. (I could have been smuggling in blotter acid—a form of LSD applied to paper—on the pages of the tablet, the pencil could have been used as a weapon, and I might have hidden contraband in the battery compartment of the tape recorder.) Joe was forced to surrender his Bible—only a slight inconvenience, since he had committed most of it to memory.

As we moved deeper and deeper into the prison, and as one steel door after another slammed shut behind me, I grew edgy and frightened—and I was only a visitor. I could only imagine what the inmates' existence was like. Then we emerged onto the open yard that separated the cell blocks from the self-standing chapel in the middle of the complex.

Suddenly, angry caged men shouted unimaginable things at us through barred windows. Men with rifles peered out from towers at the corners of the yard. I sped ahead to walk beside Joe, who was as placid and calm as ever.

"You okay?" he asked.

"You didn't lie when you promised me a powerful experience," I said. "But God, this is a wretched place."

"You got that right. These guys have run out of options, except the one that really counts."

We entered the chapel. Inside, a hundred or so inmates clad in white T-shirts or chambray, with numbers stenciled on their chests, sat shoulder to shoulder in rough wooden pews. Some sported shaved heads and tattoos. Others had scarred faces, crooked noses, and conspicuous gaps in their smiles. Some were so young that they sprouted beards of peach fuzz.

I noticed that two or three guards, armed only with walkie-talkies and Mace cans, stood at the corners. ("If there's a riot and the guards are overpowered," Joe had explained, "they don't want the inmates to have access to weapons. If that happens, and it won't, you and I become hostages.")

Joe grabbed my arm and led me to a pew toward the middle of the chapel, and as we moved through the room, the inmates greeted Joe warmly.

He looked each one in the face and said, "I love you, brother," and I believe that he did.

In a few minutes, the service began. A convicted rapist stepped to the pulpit and began to pray about forgiveness and God's promise to instill peace in the heart of the sinner.

As he spoke, the inmates around me, their heads bowed, many of them weeping, began to shout rejoinders, their voices quavering with passion and conviction: "Praise, Jesus!" "Praise God!" "Amen, brother!"

Their voices soon established a rhythm, and it sounded like one hundred men were speaking with one voice. I closed my eyes, and as I did, the cadence overpowered me, and my journalistic detachment began to erode. I felt like I was losing myself, that I was sliding into a vortex, that my spirit was merging with those of the other men in the room.

Frightened, I forced open my eyes and looked at Joe, who was rocking with the rhythm, muttering a prayer, tears rolling down his cheeks.

Though I suspected that some of those in the room were feigning devotion to God to incline parole boards to cut short their sentences, the raw emotional outpouring I witnessed—and experienced in my heart—was undeniably genuine. The power of the scene has abided through all the years since. God had filled those sinners' hearts with peace and offered them comfort in an utterly hopeless place.

At the conclusion of the hour-long service, Joe pointed to a man about my age who was rising from his seat at the opposite end of our pew. He was a well-groomed, handsome, and tanned from days spent in the exercise yard.

"Someday, when you're ready, I'd like for you to hear that man's story," Joe said. "He's a convicted mass murderer doing a life sentence. He's devoted himself to Christ."

A couple of weeks later, Joe set up an interview with the man, who spoke candidly about his crime perpetrated against victims chosen at random. He described the victims lined up on the floor and executed with a shotgun blast to the back of the head. The small trailer choked with gun smoke and the blood spreading out across the carpet. The mother, whose wig had blown off with the first blast, who was mistaken for dead and who lay still, listening as her sons were killed one by one right beside her. How after the murderers had left, she wrapped a towel around her bloody head, so she wouldn't frighten her neighbors when she went to them for help.

The man spoke of the uneasy months before the police pieced things together and knocked on his door, months of hearing all his friends talk about the horror of his crime, never suspecting that he had played a part in it. He spoke of the day he was captured and made his confession in the police station, where he was surrounded by dozens of law-enforcement officials, one of whom produced the murder weapon. He spoke of the first day in jail when he decided not to hang himself until he had given his mother a chance to tell him to go to hell and how she told him instead that she loved him despite what he had done. He spoke of that night when darkness crowded his cell and he sensed the presence of the devil beside him and how he begged God for forgiveness and how he felt it come. He spoke of the day on the stand when he testified, smiling, and how the press ascribed his smile to callousness but how it grew from knowing that God had forgiven him.

Through the interview, I held on to my journalistic detachment, but when I got home that night and played for Susan the tape recordings I had made during the interview, and the man's voice boomed out through the stereo speakers, I experienced a fear so pervasive that I soon installed dead-bolt locks but still felt thoroughly vulnerable. The forces of good and evil lay just beyond my door, and both possessed sufficient power to consume me.

The experiences with Joe provoked weeks of reflection and soul-searching. Here was a man who willingly departed his suburban home to enter one of the foulest places on earth, who had devoted his life to helping men who had violated the laws of both God and man. I found myself increasingly fascinated by love and forgiveness so unconditional and powerful that they could tame the heart of a murderer. Joe and I spent hours talking about God and the calling he had felt in his heart to lead the dregs of society to peace. On the heels of all this, I had the dream.

It occurred in the early hours of the morning, and I still struggle to characterize it. It was far too vivid and alive to be a dream, though it came to me in sleep.

It began with me full of anger, chasing someone who had wronged me in some way, trailing him down a familiar street in the darkness. He darted toward a house and disappeared into the darkened garage. As I approached, I noticed that the garage floor fell away into a deep pit, and as I peered down, I saw two glowing red eyes looking up at me.

"You can't touch me; you can't catch me," a sinister voice taunted.

I felt myself burning with rage but feeling utterly helpless. Then, I found myself sitting in an open, featureless field illuminated by dusky light, sometime just after sundown. I recall feeling remorseful about my anger, realizing that it was wrong to wish harm on another, regardless of what he had done to me. I felt compelled to turn around, and as I did, I confronted a sheer cliff of black stone that rose up hundreds of feet into the sky. I scanned upward until my gaze reached the top. Behind a row of huge boulders, three old women paced back and forth, paraphrasing the scriptures.

"He fed the hungry, he clothed the naked, he healed the sick," they said, in unison. Then they stopped and, together, pointed behind them.

"The answer is here," they said.

I looked past them and suddenly gazed on a white light that was bright beyond description, and as I looked at it, it entered my body, surged through me like a powerful electrical current, and knocked me to the ground.

My body burned and tingled as the light filled me and I recall sensing intelligence and profound power in the light, but also peace. The light seemed to say, "I am more powerful than you can possibly imagine, and I can affect your life in ways you never dreamed."

The power surged through me for several minutes in the dream, and I started moaning in my sleep. Susan nudged me awake and asked me what was wrong.

"I just had a nightmare," I said. "No, no, it wasn't a nightmare. It was . . . I don't know what it was."

As I explained the sequences to her, I had this sense that something was going to happen, that the being of light was going to demonstrate his power. Through the next day, I felt edgy and watchful.

That evening, a friend came over, and after dinner, we walked out to the front yard, which bordered on a busy road. I demonstrated the ability of my beloved black Labrador, Smudge, to catch and return a Frisbee. On each toss, Smudge dutifully came to heel and dropped the glow-in-the-dark flying disc at my feet.

When it was nearly dark, my friend climbed on his bicycle to ride home, and as he pedaled out of sight, I decided to throw the Frisbee one last time. Smudge caught it and started to return to my side but suddenly veered onto the road. She sprinted down the oncoming traffic lane, and I watched the headlights of a car turn onto the road and head straight for her. I chased after her, calling for her to stop, but she was a hundred yards ahead and seemed not to hear me.

I saw her silhouette close against the headlights then heard the impact, and I found her crumpled by the side of the road just as the car's driver hit the gas and sped around me and away. The transformation from an animate creature to a heap of torn flesh and shattered bones had taken less than a second.

I picked up the dog and walked home, full of rage, wondering if this had been the cruel footnote to the vision from the night before. "I am more powerful than you can possibly imagine, and I can affect your life in ways you never dreamed."

I grabbed a shovel and started digging a grave in the backyard. As I did, I shouted angry curses at God, and in retrospect, I realize that that marked the first time in my adult life I had ever actively acknowledged God's presence. You can't ascribe blame to something you don't believe in. I later recognized the obvious flaws in a belief system that allowed a person to take full credit for the successes while blaming God for the tragedies.

TWENTY-ONE

Logan Eyes the Big Picture

And still I wander, seeking compensation in un-
foreseen encounters and unexpected sights, in sun-
sets, storms and passing fancies.
—Charles Kuralt, A Life on the Road

How will I know when we're flying?" Logan asked, after
we had boarded the plane and buckled into our seats.
It was her first flight, and she seemed to be experiencing a
mixture of excitement and anxiety, twisting in her seat one
minute then pausing just long enough to nibble a fingernail the
next.

"Logan, when you see the ground drop away below us, you'll
know we're flying."

Logan and I had spent evenings in early September shaping
to-do lists for our father-daughter hike in the White Mountains
of New Hampshire. Challen and I had taken a similar trip two
years earlier, when she was seven, and I chronicled our trip in an
article for *FamilyFun* magazine. The article boasted a couple
dozen of my photos and made Challen into something of a
celebrity at her school. The fact that the article, and her likeness,
wound up on the magazine's Web site didn't hurt her reputation
among her peers.

Logan, seated beside me at the window, looked so damned
cute dressed in her denim jumper, yellow T-shirt, white ankle
socks, and sneakers, which would swing back and forth under
her seat nonstop until we touched down in Boston. Most of the
elderly grandparents on the plane couldn't keep their eyes off

her; she looked like the quintessential grandchild, scrubbed and decked out for a big trip.

Soon, we were airborne.

"Daddyman, this is *way* cool," Logan said, mulling the perspective for a few minutes. "If the cows down there look like bugs from up here, what do the bugs look like?"

The question reminded me of the Buddhist meditation exercise that involves contemplating the sound of one hand clapping. If you ponder such questions long enough, you either achieve enlightenment or your brain bursts into flames.

"You know, Logan, I hadn't thought about that," I answered.

Actually, I had, but not for a long time. When Steve and I were kids, my Grandma Brill took us to the observation deck on top of a skyscraper in downtown Cincinnati. Steve, who was barely tall enough to peer over the guardrail, hauled himself up and gazed down onto the sidewalk below, shaking his head in disbelief.

"Hey, Grandma," he said after a while. "If the people down there look like ants, what do the ants look like?"

Steve's question, and Logan's too, were, no doubt, part of every child's efforts to gain perspective and context, attempts to figure out exactly where they fit into the roiling world around them. It seems to me that there's value in remembering that there are vantage points from which big things look small and others from which small things look big, and the real art is learning when it's time to shift your perspective. It was a lesson worth pondering; in the months ahead Logan and I—along with Challen and Susan—would all be forced to regard things, particularly the shape and form of our family, in a whole new way.

"Logan, what you're seeing from up here is the big picture."

"Is it the biggest picture?"

"No."

"What's the biggest picture?"

"I don't know; I haven't seen it yet."

Then she turned her attention to a more mundane matter.

"Hey, Dad, what happens if you go to the bathroom in a plane? Does it get stored, or do they dump it into the air?"

"I think it's stored, but just to be on the safe side, I wouldn't have a picnic near an airport."

"Yuck!" she said, picturing the result. "That's gross."

As we approached Boston, she found it amusing that we were flying into an airport that shared her name.

"It's almost like they knew I was coming, like they were welcoming me to Boston," she said. "Did you know my name means 'little woods'? Mommy told me."

"I thought it meant 'little knucklehead.' "

"No, that's just my nickname."

Logan had initially been disappointed that our trip, unlike mine and Challen's, wouldn't generate national media attention. I had tried to sell the story idea but didn't get a nibble. But Challen had helped me convince Logan that accompanying a working journalist—even if he is your dad—can be a frustrating process.

"Logan, that's actually a good thing that Dad's not doing a story," Challen told her. "I was so sick of his camera by the end of our trip that I wanted to throw it over the side of the mountain."

"Yeah, Logan, I won't be distracted with work," I said. "We'll focus all our energy on each other and on having fun."

"But you *are* going to take pictures of me, aren't you, Daddy?" Logan asked.

"Of course, lots."

I could see her little wheels turning: Logan, the consummate actress, envisioning various poses, "Mr. DeMille, I'm ready for my close-up. . . ."

Chances were good that she, like Challen on our trip, would feature a large gap in her smile. She had called me earlier in the week to announce that she was about to lose one of her front teeth.

"I'm wiggling and wiggling it, trying to pull it out before we go on our trip, Dad," she explained. "I want to make things as easy as possible on Gwendolyn the Tooth Fairy. I don't think she could find us in a tent in New Hampshire."

Susan had penned a note from Gwendolyn the Tooth Fairy when Logan lost her first tooth. According to the note, Gwendolyn had hands the size of a period at the end of a sentence and was assigned exclusively to respond to Logan's dental sheddings.

In some ways, I was more excited about my trip with Logan than I had been about my journey with Challen. While Challen and I had always shared an unshakable bond, Logan and I had to work a little harder at staying connected.

Logan is spirited, sometimes volatile, frighteningly clever, given to occasional dramatic deliveries (she's never thirsty—she's "parched"; she's never just hungry—she's "absolutely famished"), and inclined to regard everything as a contest. (I sat on a panel at the Southern Festival of Books a couple of years earlier, and after glimpsing me seated beside the other authors at the head table, Logan approached and whispered in my ear, "Dad, I hope you win!")

She also brims with self-confidence. (Once, after I had given a talk on my Appalachian Trail experiences to a large group of hikers, three-year-old Logan stepped up on stage, craned to reach the microphone, and barked "People! People! Now listen to *my* speech!")

She's also been endowed with an energy level that's off the scale. I recently visited her gymnastic class to watch her tumble. As I entered the large gymnasium, I looked out across yards and yards of blue mats and dozens of girls all clad in leotards. Despite the throng, locating Logan was a simple matter of spotting the bouncing head.

We spent the night at a hotel in Concord, new Hampshire, and had pizza for dinner. Next morning, I bought Logan a pair of hiking boots at the L.L. Bean outlet store around the corner. By day's end, we had made camp in the White Mountains and were supping on hot dogs cooked on sticks over the fire. Early the next morning, Logan befriended a black Labrador puppy named Guinness who dived in through the open door of our tent just before sunrise and licked her on the face.

On our arrival back home, Logan's recounting of our trip to Susan and Challen would begin with meeting Guinness and transition to the fact that I let her eat chocolate bars for breakfast one morning. Her description of the mountains rated a distant third.

The next morning, we drove to the top of Mount Washington, the tallest peak in New England, renowned for having some of the worst weather in North America. Though the mountain sees snow all months of the year, and hikers have died of exposure near the summit in July, Mount Washington greeted us with temperatures in the sixties.

As soon as we emerged from the car, a single-engine plane flew directly above us, and, as we watched, it released the tow line attached to a glider that followed a hundred feet behind. As the glider caught a thermal, it soared so near the summit that we could hear the wind rush under its wings.

We trekked a mile-and-a-quarter down from the summit to Lakes of the Clouds hut, one of a series of high-elevation huts that provide bunks and meals for hikers. Challen and I had stayed at the hut during our trip, but it was closed for the season when Logan and I arrived in late September.

The hike down to "Lakes," as it's called by locals, which nestles beside two small ponds on a broad shoulder of the mountain, was no problem. The trek back up, which gains several hundred feet along steep, rocky trail, was a different matter. While Logan had mastered the art of descending, whether on a bicycle or in hiking boots or roller blades, ascending usually immobilized her and brought on high drama.

"Dad, I'm exhausted. I'm parched. My legs are aching, *aching*," she said after climbing less than a hundred yards. She collapsed beside the trail. "I can't take another step. I just can't go on." (Mr. DeMille, I'm ready for my close-up.)

At that point, fate intervened. A troop of Boy Scouts, trailed by two overweight, panting troop leaders, passed. Not to be outdone by a group of *boys*, Logan was immediately on her feet, crunching trail to catch up to them, her fatigue forgotten for the moment.

As she approached the sweat-soaked troop leaders, they seemed to be reading from just the right page in the child-motivation textbook.

"You're awfully young to be hiking in such big mountains," one of them said. "You must be pretty strong."

"Oh, yeah, I've been hiking for *years*," she said. "This is no big deal to me. Daddy took us on our first camping trip when I was one."

After a few minutes of conversation, punctuated by gasps and deep breaths brought on by the steep pitch, Logan assumed the role of master of ceremonies, telling the men much more than they cared to know about us.

"So we've been talking a long time now, and we don't know each other's names," she said. "I'll go first. My name is Logan, and I'm from Knoxville, Tennessee. The airport in Boston is named after me. This is my dad. His name is Dave. He's from Tennessee, too. My sister and Mom didn't come with us. They're going canoeing instead, with my Grandma Sis. A dog named Guinness dove into our tent this morning and woke us up. He's just a puppy. I'm wearing new boots from L.L. Bean."

As she rambled on, I braced for her to share with them the fact that her dad "says shit sometimes." She didn't. Instead, she threw the conversation back to them. "Well, okay, now you know a little about my dad and me. What are your names, and where are you from?" she asked.

"Mike."

"I'm Ken. We're from Delaware, and we'll make it home if these Scouts don't kill us first."

They had hiked up from the base of the mountain, a gain in elevation of about three thousand feet. And their tireless teen charges had set a blazing pace toward the summit, glancing back from ever-more-distant vantage points to see how the old guys were doing.

Once back on the summit, Logan asked if I'd take her picture. As I focused the camera, she assumed "the mountaineer-who-has-reached-the-summit pose," made famous by Sir Edmond Hillary and every other climber whose image has been captured at the moment of triumph.

Arms thrust up and outward, fists clenched, broad grin, terra firma dropping away in every direction below her. As I snapped the picture, I realized that she was aping the shot I had taken of Challen in about the same spot, which graced the opening page of the article about our trip.

After another night in the tent and a morning wake-up call from Guinness, the black Labrador, we set out for Boston and home. Though we didn't cover many trail miles, we had traveled far in terms of our relationship, and as Logan laid her head on my shoulder and gripped my hand during the flight home, I realized we had bonded in a way we hadn't to that point. She had proven a most worthy—and thoroughly amusing—traveling companion.

Over the coming weeks, I would spend time with other worthy travelers, and our sojourn would carry us deep into the world of spirit.

TWENTY-TWO

Embraced by the Brotherhood

They will lay hands on the sick, and they will recover.   —Mark 16:18

I'm getting to the point where I can't bear Susan's anger any-more," I said, staring into the campfire and leaning against a stout log. I was surrounded by the Christian Brotherhood, who had traveled from Cincinnati to Tennessee for our annual fall backpacking trip. We had "camped out" at the cabin the night before and departed early in the morning for Big South Fork National River and Recreation Area, about an hour north.

I valued the Brotherhood's perspective on things because it grew from deeply held spiritual beliefs and differed so vastly from the more practical advice—to seek legal guidance, to stand my ground when Susan pushed too hard, to prepare myself for the showdown that was sure to come—I had received from my secular friends. I had hoped that both perspectives would help steer my course over the coming months.

"I believe that life is supposed to be a celebration, and when circumstances you can't change have you by the throat, it's time to try something else," I continued. "I think it's time for me to give Susan what she wants and move out."

"That's a cop-out," Dave said. "Life is not supposed to be fun. Life is a struggle sometimes, and God doesn't want us to duck for cover when things get rough."

"I don't agree," Jeff said, identifying himself as an ally among a group of hard-liners. "I think we have one chance at life. Why stay married if it's making you miserable?"

"Because marriage is a holy union, a lifelong commitment," Dave responded. "If for no other reason, consider the fallout from divorce. Children of divorce are much more likely to get divorced."

Dave had just articulated my greatest fear, that, if Susan and I split, we'd be setting Challen and Logan up for a lifetime of failed relationships.

"I've wrestled with that issue more than you might imagine," I said. "But I really don't know which outcome will be more harmful for the kids in the long run: being raised by parents locked in a bloodless marriage or seeing us find happiness on our own."

"Dave, we're all sorry for the hurt you're experiencing," Russ said.

"You guys are luckier than you realize," I said. "And I hope you thank God every night for your marriages, for the women who love you and can forgive you your failings."

In the past, the conversation would have cut close to my emotional core, left me vulnerable and fearful, but instead my heart felt like deadwood.

"Through this whole process, I've felt my emotional margins shrinking, and I've felt my heart hardening," I said. "It really doesn't hurt much anymore, and I realize that this emotional numbness isn't specific to my marriage; it's deadening my emotional responses to other experiences, too. Maybe even my kids."

Silence settled over us. In some ways, I was on a parallel path with one of the other members of the Brotherhood. Like Susan, his wife had drifted from their relationship. She told him that she didn't love him, never really loved him, and wanted out—or rather, wanted him out. He and I had both assumed the passive role of hanging tough, refusing to leave, and hoping—and praying—that our wives would return to their senses and to us and our families.

Over the two years I had known him, my Cincinnati friend seemed to be slowly dying as a result of the emotional beating he was taking. On each visit, he seemed less hopeful, more deeply wounded, but no less committed to staying his course, no less inclined to trust God to sort things out. It occurred to me that the admonishment that, when you pray, you should "move your feet," had application in his case. Did God really want us to wait passively for his intervention, or did he want us to become proactive in resolving our own problems? But then, exactly *how* does one go about changing another's heart?

During the previous night at the cabin, the mood had been much less solemn. In fact, it had been celebratory. None of the Brotherhood, except Russ, had seen the cabin, and it assumed the role of clubhouse for a bunch of forty-something kids.

My high-school buddy Kent built a campfire. Jeff strummed his vintage Gibson guitar. Benton tore through the woods then collapsed, panting, by the fire pit. I served up a pasta meal alfresco. Appropriately, the Christian Brotherhood provided the wine.

At midnight, we hiked down to the creek and stood on the bank, watching shooting stars arc across the sky. Though the temperature was plunging into the thirties, Russ-the-Gentle-Giant couldn't pass up an opportunity for a dip. We occasionally caught his lanky form in our headlamp beams as he stroked to the far side of the river.

He emerged from the creek a few minutes later and stripped off his wet shorts. His body steamed in the chill air.

"Don't be surprised if you notice some significant shrinkage," he said, officially initiating three days of intermittent penis jokes.

The next morning, we hiked an easy two miles from the cars to a campsite on the shores of the Big South Fork River, and we spent the afternoon swimming and rock-hopping. At sundown, I cooked up a huge pot of lentil stew, dosed with enough Tabasco sauce to cause grown men to weep. But we were hungry hikers bereft of other culinary options, and we emptied the pot.

After sundown, we gathered around a campfire, and the conversation lingered on beleaguered marriages.

"Can we pray over this guy?" Dave asked at one point, rising from his seat by the fire. The Brotherhood gathered close around me, laid their hands on my shoulders, stroked my back. I lowered my head and surrendered to the moment.

"I thank God for my friendship with Dave," Kent began. "I love him like a brother. Closer than a brother. Help guide his path."

Each, in turn, touched me, prayed over me, affirming their love for me, expressing their sorrow over my situation, asking God to intervene and save my family. Human touch, beginning with a mother's first caress and continuing through a lifetime of handshakes and hugs, communicates more effectively than words ever could and possesses profound power to calm and soothe. It reminds us, on some deep level, of the essential connection we have to the people who love and care about us.

After it was over, I glanced at the fire through tears. I had spent fewer than five days in the presence of some of the members of the Brotherhood, though I had known Kent for most of my life and Russ for several years. But the depth of their love and concern for me was apparent, and I felt closer to each of them than I did to friends I had known for decades.

TWENTY-THREE

Deer Cocaine and a Full-Immersion Baptism

Lives like a drunken sailor on a mast,
Ready with every nod to tumble down
Into the fatal bowels of the deep.
—William Shakespeare, *Richard III*

My land, this is nice!" said Sis, Susan's mom, in her thick Alabama accent. "Y'all have done real good."

Sis had visited the property a year earlier, before construction began, and seemed to appreciate the finished structure, partly because rustic cabins had been a big part of her family since she was a kid. When Sis and her brothers, Bud and Gerald, were young, they spent summers at their family's cabin on the Tennessee River in northwestern Alabama. When Susan and her brothers came along, they did the same. Later, Susan's Uncle Bud kept a rough cabin, called River Hill, on the bluff overlooking the river.

But I also sensed that our cabin made Sis uncomfortable because she wasn't sure what role it would play in her daughter's life. I knew that Susan had shared with her some information on where our relationship stood.

Midafternoon, while Susan and her mom sat inside sipping wine, I started to remove brush from behind the cabin in preparation for our upcoming Halloween party. I knew we'd have a dozen or more kids charging through the woods, and I didn't want to leave the snakes too many places to hide.

Logan stepped onto the deck, saw me hauling off brush, and charged out to intervene.

"Stop! Stop!" she said. *"Dad, you have all this space. Why do you have to destroy Toad Hall. Where will all the toads live if you remove their homes?"*

We had dubbed Logan the "fairness police" because of her preoccupation with the world's injustices, both large and small. Even the plight of displaced toads didn't escape her notice.

"Logan, poisonous snakes can live here, too," I said. "And I don't think you want to tangle with a copperhead."

"It's just so unfair. The toads will be homeless. And you don't care!"

"Yes, I care. But I care more about you and Challen and all your friends who will be up here for the Halloween party. I don't want to have to rush anybody to the hospital for a shot of antivenom in the middle of the night. Besides, I haven't seen a single toad."

"That's because they're running for their lives. How would you like it if a gigantic creature started tearing the cabin apart?"

Just then, Challen emerged from the cabin, listened to part of Logan's impassioned appeal, rolled her eyes and shook her head, and ducked back inside.

I worked for an hour dismantling Toad Hall and felt somewhat discouraged when I peered around me and saw similar heaps of brush and construction debris off in every direction.

Later, I cooked dinner for the family and while Sis and Susan were doing the dishes, I went out onto the deck to whittle.

When the dishes were done, Susan approached me. "Why don't you come inside and spend some time with us?"

"I just cooked dinner for you guys."

"Cooking is not interacting. Now you're withdrawing."

She was right. I was withdrawing, and I realized that withdrawing had become my modus operandi. I had convinced myself that just by being in the house with the family, I was engaged with them. But being present and being involved were two different things, and I realized how remote I had become, particularly to Susan. I had often seen a look in Susan's eyes that told me she was miles away and not registering what I was saying. It pained me to see it because I knew we weren't connecting—two warm bodies sharing space but little more. Now she was seeing that same look in my eyes.

I folded up my pocket knife, swept the carvings off the deck, and went inside. The girls were in their pajamas reading to Sis on the couch. Susan and I sat and watched, proud parents savoring the rewards of family. I realized that wherever our relationship ended up, we'd always be united through our shared love for the girls.

Tim Steelman, the county clerk who lives a quarter mile up the road, pulled up Sunday morning with his wife, Trish, and daughter on their ATV—an open, four-wheel-drive vehicle just slightly larger than a go-cart. ATVs are a favored mode of travel in the county, particularly among the area's hunters, who can navigate them deep into the forest in search of game.

I walked out to greet them.

"Seen any deer?" Tim asked. "Hunting season is about to start."

"Quite a few. All does, no bucks, though."

"Know what this is?" he asked, holding up a clear plastic jar filled with white powder.

"No idea."

"It's deer cocaine," he said. "It's a blend of minerals that attracts deer. Don't mind if I sprinkle some back in the forest toward the bluff, do you?"

Fact was, I was fine with Tim and his family visiting the property. They were nice folks who had made a point of welcoming us to Morgan County.

"No, sprinkle away, and you're welcome to hunt back here, too, provided we're not in the cabin when you start shooting."

"Hey, I hear that you've got a pretty good path down to the creek. Want to show it to me?"

"Sure, let's get the kids and hike down."

As we descended the bluff, Tim mentioned that our path was much easier than the route he had been following down to the creek since he was a kid. At the bottom, I edged toward the creek and stepped down on a damp rock on the shoreline.

"Hey, girls, be careful, these rocks are . . ."

Before I could finish the sentence, the lug sole of my hiking boot glanced off the rock, and in an instant, I was airborne, hurtling headfirst toward the water and a jagged, upturned rock jutting above the surface. I raised my forearm to deflect the blow and somersaulted into the creek.

I had just enough time to yell "Shit!" before I plunged into the water.

The first sound I heard when I surfaced was Logan and Challen, in unison: "Ah, ah, ah! Daddy said a bad word." I could hear Tim laughing in the background.

My forearm had been scraped nearly down to the bone. The rock had raked across my back and torn my shirt. And the October water was freezing. But what concerned me more than my wounds or the risk of immersion hypothermia was my reputation. I could just imagine Tim at the table in the front of Williams market on some Saturday morning during hunting season, sharing the details of my tumble into the creek with the camouflaged multitude.

"You know that city fella who lives up on Walczak's place? He took a heck of a fall into the creek. Just tumbled right in. Yelled *shit* as he was falling. Felt bad for him, but it was kind of funny."

I feared that in Morgan County, as in the movie *Dances with Wolves,* the native population would bestow names on outsiders based on the observed conduct. Would I, henceforth, be known to the locals as "Falls-in-Clear-Creek"?

TWENTY-FOUR

A Haunting in Morgan County

*I saw a werewolf drinking a piña colada at Trader
Vic's. His hair was perfect.*
    —Warren Zevon, "Werewolves of London"

I stood on the deck, looking out over thirty children and parents—suburbanites right down to their Rockport boat shoes and perfectly manicured fingernails. I saw yuppie moms with dirt-smudged knees sitting on pine logs and meditating on quiet woods. I saw kids crouching among the trees, studying bugs and rocks. I saw my daughters hand in hand with their friends, sharing with them lore from the short history of Benton's Run, about swimming in the creek, about bounding toads, about curling in their sleeping bags in the loft.

I realized at that moment that building the cabin was the right thing to do and that it would become even more precious the more we shared it. The cabin had offered me a measure of peace and calm through a period of my life that should, by all rights, have been fraught with tension and dread, and it was having a similarly soothing effect on our guests. They might not have known it, but they were decompressing right before my eyes, a process I'd witnessed in so many visitors to Benton's Run.

It was October twenty-fourth, and we had staged a haunting in Morgan County in observance of Halloween. While the suburbs are *never* scary (eerie, perhaps in their manicured perfection) the cabin's environs—primarily acres and acres of dark woods populated by owls and howling coyotes—boasted considerable potential for playing on visitors' imaginations. We decided to throw the party the week before the official event, because the kids would likely have balked if attending our party meant missing trick-or-treating in their neighborhoods.

Russ-the-Gentle-Giant had shown up midafternoon on Friday to help me prepare. We had cleared brush, cut and stacked wood for the bonfire, taped cutouts of jack-o'-lanterns and black cats to windows, strung black and orange lights around door frames, hoisted a sound-activated witch into the trees around the fire pit, and made a trip into Wartburg to buy supplies.

We returned an hour later with soda (house brand at the Save-A-Lot grocery is Bubba Cola), inexpensive toys to give out to scavenger hunt winners, chocolate bars and marshmallows for S'Mores, serving bowls, salt-and-pepper shakers, a grill, and a large garbage can. I got a bargain on frozen meat patties—twenty for $3.99—and I thought it too good to be true. It was. I didn't realize the error until we got home and I read the ingredients. Listed first was water, second was cow hearts, third monosodium glutamate.

Each patty was cadaver gray and contained 100 percent RDA of saturated fat and enough sodium to bring on strokes in otherwise healthy people. I wanted to feed and entertain people—maybe even frighten them—not kill them. I decided to zip into Crossville the next morning and buy some 100 percent ground beef.

We stoked a campfire, and while I assembled my new grill, Russ drafted clues for the scavenger hunt. He would return the next day with his family and fifteen copies printed from his computer.

A sampling of his work:

There's no time to sit and groan;
Find a perfect pine cone!
In fact, find three
And let us see.

Autumn's here, with pumpkins and cider;
It's not too cold for bug or spider.

Find one each; you've got the knack—
Perhaps one's crawling on your back.

The forest is full of towering trees.
They wear their coats so they don't freeze.
Bring three different kinds of coats;
Be sure to name them in your notes.

Once we had completed our chores, just after midnight, we walked with Benton up to the field. The stars were brilliant, and Orion guided us along the last few hundred feet to the open meadow. As soon as we settled onto the ground, the heavens greeted us with shooting stars. We laid in the dewy grass for a long while. Beside me, I could see Benton's handsome profile silhouetted against the sky.

Soon, a pack of coyotes began to howl. I was a bit disappointed that they had been miscued and might have saved their performance for the following night. Their yowls were more impassioned than usual; they clearly were excited about something. Then we heard a cow unleash a powerful and seemingly defensive *"Moo!"* from a nearby farm. It occurred to me that the coyotes had probably taken a calf and its hapless mother was using the only weapon she had to drive them off.

Benton sat in the darkness, his ears peaked, the fur on his back erect, growling softly. Like Buck in *Call of the Wild,* he wanted more than anything to go run with the wild dogs. I was glad I had him on the leash.

"Hey, Dave, what's that," Russ said, pointing to the sky just above the horizon. "Is that a star or a planet?"

"I see it. It's moving erratically and it's changing color from blue to red. I think we're about to be abducted and anally probed by aliens," I said. "I *hate* it when that happens."

"I just hope they're gentle."

Though we both knew that we were viewing a planet whose light was being refracted by the atmosphere, we still enjoyed speculating on aliens hovering out there, waiting for the perfect moment to snatch us up and shuttle us up to the mother ship. The fact that our imaginations had been primed by a few beers didn't hurt.

"Eerie," I said. "I'd love to meet their leader, but I'd hate to miss the party."

"Maybe we should invite them."

"Perfect costumes."

The next day, by midafternoon, eight vehicles—most of them suburban SUVs that had rarely, if ever, been operated in four-wheel drive—wedged onto the tight gravel pad in front of the cabin. Sixteen kids ranging in age from just under two to fifteen scampered through the trees, and their parents settled on the deck or by the campfire sipping beers and getting acquainted.

Two of the guests—die-hard Tennessee Volunteer fans—spun the radio dial until they found a station broadcasting the game, and announcer John Ward's voice soon boomed out through the speakers. The Volunteers were on the way to winning the NCAA football championship, and fan loyalty in east Tennessee bordered on religious zeal.

Support for the Vols had fully penetrated the rural reaches of Morgan County, and on game days, orange banners appointed porches and decks, orange and white pompons flapped from car windows, and the little man who lives at the railroad crossing in Lancing and who tinkers endlessly with the scattering of auto parts and discarded appliances in his front yard observed Volunteer game days by sporting a bright orange Vols T-shirt. Several of the pre-Halloween revelers arrived clad in Volunteer orange.

As the guests emerged from their cars, they sized up the cabin and its setting and offered varied assessments.

"This place is a lot less rustic than I thought it would be," one guest told me as she scanned the interior. "We were expecting something pretty primitive. Where's the microwave; I want to heat up some dip."

I confessed that we slow-cooked things at the cabin.

"No microwave?" she said, incredulous. "How could anybody get along without a microwave?"

"Nice place, but I'd miss the mall," said one impeccably coifed and outfitted suburban mom. "If I lived out here, I'd go through shopping withdrawal."

One guest asked, "How in the world did you ever find this place?"

A mother of two young children asked, "Aren't you terrified out here after dark?"

Another guest, an avid hunter, said, "If I had a cabin like this, I'd *never* go back to the city."

I watched Logan and Challen, playing host to their friends, proudly describing the cabin's many charms. At one point, I saw Logan pointing to the cleared ground that once housed Toad Hall, and I was fairly certain she was explaining that her father had created a population of homeless amphibians.

Russ, who always welcomes an audience, settled into the role of chief camp counselor and began organizing the events.

The festivities started with pumpkin carving. Parents and kids soon knelt together under the hemlocks, scooping out gobs of pumpkin guts and tossing them into the woods where birds and other forest creatures would enjoy the bounty. By 4:30, jack-o'-lanterns ringed the fire pit, some boasting basic toothless grins and triangular eyes; others more elaborate creations featuring silhouettes of witches on broomsticks, spiders, and cats.

Russ then initiated the scavenger hunt and divided the kids into six teams. Towering above the crowd, topped by his trademark Australian bush hat, he explained the rules: Each team would have to return with each item in turn to gain the approval of the "ultimate authority" (Russ) before they could continue.

"Do I make myself perfectly clear?" he boomed.

"Yes!"

"Okay, *go!*"

The kids tore off, scattering through the woods, crawling on hands and knees, leaping up to grab leaves from trees.

Susan approached me, smiling.

"Dave, this is a *great* party," she said. "A bunch of people have asked me if we're going to make this an annual event."

"I think we should. If for no other reason than to pay back all the people who have invited us to their homes. We've been a little remiss in that regard."

Over the previous three years, we had entertained little, partly because our suburban house was in a constant state of remodeling, partly because our efforts to remain civil were eroding. All of the families at the party had hosted us at their houses on many occasions, and I was thankful to have the chance to return the favor by exploiting the somewhat neutral ground of the cabin.

A couple of hours into the party, just before we began preparing for dinner, Susan asked, "Where is your cutting board?"

I didn't even bother to suggest that *our* cutting board was in the cabinet to the right of the stove. For the time, it was sufficient that she was enjoying herself, even if her status seemed to be that of "guest" rather than "resident."

Through the evening, we orbited widely but our paths rarely intersected. When they did, I often found myself at a loss for what to say, feeling cursed that we had been reduced to swapping pleasantries when there were so many themes and topics burning with urgency. But a party wasn't exactly an appropriate venue for addressing them.

I couldn't shake the irony that I was struggling to make conversation with a person I had lived with for eighteen years. Meanwhile, I palavered effortlessly with other people, some of whom I had known for only a few months.

As I watched Susan, animated and laughing, interacting with friends, I recalled the night we had met, at another Halloween celebration, and the conversation that had completely absorbed us for seven hours. I remembered her energy, the sharpness in her eyes that penetrated right through me, and the incredible feeling of being awash in her pheromones.

Watching her from the far end of the deck, which might as well have been two hundred yards away, I wanted to ask, "What the hell happened to us?"

Instead, I contented myself by watching a gathering of people loosen up in the embrace of the forest. It gratified me to watch them, reluctant at first, rub themselves up against nature. Before we built the cabin, I had hoped it would become a place where people could shake off the stress of the city, relax with new friends, and have fun.

I had talked this through a few years earlier with my friend Elmer, back in Hot Springs, on that ten-day break from the trail. I had visited Hot Springs to speak to a gathering of Appalachian

Trail hikers who were passing through town. At the time, my plate was brimming with far too many gotta-dos, my blood pressure was spiking into the red zone, and I was about as edgy as I'd ever been.

After a few hours in Hot Springs, interacting with Elmer, the AT hikers, and the hippie servers at Elmer's inn—people so laid back they barely registered a pulse—I started to respond to the calm of the setting, and only then did I fully fathom just how stressed out I had been when I arrived.

It's ironic that as long as you stay anchored to a place charged with tension and as long as you surround yourself with type-A people, you can't fully grasp just how far gone you really are. You're just one stressed-out cow in the madding herd. It takes a trip to Hot Springs or Benton's Run to gain the necessary perspective.

"People show up in Hot Springs just ragged from all the stress in their lives," Elmer said. "But they don't realize it; they think they're coping. After they've spent a few days here, they start to relax, they recognize just how tense they really were, and when they leave, they swear they'll never let their stress load build up like that again. Few of them succeed, because they go home and return to the same stressful jobs and relationships."

I sensed that the same was true of our party guests, but I hoped that when they left, they'd recognize that stressed-out city life is one way, not the only way, to live and that a few hours spent in a cabin without a microwave can work a little magic.

The sun went down, the campfire blazed, and thirty people gathered on the pine seats in the amphitheater Russ and I had built a few weeks before. Russ donned his headlamp, grabbed several volumes of ghost stories, and settled into the role of sinister raconteur.

"And they never found her head!" he'd shout, and punctuate his delivery with a maniacal laugh, which would trigger the howling, sound-activated witch hanging in the trees.

It occurred to me as I listened to Russ organize events and read ghost tales that his affable personality and outgoing nature more than likely resulted from his height. When you're six-foot-eight, you can't very well blend into the background. During one of his visits to our home in the city, the girls ran and grabbed their friends to show them the "giant," as if he were a sideshow attraction. I suspect it happened often. Perhaps Russ had just determined to make the most of being the center of attention.

Soon, one by one, the kids started to share their own ghost stories from years of summer camps and Scouting trips. There were numerous variations on the theme of vengeful spirits intent on tormenting the living:

"And to this day, every time there's a storm, you can still hear Hangman Harry's dead body thumping against the side of the house. . . ."

"And just when they thought they were safe, blood started dripping down from the roof of the car. . . ."

"And the wolves still haunt these woods, feeding on little children. . . ."

Just before it was Logan's turn to regale the crowd with her ghost tale, she pulled me aside.

"Dad, I'm going to tell a ghost story about a guy who got all hacked up with a chain saw," she said. "Can you help?" She asked if I'd provide sound effects by yanking the starting cord on my saw at just the right moment.

I hid in the trees beyond the glow of the campfire. As she reached the climax of her story—"and they found his body chopped up into tiny little pieces by a chain saw!"—I yanked the cord. Logan was disappointed when everyone started laughing.

"I wanted them to be scared," she confessed later.

"They were; that was *nervous* laughter," I said. "They were frightened out of their wits."

"Really?"

"Sure. Bodies being hacked up by a chain saw is pretty creepy stuff. These people won't sleep for days."

"Cool."

V

WINTER

TWENTY-FIVE

Yule Lament

"I am the ghost of Christmas Past."
"Long past?" inquired Scrooge. . . .
"No. Your past."
—Charles Dickens, A *Christmas Carol*

As I coursed through the sporting-goods superstore search-ing for bicycles for the girls' Christmas presents, the store's Muzak system was cycling through the Christmas classics. Despite the music, I wasn't in a particularly festive mood. My marriage was disintegrating before my eyes, and my father had called me a few days earlier to tell me that his prostate cancer may have become active again. I kept trying to tell myself that neither condition was necessarily fatal, that both flagging marriages and diseased organs could be treated. But I wasn't convinced.

Six years earlier, when Dad's cancer was first diagnosed, he had opted for radiation rather than the more aggressive treatment—removal of his prostate gland—citing the possible side effects, including incontinence and impotence.

"The risk of impotence doesn't bother me that much," he said. "Your mother and I have had a good thirty-some years of great sex. But I just don't want to spend the rest of my life peeing into a diaper."

The radiation treatment had brought him six years of good health, but even Dad realized that it wasn't a cure and that the cancer might eventually return.

When he called me at work the week before Christmas, I

knew immediately that something was wrong. The tension in his voice gave him away.

"Dave, I've got some news, and I wanted you to hear it from me before you heard it from someone else," he said, and cut right to the chase. "My prostate cancer may have come back."

"Oh, Dad, I'm sorry," I said. I balked when I tried to offer reassuring words. "Are you sure?"

"Well, the result of my most recent PSA test is about double the previous reading, so something seems to be happening," he said.

"What are your options?"

"Well, surgery is out, and so is radiation; I already played that card," he said. "Next step is hormone therapy."

I cringed. Though the treatment sounded innocuous enough, I knew generally what it entailed. Testosterone tends to feed prostate tumors, so injections to neutralize the testosterone tend to shrink them. For the rest of his life, Dad would be perhaps a little too in touch with his feminine side, as the injections worked to slow the growth of his tumorous prostate. While a man's testicles are his closest allies in the mating game, maybe all those rabid feminists out there are right. Testosterone *is* a killer.

"How you doin' with all this, Dad?" I asked.

"Well, I may have to change my bra size," he joked.

We spoke for a few minutes and he explained that the next steps would be a bone scan and CAT scan, which would indicate whether the tumor was still confined to his prostate or had spread.

"I'm just going to take this one step at a time," he said.

I wished him luck and told him that I loved him.

"Don't worry," he said. "I haven't even begun to fight this thing yet."

Though I realized that Dad's cancer and my marriage were separate issues, there were some glaring—though admittedly hackneyed—metaphoric similarities. Dad's body was diseased; so was my marriage. To enable him to survive, Dad's doctors might have to engage in some aggressive treatment. Could Susan and I survive our diseased marriage, or would we have to resort to radical procedures and commence separate lives?

I didn't want to diminish my dad's hopes for survival or perform last rites on my marriage, but the combined misery of both began to work on me, and I experienced a moment of fear and self-loathing as I stood shoulder to shoulder with the cheery-faced holiday shoppers at the sporting-goods store. My dad may be dying, I thought, and here I am poised to fragment his family and become the first Brill in history to go through a divorce.

As the line in the sporting-goods store slowly nudged me closer to the cash register, I could feel my thigh muscles tighten. I wanted to run like hell, all the way to Morgan County and to the cabin.

My flight would have to wait. There were more Christmas presents to buy and obligations to fulfill at home before I could kindle a fire in the woodstove and collapse on the couch.

Though I was surrounded by other people at the store, I felt completely isolated and alone, and I realized that the haphazard belief system I had patched together over the years may have been adequate for good times, but it was woefully inadequate to buoy me through the twin crises I now faced. I had deferred nurturing my spiritual self during times of plenty, and now that my life was falling apart, I had no idea where to turn. I was, in the lexicon of the theologian, about to become a "foxhole Christian" but one, I hoped, whose devotion would endure after the shelling had stopped.

In the past, Christmas had always brought a bit of joy to my heart, owing more to the notion that I would enjoy a few days of sleeping late and overeating than to the "reason for the season." Truth was, Christmas in our home was primarily a secular holiday, where Santa, not Jesus, was the reigning figure.

My family's holiday orientation was more the result of Susan's and my spiritual neglect than an outright rejection of religious tenets, be they Christian or otherwise. As I'd halfheartedly pursued my own internal search for spiritual meaning, I realized that I'd failed to involve my children in my process or to invite them to engage in their own searches. In fact, the only advice I'd offered them was to look inside for the answers before they began to conduct an external search for God.

A few days earlier, Logan had reminded me, indirectly, of how remiss we had been in paving the girls' spiritual path.

She had been assigned the task of drafting a letter to a pen pal a week before Christmas break, and she was struggling with what to write. I sat down on the floor in her bedroom and helped her explore options for the letter's content.

"You know, you could ask your pen pal questions about how she's preparing for the holidays," I suggested.

"Yeah, that's a good idea," Logan said, gripping the pencil and beginning to write. Her tongue protruded from the side of her mouth as it always does when she's concentrating.

"Dear Sarah: Are you ready for Christmas?" she began, sculpting the large, rounded letters of a second grader.

I quickly pointed out that it might be a little presumptuous to assume that her pen pal would be celebrating Christmas.

"Christmas is a Christian holiday," I said. "It's in observance of the birth of Jesus Christ. You don't know for sure that your pen pal is a Christian."

"Dad, I'm sure she is," Logan answered with complete confidence. "She's an American."

I struggled not to laugh. Truth is, Logan was only echoing a popular assumption in this country, reinforced in churches that place the cross of Jesus and the American flag side-by-side in their sanctuaries. I see them as completely incongruous elements, the former representing spiritual awakening and salvation, the latter a symbol of secular laws and strictures that stave off anarchy, keep the schools open, protect us from outside aggression, and ensure that the interstate highway system doesn't collapse.

"Well not all Americans are Christians," I said. I pointed out that the girls' babysitter is Hindu and that Logan's friend Pauli is Jewish.

"You might want to ask your pen pal if she's ready for the *holiday* instead," I suggested.

"Oh, yeah," Logan said. The tongue reappeared as she began to write. Then after a few seconds, she stopped and her brow furrowed.

"Dad, what are we?" she asked.

The question threw me, largely because I didn't have an answer, at least not a simple one. I had spent the better part of my adult life trying to find a spiritual doctrine that didn't feel like dogma, one that liberated my soul rather than encumbered it. That was no simple task here in the Bible Belt, where being Christian is sometimes synonymous with intolerance and where faith is often predicated on fear and a perversion of Christ's message of love and acceptance.

I had recently passed a sign in front of a church in our area. The message was both terse and troubling: AVOID HELL, it admonished.

Before I made a leap of faith, I wanted to be sure that the ground under my feet was stable, a prospect that I knew would take time. But my own internal questioning was of little value to Logan, particularly if I failed to share it with her. I had been waiting until I had resolved the uncertainty in my heart before I involved her and Challen in my spiritual quest. That, I realized, marked a lapse in my conduct as a parent.

"Logan, we are what are called *seekers*," I said, "people who are searching for answers but haven't quite found them yet.

"This search is about the most important thing we will do in our lives, and it's also one of the most difficult. It's something we all need to think about and work on," I continued.

Someday soon, I'd help her begin her own search, but now wasn't the time. It was past her 8:30 bedtime, her homework wasn't finished, and Christmas was nearly upon us.

Over the next several days, as I made my way through one checkout line after another, the refrain " 'Tis the season to be jolly" began to sound more like a legally enforceable mandate than a description of seasonal cheer.

As I studied the faces of the other last-minute shoppers, their arms and shopping carts brimming with Rollerblades, computer games, soccer balls, ski suits, and golf clubs, I imagined an entire community of traditional families unfettered by marital conflict in homes where the major points of contention involved whether to put the Christmas tree lights on flash or have them shine steadily.

I imagined fathers and mothers smiling across the room at one another as their children scribbled the last few entries on their Christmas lists, knowing that they had covered all the bases and that Brian would get his hockey skates and little Lisa would find the Furby she wanted nestled under the tree come Christmas morning. I imagined families gathered in church for the midnight candlelight service, singing Christmas hymns and experiencing hearts full of love rather than resentment.

I remembered Christmases at home as a kid. Dad would make a batch of eggnog, Mom would bake cookies, and my brother, Steve, and I would lie on our twin beds and listen to a recording of Charles Dickens's *A Christmas Carol*. We always cried together at the end, when Tiny Tim recited his now-immortal line, "God bless us every one!"

But now, the cynic in me kicked in. I pictured housewives in our affluent neighborhood sobbing inconsolably over Christmas cookies left a moment too long in the oven or lamenting their unsuccessful sorties to find wished-for toys for their children. I imagined fathers in the grips of despair over not being able to take their families to Aspen for a ski vacation over the holidays. And suddenly I felt very, very sorry for myself and my family. We had real problems, ones that even Santa couldn't fix. In fact, we had enlisted the expert assistance of some of the best marital counselors in Knoxville, but none helped much.

This year, as Christmas approached, the friction between us seemed to escalate, though no one, except for a few close friends, had any grasp of the trouble we were in. While we'd succeeded in buffaloing the outside world, we had failed miserably at our attempts to insulate our children from our problems.

I could only wince when Challen burst into tears a few nights before Christmas when Susan and I quibbled over whether or not to disconnect the smoke detector, which had been activated when a forgotten loaf of bread immolated in the oven.

Challen had been in her room reading, a pastime that I'd come to realize served as her escape from a traumatic home life. She had her face buried in her pillow when I entered her room.

"You and Mommy hate each other!" she sobbed into the pillow. "You hate each other! You know you do!"

At that moment, I grasped that our charade was over and that Susan and I had been busted. And as I stammered for a suitable response, one that might have been tinged with denial and grounded in a complete lie, I found myself for the first time uttering the truth to Challen.

"Sweetie," I said, rubbing her back, "Mom and I are really struggling, and I'm afraid we don't love each other very much right now, but I don't think we hate each other."

"Yes, you do!" she said. "You fight all the time."

"You're right, we do," I said. "And I dislike it as much as you do."

"I'm afraid you're going to get divorced," she said. "Please, please don't get divorced."

I caught myself before I offered her the flimsy reassurance I had proffered in the past, and I leveled with her.

"Challen, the truth is we might get divorced," I said. "I really hope that doesn't happen, but it might."

"Oh, Daddy," she cried, and I knew her secure little world was being rocked to its foundation.

"Challen," I continued, "whatever happens between Mommy and me, you need to remember something: You and Logan have always been, and will always be, the very center of my universe. That will never change. Can you remember that?"

"Yeah, but I don't want you to get divorced," she said, now sitting up and hugging me.

I waited for the twisting in my gut that always arrived when I contemplated divorce, even if the thought lingered for only a second. But it never came. After the past few weeks, weeks filled with icy stares and a brutal aloofness between Susan and me, I had begun to fantasize about the relief that divorce might bring.

"Challen, I promise you everything will be okay," I said. "It may not work out exactly the way we want it to, but it will be okay. Sometimes we just have to trust God to sort things out. Good night, sweetie."

"Good night, Daddy," she said. "I love you."

"I love you, too, kid. Try to get some sleep."

TWENTY-SIX

The Ice Storm Cometh

The immortals will send you to the Elysian plain at the ends of the earth, where fairhaired Rhadamanthys is. There life is supremely easy for men. No snow is there, nor ever heavy winter storm, nor rain, and Ocean is ever sending gusts of the clear-blowing west wind to bring coolness to men.
                              —Homer, *The Odyssey*

December twenty-second marked my last day at work before a three-week break, and I was hoping to spend most of my downtime at the cabin. Susan seemed to welcome my decision. A couple of days before, she had told me that she needed some time apart, and she didn't protest when I shared my holiday plans with her.

I would return to Knoxville on Christmas Eve, spend Christmas day there, then head back to Morgan County. Susan and the girls would arrive at the cabin on New Year's Eve for our annual party and spend New Year's Day before returning to the city. Though I didn't realize it at the time, my holiday was going to include some difficulties beyond separation from my family, and I was about to experience mountain living at its most primitive.

After I left work, I loaded a few changes of clothes into the car, and Benton and I headed for the woods. Work had been particularly stressful in the days before the break. I had rushed to get two publications out before the holiday, my dad had called me with the news about his cancer, and Susan, plagued by pre-holiday stress, had seemed more unhappy with me than usual. I needed space and wanted to put some distance between the two of us, and I knew the cabin would provide both.

The cabin had been vacant for two weeks, and when I arrived, the air temperature inside hovered at thirty-five. It would take an hour or more for the woodstove to heat the space, I realized, as I watched my breath trail away in white mist. As soon as I had crossed the threshold, I realized I was getting sick. The stomach bug that had been making the rounds among Challen's and Logan's friends had established a colony in my gut, and after I had turned on the well pump, I raced to the bathroom.

I spent the rest of the evening alternating between shivering under a blanket on the futon and getting sick in the bathroom, but the isolation of the cabin and the warmth of the woodstove somehow felt soothing.

I spent the next day lying on the couch reading by the stove and watching freezing rain fall outside. Though I hadn't heard a weather report, I suspected that Morgan County was about to be blasted by an ice storm. Wednesday evening, Susan called to alert me of the approaching front and urged me to make for home.

"You don't want to be stuck in the cabin for Christmas," she said. The truth was, though I didn't want to disappoint my kids by being absent on the most important holiday of the year, being in the same living space with Susan was becoming more and more strained. No matter what I said or did, it seemed, I always managed to rankle her. The cabin was isolated, and at times lonely, but it was always calming.

Besides, my stomach was still turning cartwheels, and I was weak and shaky. And if a storm was going to damage the cabin, I wanted to be present to witness the carnage firsthand. But I also realized that if the storm hit, I'd be stuck in place for God knows how long before I could make my way home. I'd lived in the South long enough to take winter storms seriously.

Southerners are often maligned because of their lack of finesse when it comes to handling winter weather, but part of the reputation is undeserved. Granted, threat of winter weather inclines Southerners toward panic, and you'd be hard-pressed to find a single loaf of bread or a pint of milk at local grocery stores in the hours following a winter weather advisory, but the nature of winter storms can be particularly menacing in the South.

Winter typically blankets Northern towns with soft snow that becomes hardpack on the highways and provides a navigable base. The South gets slammed by ice storms that turn twisting mountain roads into deadly toboggan runs and cause top-heavy, shallow-rooted pine trees to topple like fifty-foot-tall toothpicks.

The cabin, nestled among towering Virginia pines, was particularly vulnerable, I realized, as were the power lines, which followed a twelve-foot-wide cut through the forest from the field to circuit box on the end of the cabin.

As I settled into bed on Wednesday night, the rain began to form icicles where it dripped from the eaves. At 10 P.M. the space heater by the bed stopped oscillating, and I realized that I had lost power—a common occurrence in rural counties. I drifted back to sleep.

As I slept, I experienced a recurrent dream that always corresponds to periods of stress in my life. In the dream, I'm on the snowy flanks of Mount Rainier.

I'm fit and strong and ready to push for the summit, but I'm with a party of poorly prepared and out-of-shape people who have forgotten critical gear items. They seem unfocused and helpless. I keep peering ahead toward the summit, knowing I'm strong enough to reach it, but I feel responsible for the others and can't bring myself to leave them behind.

I delve into my own pack and start handing them articles of clothing, in the process making myself vulnerable to the harsh mountain weather. In the dream, I realize that the others on my climbing team are ruining my chances for success, but I'm tethered to them by a rope—I can't reach the top unless they do, too. In the dream, our summit bid always fails.

Though I'm not a Jungian scholar, I suspected that my subconscious had bundled my anxieties regarding my marriage into a dream. I was emotionally and financially tethered to Susan. Where she went, I went. Traveling solo meant success, but it also forced me to sever connections and leave people behind.

It occurred to me that the mountain represented a perfect metaphor. Human passion and drive compel us to scramble for the top and disentangle ourselves from painful connections, but human failings often cause us to cling to destructive relationships and destine us to fail in our attempts to find success and happiness. Far too often, we languish on the lower flanks of the mountain and can only imagine what it might feel like to be on top.

In the most recent version of the dream, I was pleading with my climbing partners to focus their energy and prepare to set out for the summit, but they were lost and confused, and in their confusion they ignored me. I was trying to unclip myself from the rope and head out alone, when a loud crash shook the cabin and wrenched me back into the wakeful world. Benton sprang, barking, from his mat in front of the woodstove, and I staggered to my feet and looked at my watch. It was 3 A.M.

In my groggy state, all I could imagine was that a toppling pine had creased the metal roof. I felt my way through the darkened greatroom and found a headlamp in a drawer in the kitchen. I opened the front door and glimpsed an ice-shrouded world—stark and beautiful—shimmering in the headlamp beam. The roof was clear, but a fifty-foot pine had fallen six inches from the back of my Jeep, which I, in error, surmised had accounted for the crash.

The pines around the cabin were bowed in a posture of supplication, with the tufts of their upper branches drooping under the weight of the ice. From beyond the Jeep, I heard the slow splintering of wood and a showering of ice crystals, and I knew that another pine was meeting its fate off in the darkened woods.

I was cold and didn't see much use in exploring further; I could wait until dawn to assess the damage. So I crawled back into bed and slept fitfully, anticipating another crash. I rose just after daybreak and peered out the bedroom window. As I did, I solved the mystery of the predawn commotion. About seventy-five yards distant, the root ball of a massive pine pointed toward the cabin. The tree had popped its roots and fallen across the power lines, pulling over the power pole and tugging the wires—and part of the framing—out of the side of the cabin. The electric meter lay on the ground, and cold air blew into the bedroom through a hole that had been occupied by the plastic conduit that led the wires into the circuit box.

Two now-bare wires lay on the ground, and I hoped that somewhere up the line, someone had had the wisdom to cut off the power. I could only imagine Benton running to investigate the damage and having 220 volts surge up through his wet nose as he pressed it to the ground. As it turned out, I had little to worry about. The whole county was without power, and many of its residents shared my dilemma of a yard full of toppled trees.

It was Christmas Eve, and I was expected back home in the city, provided I could negotiate the gravel road to the highway. I packed my gear, topped off the fuel tank on my chain saw, locked up the cabin, and shifted the Jeep into four-wheel drive. It took me nearly an hour to cut my way through the tangle of downed pine trees out to the main road. As I made my passage out, I noticed that two pines rested on the Reeds' cabin, and a single pine had fallen across Jimbuddy's roof, barely sparing his power lines and chimney. It took me another two hours to navigate the icy roads home.

When I arrived home, the girls ran to embrace me. Susan offered me a cold greeting and a perfunctory inquiry about the cabin. I spent most of the afternoon occupying myself in the garage, adjusting the gears and brakes on the new bikes I had purchased for the girls. I had also bought a mountain bike for Susan—hoping, foolishly, that a handsome and useful gift would incline her to give our relationship another chance—and had stowed it in the shed in the backyard.

For the first time, the house I had lived in for eight years felt like someone else's home. The cycle of waking and sleeping and eating, I realized, would continue in my absence, and the house would become more and more foreign to me, until one day I would enter a house that no longer contained the artifacts of my life, though it would always hold my memories. Memories of two-year-old Challen stacking blocks on the living room carpet while Susan breast-fed newborn Logan on the couch nearby. Of the girls swooshing past each other on the swing set and calling to me to watch as they leaped off and landed squarely on their feet. Of warm spring evenings on the front porch, strumming my guitar as I watched the sun set. Of days spent by Dad's side, tearing down old walls, erecting new ones, laying hardwood floors, installing bay windows, building a deck, and transforming a shabby ranch-style house into a comfortable home. Of early days in the house when Susan and I still treated each other kindly and held each other close in bed at night.

The sensation of entering a house that no longer felt like my home reminded me of the feeling I had experienced when I returned from college to my parent's house for summer breaks. The same furniture occupied the same space in the same rooms, the same paintings hung in the same places on the walls, but I entered the house as a stranger.

Through the evening, we nibbled smoked cheese and crackers, Susan and I split a bottle of chardonnay, and we watched *It's a Wonderful Life* on TV.

Just before bedtime, Logan fell into a panic, when she realized that she hadn't made a list for Santa.

"Santa has no idea what I want for Christmas!" she shouted. *"I forgot to send my list!"*

"Logan, it may be a little late for that," I said. "Santa's already on his way. But he probably already knows what you want."

"I don't want to take any chances," she said, disappearing into her room. She emerged a few minutes later clutching a hastily scrawled list. She handed it to me, and I was relieved to see that we had covered all the bases: *Nancy Drew* books, Celine Dion CDs, and a new bike.

"Logan, how are you going to get this to Santa?" I asked.

"I was thinking we could fax it to him," she said with complete conviction. "But I don't know his fax number."

"Kid, don't sweat it," I said. "Santa can read minds. He knows what you want. Trust me on this one."

I could tell that she wasn't thoroughly convinced, but she dutifully helped Challen prepare the plate of cookies and glass of milk to sustain Santa through his long winter's night. The girls hit the sheets by 9 P.M., and Susan went to bed at 11 P.M., after we had placed the girls' gifts under the tree and penned a note from Santa, thanking them for the milk and cookies.

I felt restless and sad, and after I wheeled Susan's new bike into the family room, I switched on the TV. My channel surfing led me to a live broadcast of a Church of Christ midnight service set somewhere in New England. In his sermon, the minister talked of Christ's gift of grace. He talked of inner peace and forgiveness, and I found myself wanting both very badly. By the end of the service, as the choir sang "O Holy Night"—my Grandma Brill's favorite carol—tears streamed down my face. I felt utterly lost and empty and frightened.

I reflected on the core message of the life of Jesus, and of all the secular Christmas stories, too, including *It's a Wonderful Life, A Christmas Carol, How the Grinch Stole Christmas,* and realized they were all predicated on the hope for redemption and the power of love.

I switched off the TV, and before I started back toward the bedroom, I knelt and prayed. It was the first time in my life I was driven to my knees by fear and desperation. My head was a jumble of regrets and hopes and fears, and there were many specific things I hoped God would do for me—not least of which was to incline Susan to return to our relationship—but I articulated the one and only prayer I've ever uttered.

"God, guide me," I whispered. "*Please,* guide me."

I've always thought it presumptuous to ask God for specific favors—healing sick people, providing new jobs, granting wished-for material possessions, repairing damaged marriages. If God truly has a plan for the world and all of its creatures—and I believe that he does—he's way ahead of us in terms of anticipating our needs. Sort of like Santa knowing in advance what Logan wanted for Christmas. But on a much higher plain, in asking for guidance, I deferred to God's wisdom and trusted him to handle the particulars. It all came down to trust and faith. There was doubt in my mind as I prayed: Perhaps God and Santa were both characters of myth, I thought, and I'm totally on my own to navigate through the crisis.

I rose from my knees, and waited for the feeling of peace the minister had promised to settle over me, but I still felt ragged and sad. I realized that the path leading from where I now stood to whatever lay in my future was going to be a difficult one. I tried very hard to believe that grace and peace lay at the end of my journey, if not somewhere along the way.

*   *   *

The next morning, the girls sprang from bed at 7 A.M., and hovered at our door, disinclined to wake Susan and me but also reluctant to venture into the family room and risk encountering Santa as he doled out their presents. I told the girls to wait in our bedroom until I had downed a cup of coffee and grabbed the camera, then I gave them the go-ahead.

I remembered from my childhood the magical transformation between Christmas Eve and Christmas morning, from an empty floor to one brimming with gifts, and I knew that as they entered the family room and beheld all the presents, the girls were believing in Santa with all their hearts.

We spent the morning playing board games and scanning new books and set out for a short bike ride just after noon. The girls struggled with cold fingers and highly complicated bikes that had grip brakes and twenty-one gears—far more complex than their single-speed models that were so small for them that their knees banged their chests as they pedaled. Logan was particularly unnerved when I explained why she should always hit her back brake first.

"If you're moving fast and you grip the front brake first—the left one—you'll wind up doing a somersault over the handlebars," I explained, feeling a little like J.J., Mr. Health-and-Safety Man. "Always brake with your right hand first."

"Like this?" Logan asked, crimping the left brake lever.

"No, Logan, your *other* right hand," said Challen.

"Oh, yeah," Logan said.

Through the afternoon, the girls sorted through their toys and headed out with Susan to visit friends in the early evening. I wasn't in the mood to be around cheerful people and stayed home and languished on the couch. While Susan and the girls were out, I watched the remake of *The Parent Trap* for the second time. I was certain that the girls had watched the movie with Susan and me in mind, believing that, despite our differences, we'd wind up staying together in the end. Dangerous expectations, I thought.

The next morning, I said good-bye to the girls and headed out to Morgan County with Tom Smith, a.k.a. "Mister Build It, Mis-

ter Fix It," a general handyman who had undertaken a few remodeling jobs for us in the past. Tom had agreed to repair the
damage to the circuit box and get us ready to be hooked into
the power grid after Plateau Electric Cooperative had cleared the
trees from the wires on the main highway and started working
the back roads.

When we arrived at the cabin, Tom assessed the damage.
"Based on your description, I was expecting much worse," he
said. "We can fix this today if we can find the right parts."

We made a trip to the hardware store and ran into our
builder, Joe Sexton, who was helping the store manage the crush
of customers trying to recover from the storm damage. Joe and
Tom talked in contractor-speak—which was indecipherable to
me—in describing the damaged items from the circuit box, and
we left in fifteen minutes with thirty-eight dollars in parts.

Back at the cabin, Tom and I began making repairs, and Jimbuddy, who had just arrived from L.A. via the Nashville airport,
pulled up in a rented blue pickup truck. He was in town for the
week and hadn't anticipated being without power—which meant
no running water, heat, or lights. Jim, a big-city boy who loves
his creature comforts, was clearly rattled.

"My cabin is cold," he said. "I don't have any wood for a fire
in the stove, and I really need a shower."

"Aside from that, are you doing okay?"

"I guess, but I didn't exactly expect to spend my week of vacation living like Daniel Boone."

"Hey, this is rural living at its finest and great preparation for
Y2K."

"Did I mention that my cabin is cold?"

I pictured ten acres of forest surrounding Jim's cabin, and
found it hard to believe that he couldn't lay his hands on some
wood. But then I realized that stoking woodstoves and harvest-
ing oaks and maples while avoiding pine—which coats
stovepipes with creosote and causes chimney fires—are acquired
skills that a vice-president for CBS in Los Angeles doesn't necessarily cultivate on the job.

"Tell you what, Jim," I said. "After Tom and I finish making
repairs, we'll head into Knoxville and stop by my house. I need

to pick up a few things for the next few days, and you can take a shower."

Suddenly, Jim's disposition brightened.

We traveled into Knoxville, picked up some groceries, and Jim got his hot shower. We returned after dark to our cabins. Inside Jim's woodstove I spotted a six-inch-thick pine log laying on three or four pieces of kindling the size of my pinkie and realized that he was in for a cold night. Before I left, I kindled a fire for him.

I entered my cabin, lit two oil lamps, built a fire, and basked in primitive solitude. The phone line had been tugged out of the side of the house along with the power lines, and I didn't own a cellular phone. Until the power company reconnected me to the grid—and I had no idea how long that would take—I was living a pioneer life in a cabin in the woods, reading by lamplight and warming bean soup on the woodstove. My spin on the whole situation was the opposite of Jim's. I was sublimely happy; Jim was miserable. Though his builder had removed the tree from his roof, he still had no water or power. The next day, he opted to head into Knoxville and stay at the Hilton.

The following three days were blissful. I was alone with my dog, my woodstove, and a chest-high stack of split oak logs. My acoustic guitar provided music. I had no obligations and had no contact with the outside world. I had no notion of the events that were shaping local and world news—I assumed that Clinton and Sadam were competing for headlines—and I really didn't care. If it didn't directly affect my life, it was of no importance to me.

I had experienced a similar lack of interest in news and politics while I was on the Appalachian Trail. During our days in the woods between supply stops, we had no access to news, and when we arrived in town, we typically walked past newspaper stands without even scanning the headlines. We had left the world behind and had little interest in anything that didn't affect us directly.

During the summer of 1979, for instance, the big news was the oil embargo and skyrocketing gasoline prices. We had heard about gas rationing and the occasional act of violence that resulted when someone butted in line at the pump, but to us, the embargo meant little more than that it cost eight cents rather than five to fill the fuel bottles for our camp stoves.

Now, during my days of isolation at the cabin, I read Thoreau and Whitman, walked through silent woods with Benton, whittled a walking stick, waterproofed my boots, and wrote in my journal. I ate cold beans out of a can and drank beer left to chill on the porch. I heated tea on the woodstove, and I slept snug in a cabin rendered primitive and reclaimed by the forces of nature.

On Tuesday, after Jim had returned from Knoxville, he called the power company on his cell phone to remind them that we were still without electricity.

"Oh, we forgot about you," said the woman on the other end. "We'll send someone out right away."

The boom truck showed up an hour later, and by early afternoon, the space heater in the cabin's bedroom again began oscillating. If I was going to be reconnected to the world, I figured I might as well complete the connection by repairing the phone line. I grabbed a pair of pliers and a screwdriver, sorted through a tangle of colored wires dangling from the severed cord, and somehow managed to produce a dial tone. The phone rang a few minutes later—jarring me from my reverie— and I realized that my primitive interlude was over: I was once again linked to the power grid and hardwired to the civilized world.

I'll confess, I enjoyed a hot shower—my first in several days— but I knew I'd miss the simplicity of a Spartan life in the forest. Though I realized that I could re-create the conditions brought on by the storm by turning off the lights and inactivating the well pump and water heater, it just wouldn't be the same. Modern conveniences are aptly named, and it takes a powerful yen for simplicity to turn away from them for good.

My friend Randall, who lived in that primitive cabin outside Hot Springs, North Carolina, had chosen such a life. He had no power, no inside plumbing, and no running water except for the spring water he piped down from the mountainside and let tumble into a wooden barrel on his front porch. I'd often wondered if, on the coldest winter nights or in the depths of loneliness, Randall would have reached for a wall switch, if he could have, and flooded his house with heat and light and sound. I liked to think that he wouldn't. He knew better than I how distracting modern conveniences were and how sublime a life of utter simplicity can be. Perhaps, someday, I would, too.

TWENTY-SEVEN

Auld Lang Syne Alfresco

*The beginnings and endings of all human under-
takings are untidy, the building of a house, the
writing of a novel, the demolition of a bridge, and,
eminently, the finish of a voyage.*
      —John Galsworthy, *Over the River*

For months, I had looked forward to spending New Year's
Eve at the cabin, in part because it represented a perfect
place to host a party. All guests would be overnighters, meaning
that should anyone overindulge—a reasonable risk with some of
my friends—the most perilous journey would lead from the outside fire pit, up the porch stairs, into the cabin, and onto the
floor by the woodstove.

No one would have to spend the evening tabulating fluid
ounces of booze and calculating elapsed time in an effort to
gauge sobriety. Driving under the influence wouldn't be an issue,
though I did have concerns that someone with impaired judgment would try to stagger down to the creek for a postmidnight
dip in forty-degree water. I hadn't anticipated that the culprit
might be me.

But more important, the cabin provided a way for our family
to continue a long-standing tradition of camping out on New
Year's Eve with the added luxury of heated indoor space, should
anyone decide not to contend with outdoor temperatures that
threatened to plunge into the teens.

In the past, in the waning days of each year while most of our
friends were cursing winter and languishing indoors beside the fire,
you'd find the Brill family compiling a grocery list, waterproofing

hiking boots, fueling up camp stove and lantern, and hunting for the lost mates to gloves and mittens. It was all part of the preparation ritual that preceded our annual New Year's Eve camping trip. We established the tradition in 1992, when Logan was a couple of months shy of two and Challen was about to turn four.

It started as an impulse a few days after Christmas. For months, Susan and I had discussed the right time to introduce our daughters to camping—a favored pastime we had put on hold after their arrivals—but the prospect seemed a bit daunting for two reasons. First, neither of us was completely confident of our ability to respond to the girls' needs away from the comforts of home. And second, though our basement boasted enough gear to stock a small outdoor shop, we didn't really have suitable equipment for family camping. Instead, we were equipped for Spartan hiking excursions that required us to pack light and forgo weighty luxury items in favor of the bare essentials: shelter, food, and clothing.

We eventually quelled the former concern by determining we could change Logan's diaper even with numb fingers and that camping beside our car gave us an easy avenue of escape should things turn ugly. I quickly—and unilaterally—resolved our concerns about gear.

With a few slack days between Christmas and New Year's Eve and some holiday money jangling in my pocket, I visited a local camping store. Just to look, mind you. I left a half hour later with a huge purple dome tent we later dubbed the Taj MaBrill, a Coleman two-burner stove, and four camp stools. Within an hour, I had erected the new tent in our living room. The girls were soon ensconced inside, happily playing with their dolls and refusing to budge.

"Hey, how would you guys like to sleep in this tent on New Year's Eve . . . out in the woods?" I asked, hoping to capitalize on the energy of the moment.

The girls responded with shrieks of delight; Susan's response was a bit more guarded. After some persuading, she bought into the idea, on two conditions: I would share the diapering chores, and if anyone complained of being too cold, we'd break camp immediately and make for home.

Over the next couple of days we communicated our plans to friends and relatives and encountered a welter of reactions, most of them disapproving. My parents, only half joking, accused us of child endangerment, fearing that, at worst, the girls would lose fingers and toes to frostbite or, at best, they'd have such a miserably cold time they'd never want to venture outdoors again.

That was seven years ago, and I'm happy to report that both girls are still possessed of all their digits and can't imagine spending New Year's Eve anywhere but in the woods. Though the girls and I continued to cherish our New Year's Eves alfresco, Susan began to lose her enthusiasm for the outdoor ritual the year the daytime high on December thirty-first peaked at thirty-two degrees and plunged through the evening to a low in the teens. Among the four of us, she possessed the least body fat, and she endured a sleepless night curled in a fetal position, while the girls and I slumbered peacefully in our sleeping bags in the Taj MaBrill.

"Next year, why don't we rent a cabin somewhere?" Susan had asked as she emerged from the tent. "Freezing my fingers and toes isn't fun for me."

"But it's a tradition," I protested. "It's a source of pride for the girls, something they can brag about to their friends. And it's just one night a year."

In an effort to keep Susan within her comfort zone without scuttling the tradition outright, I bought her a down sleeping bag rated to 10 below zero. The measure kept her cozy while she slept, but the waking hours still posed a problem the next year when temperatures again dipped below freezing. Susan kept the engine idling in the minivan and retreated to it frequently to warm her fingers.

This year, by default, Susan got her wish, and our new cabin provided for her need for warmth, and the ten acres of woods surrounding it allowed the more hearty revelers to sleep in the great outdoors. Though frostbite was no longer an issue for Susan, our relationship was chilling in the deep freeze, and through the evening, despite our efforts to remain civil, our guests caught glimpses of the full-blown tension between us.

I had been writing at the cabin since the day after Christmas, and Susan and the girls arrived midafternoon on December thirty-first. Over the few days I had been alone there, the space had begun to feel like home—I was sublimely happy even through several days without power and water following the ice storm—and I realized that I was beginning to make the physical transition that would accompany the emotional shift I'd face if, or more like *when*, I moved out of our house in the city for good.

Before the van had come to a complete stop in the driveway, the girls emerged from the sliding door and ran to hug me. Logan clung to my waist for a few seconds before sprinting off to scope out the campfire. Challen refused to let go and buried her face in my chest.

"Daddy, I missed you so much," she said. There was desperation in her tone that I hadn't heard before. "Why weren't you at home with us?"

You better get used to this, Challen, I thought, *'cause things between your mom and me aren't getting any better, and these may be the living arrangements you and I both have to accept.*

But I didn't say that. Instead, I explained to her that, as a writer, I sometimes have to go away to work.

"Some dads travel with their jobs," I explained. "Writers have to go away, too, sometimes, to a place where it's quiet, where they can concentrate."

I held her close, and she peered up at me. "I love you so much, Daddy," she said. "And I miss you when you're gone."

She and I were talking around the truth, and I suspect that we both knew it. Her parents were drifting further and further apart, her world was being torn asunder, and there was nothing she could do to fight the emotional inertia that was nudging us toward a very sad finale.

I knew that both my kids would be hurt deeply if Susan and I divorced, but Logan seemed to possess Susan's emotional toughness. Like Susan, she was quick to anger and readily gave vent to frustration when things didn't go her way, but she rarely seemed knocked off balance by the emotional buffeting that reduced Challen to tears.

In fact, Logan's day care teachers had nicknamed her "Logan

the Assertive" several weeks after she had entered their nursery. I knew that Logan's temperament would see her through a lifetime of challenges, but I tried to keep in mind that a calm exterior often hides churning insides.

Challen emerged into the world a sensitive vulnerable creature who wanted more than anything else to make people happy—a character flaw I had spent years battling in myself. She berated herself over her occasional angry outbursts and frequently revealed an ego as fragile as an eggshell. Though I've wished she had been imbued with some of Logan's and Susan's chutzpah, most people find Challen's easygoing nature and willingness to let others lead endearing traits.

My absence over the days prior to New Year's had been particularly hard on Challen, and once we were reunited at the cabin, she didn't let me out of her sight and gripped my hand whenever it hung idle at my side. She clearly needed me in her life, a notion that both comforted and disturbed me. It comforted me because I knew that our relationship would endure the end of the marriage and we would always enjoy an unshakable bond, but it troubled me because I realized that there was nothing I could do to protect her from the hurt that was to come—a hurt I would be partially responsible for.

I drifted through the evening making sure the chili pot stayed hot on the camp stove and that our guests had full mugs of whatever they were drinking. Unlike years past when our New Year's Eve party boasted several other families, this year's revelers primarily represented my friends. Susan had agreed to attend the party but had opted not to invite anyone.

Kit and Candy had driven up from south Florida to join us. The rest of the partyers—including Sam, J.J., and Ed, a geographer and colleague from the university—were regulars at Wednesday Night Prayer Meetings at the Knoxville pub.

A couple of weeks before the New Year's Eve party, Sam had returned from a month in Japan, during which he snacked on deep-fried crickets and began to assimilate some Japanese idioms and catchphrases. Through the evening, every time I called his name, he responded with a sharp "Hi!"—the Japanese equivalent to "I'm here!"—and I always expected to see him crouched in a defensive jujitsu stance. We henceforth called him by his Japanese moniker, Sam-san.

Sam spent the better part of the evening pushing Challen and Logan on the new rope swing Kit and I had rigged up a couple of hours before the other guests arrived. Though Sam had experienced more than his share of dead-end relationships with adult women, by the end of the evening, my two girls were convinced he had hung the full moon that illuminated the forest around the cabin. After she had tired of the rope swing, Logan laid her head in Sam's lap and gazed contentedly at the campfire.

Ed had arrived with J.J., who had left his girlfriend, Susan, back home in Oak Ridge. His plan was to spend a couple of hours at the cabin before returning to uncork a bottle of champagne with Susan at midnight. At 10 P.M. J.J. went out to warm up his car, but by 10:15 had succumbed to the lure of the campfire and Kit's offer of a Honduran cigar. He called Susan and returned to the fire ring a few minutes later.

"You have room for two more overnight guests?" he asked, cracking open a beer.

"Hey, are you kidding?" I said. "I'm the proud owner of a ten-acre campsite."

After the overnight guest list had been finalized, Susan pulled me aside and asked, "Where are all these people sleeping?"

"Well, I thought Ed could sleep on the futon with you," I joked. "He's pretty drunk, so I don't think he'll give you much trouble."

She wasn't amused. "No, really, where are all these people going to sleep?"

"Well, Candy will sleep on the fold-out couch, and the rest of us are going to sleep outside. You've got dibs on the futon," I said. "And I'm pretty sure Logan is going to want to sleep inside with you."

Challen's roost for the night was still being negotiated. Earlier in the evening, she asked me if I was going to sleep outside.

"Kid, if this is New Year's Eve, you can bet I'm sleeping outside," I said.

"Daddy, I want to sleep in the tent with you," she said.

"I wouldn't have it any other way," I said. "You want to help me set up the tent?"

"Sure," she said. "Are we going to sleep in the Taj MaBrill or the little green tent?"

"Big tents get mighty cold in the winter," I said. "Let's sleep in the green tent; it's smaller and will keep us warmer. We'll get Benton to sleep with us, and he'll throw off some added heat."

We walked a few yards from the fire pit and started erecting the tent while the rest of the revelers clustered around the fire.

Soon, Susan emerged from the cabin. "Dave, Challen is *not* sleeping out here," she said. "It's freezing, and this morning she said she felt sick. She slept over at Faith's house last night and didn't get to sleep until after midnight."

I noticed that conversation around the fire had stopped. My friends knew that Susan and I were struggling, and our exchange was too tempting to tune out.

"Susan, this means a lot to her," I pleaded. "And she'll be snug in the down sleeping bag. She'll be fine. I promise."

"No, she won't be fine," Susan said. "She's going to get sick."

"She'll be fine," I repeated. "If she gets cold, I'll have her inside in a heartbeat."

"Mommy, I want to sleep outside with Dad," Challen said. "Please?"

Susan turned and walked back inside.

After the tent was up and we had rolled out mats and sleeping bags inside, I returned to the fire, and Challen went back inside to get her sleeping companion, a stuffed cat.

"Guys, I'm sorry you had to hear that," I said.

"She's just being a mother," J.J. said. "It's a mother's job to overprotect her kids."

"Yeah, I suppose," I said. "But sleeping in a tent isn't a hardship; it's an adventure."

I had never been one to coddle my children. In fact, I had encouraged them to push their limits from time to time by trying new things, and I found that each new challenge bolstered their sense of competence. My own adventures—including hiking the Appalachian Trail and climbing Mount Rainier—had forced me to confront fears and develop a perspective that helped me wrestle with problems back in civilization.

Though Susan and I never officially resolved where Challen

was going to sleep, I got the impression that she was going to yield on this one. But Challen was left a little shell shocked, thinking that wherever she opted to sleep, she'd be letting one of her parents down.

"Challen, this is your call," I said. "But don't worry about Mom and me. Whatever you decide is okay. It *is* cold out here, but I'd love to have your company in the tent."

I put my arm around her and started to lead her back to the fire, but she pulled away. "Hey, kid, come hang out with the boys," I said.

"I just want to walk around the cabin for a while," she said, and I could hear a tremor in her voice.

"Challen, if you need space, you can have all you want," I said. "But if you're upset, I sure would like to talk about it."

"I don't know what I'm feeling," she said. "I don't know what's wrong."

It occurred to me that a walk from the cabin up to the field might do us both some good. It was 10:30 P.M., and we had plenty of time to return to the fire for the rendition of "Auld Lang Syne."

The moonlight illuminated the gravel road to the field, and we settled onto the rock pile at the edge of the forest and peered up at the night sky. I put my arm around her shoulder and pulled her close.

"Challen, can you tell me what's working on you?" I asked.

"I don't know," she said. "I just know I feel sad." I knew many adults who were incapable of putting feelings into words, and it occurred to me that by expressing sadness, Challen, a nine-year-old whose emotional vocabulary was still being formed, was adequately in touch with herself.

"Sometimes when I get really stressed out and edgy," I said, "I try to separate out all the things that are bothering me and think about them one at a time. Otherwise, they just get mixed all together, and it's tough to work through them. Can you do that?"

"I don't know," she said. "I feel really confused."

Amen, I thought, me, too.

I shifted gears. "Have you thought about your New Year's resolution?"

"Yeah," she said. "I've got three: I'm going to be nicer to Logan. I'm gong to spend more time at the cabin. I'm going to do a better job of picking up after myself at home."

"Good resolutions," I said. "But I'd suggest one that you didn't mention. How about going easier on yourself and letting yourself be snitty every once in a while?"

"But I don't like to make people mad," she said. "I'm afraid they won't like me."

"Challen Brill, you don't ever have to worry about that," I said. "You've got what's called a 'magnetic personality.' "

"What's that?"

"You know those refrigerator magnets you got for Christmas?"

"Yeah."

"You know how metal is attracted to the magnets?"

"Yeah."

"Well, your personality is like that magnet," I explained. "People are just drawn to you because you're such a great person."

"But I feel like I always have to be nice," she said.

"That's a major trap, kid," I said. "Does Logan ever get mad?"

"Yeah."

"Do you still love her?"

"Sure."

"Do Mom and I ever get mad?"

"Yes."

"Do you still love us?"

"Sure."

"Have you ever gotten mad at your best friend, Rachel?"

"Yeah."

"Does she still love you?"

"Yeah, she actually smiled once when I got mad at her."

"Well, then, there you go. Why don't you make another resolution that you'll let yourself get mad from time to time, be a total snit, and throw a regular old temper tantrum?"

"Okay, Daddy, I'll make four resolutions."

We sat for a few minutes and watched the stars, and I remembered my own resolution from the few days before Christmas to nurture the girls' spiritual journeys. This seemed like a perfect time to start.

"Challen, when I'm out in the woods and I look up at the perfect night sky, it feels natural to think about God," I said. "Do you ever think about God?"

"Yeah, sometimes," she said. "Remember when we were in New Hampshire? When I was up that high in the mountains, I felt like I was closer to God."

"I feel the same way in the mountains," I said. "And I feel that way here, too."

We sat in silence for a while.

"Do you think that God has a plan for the world and for you and me?"

"I don't know," she said. "Sometimes it doesn't seem like it."

"Do you think you need to understand the plan for it to be real?"

"I'm not sure."

"See that tree out in the field?" I said, pointing to a lone oak that had been spared when the field was cleared.

"Do you think that tree has a purpose?" I asked. "Do you think it's part of God's plan?"

"Yeah, I guess so."

"Do you think the tree knows what its purpose is?"

"No, Dad, it's just a tree," she said. "Trees can't think."

"Well, maybe people are like trees. We have a role to play, but we're not sure what it is," I said. "You know, sometimes it doesn't seem like there's much purpose to things, like what's happening with Mom and me. But you just have to have faith that things are going to work out, that everything is going to be okay. God manages our lives the way he manages this forest. You just have to trust God to take care of things in his own way. Can you do that?"

"Dad, that's really hard right now," she said.

"I know it is. But we can get through this, and we're all going to be okay. We just have to trust."

"I'll try."

"Listen, you and Logan are my best buddies, and I want you

to talk to me about what you're feeling," I said. "And I'll do the same. Okay?"

"Sure."

"Let's get back to the campfire," I said. "It's getting close to midnight, and we don't want to miss the countdown."

We held hands and walked slowly back to the campfire, and I was worried for all of us. Trusting is the only option left when you're powerless to shape circumstances to your advantage. If Susan had decided that she wanted out of the marriage, there was nothing I could do to pull her back. I had tried the groveling routine, and it had fallen flat.

When Challen and I arrived back at the campfire, Sam and Ed had their arms draped around each other's shoulders, and I noticed that the bottle of Captain Morgan's spiced rum was nearly gone. Kit and J.J. were smoking Honduran stogies. Susan and Logan were asleep on the futon in the bedroom, and Candy was nestled in her sleeping bag on the fold-out couch.

"I'm worried about those guys," J.J. whispered to me, pointing to Sam and Ed. "I think they're falling in love."

"Just a little innocent male bonding," I said. "Intensified by demon rum."

I had known Ed, J.J., and Sam for years but had never once seen them over the edge. Though Sam seemed fine, Ed was adrift in the twilight zone. I thought the situation might warrant an explanation to Challen, who had never seen a drunken person before. My friends weren't setting a very good example, but they were all kind, gentle souls, drunk or sober.

"Sometimes, adults drink a little too much," I said. "Particularly on New Year's Eve."

"Like me!" Ed said, suddenly alert. "I'm . . . really . . . trashed. Don't ever do what I'm doing."

Kit, a captain for Palm Beach County Fire and Rescue, who has to keep several squads of macho thrill-seekers in line, isn't known for having a particularly light touch. "Ed's a mess," Kit whispered. "What are you going to do with him?"

"The loft's empty."

"How in the *hell* are you going to get him up that ladder!"

The ladder to the loft is the cabin's only glaring hazard. Two parallel two-by-sixes pitched at a near vertical angle are connected by seven slick wooden steps leading to the edge of the loft—eight feet above the main floor. I suddenly had a vision of Ed, plagued by a full bladder or restless legs, reeling toward the opening, and taking one long tragic step down into the great room and landing unceremoniously on Candy, who was asleep on the couch.

It was 11:40, so we had at least twenty minutes before we had to figure out where to deposit Ed. I peered around the fire at my friends who had patiently counseled me through months of marital cancer, and as I studied their faces aglow in the firelight, I realized how much I loved all of them. Maybe the rum was working on me, too.

J.J., who had just completed his first marathon, was encouraging Challen to take up distance running.

"Running a marathon is just like running around the block," he said, "but it's a twenty-six-mile block."

Ed and Sam were still arm in arm, sodden grins on their faces, perched on a pine log staring at the coals. Kit was sucking hard on his cigar, laughing and shaking his head, clearly amused by the two rummies' undying devotion to one another.

I checked my watch. "Five minutes to midnight," I said.

"Un-uh," said Ed. "Ish eight minutes to midnight."

"I've got three," said J.J.

"It didn't occur to me to synchronize our watches," I said. "Hey, should we hang Ed from a tree and set fire to him and lower him like the ball on Times Square?"

"You're a sick puppy," said Kit, who, as a firefighter, didn't see much humor in the suggestion.

In a couple of minutes, I started the thirty-second count. When I got to zero, we spontaneously broke into a rendition of "Auld Lang Syne" in at least four conflicting keys.

When the song ended, we all sat quietly, reflecting on the past year and shaping plans for the next. It was the first New Year's morning in eighteen years that hadn't started with a kiss from Susan. I imagined myself beginning 1999 as a single dad and permanent Morgan County resident, and I wondered how we'd all weather the journey of the coming year. Would 1999 be one of those years the four of us would forever look back on and wonder how we ever got through it?

I let Challen stay up until 12:30 and then tucked her into the tent. She clutched her stuffed cat and disappeared into the sleeping bag.

"I like your friends," she said. "They're funny."

"Yeah, they were in rare form tonight," I said. "Good night, kid. I love you."

"I love you, too, Dad," Challen said. "Thanks for letting me stay up with you guys."

I hoped that putting Ed to bed would be as effortless.

I returned to the fire to find Sam and Kit already in their sleeping bags by the fire. J.J. was still puffing on his cigar. I grabbed Ed's arm.

"It's bedtime, Edward," I said, leading him up the steps to the cabin. He did fine until he reached the deck and stuck his foot out, reaching for a phantom step that only he could see. Before I could catch him, he flipped forward and tumbled into an overturned washtub.

Once inside the cabin, I led him to the bathroom, turned on the light, and nudged him in.

"Ed, go to the bathroom," I said, keeping my instructions as simple as possible. "And aim *carefully*."

" 'Kay," he said, disappearing into the bathroom.

The scene reminded me of the days before the girls could sleep through the night without wetting the bed. I would awaken them just before I went to bed to let them use the bathroom. At least I didn't have to unbuckle Ed's pants and point his body in the right direction.

He emerged a minute later.

" 'Kay," he said, awaiting the next command.

"Ed, stay!" I said, gripping his shoulders. I noticed that Benton immediately lay flat on the floor, unaware that such commands could be used on humans as well as dogs.

" 'Kay," said Ed, standing still as a statue while I scrambled up the ladder and grabbed a sleeping bag and mat.

J.J. entered the cabin and stoked the woodstove for the evening while I helped Ed slip into the sleeping bag, which I had laid out by the kitchen counter. Within two minutes, Ed, in the embrace of both Morpheus and Captain Morgan, began to snore softly.

"He'd better not snore all night!" said Candy, suddenly awake. "Does Kit have our tent set up?" She was thinking of joining her husband outside, despite the sixteen-degree temperature.

"No, he's sleeping by the fire under the stars," I said.

Just then Ed's snoring stopped and he broke wind.

"Oh, God," Candy muttered.

J.J. and I crouched by the woodstove, trying to stifle our laughter, but it was no use. We trailed outside, howling at the hilarious irony of a thoroughly disoriented geographer with gas sleeping in the same room with a woman whom he had met only five hours earlier—a woman who was a notoriously light sleeper with no tolerance for nocturnal sound effects.

J.J. and I sat by the fire for another hour or so, whispering to avoid waking Kit and Sam, who were sleeping at our feet. We were successful until a large ember lofted out of the fire ring and landed on Kit's sleeping bag. Without thinking, I jumped up and slapped it out with my hand.

"Holy shit!" shouted Kit, now thoroughly awake.

"Sorry, man," I said. "You were on fire."

At 1:30, J.J. said he was going to turn in, and I decided to bushwhack down to the creek. J.J. and I had been hinting at a midnight swim all evening—the adult equivalent of two kids in the schoolyard daring each other to send a spitball hurtling toward the back of their math teacher's bald head—never thinking that the other would actually follow through.

"I'm going swimming," I said.

"No, you're not."

"Oh, yes, I am."

"Then I'm coming with you."

We trailed off into the woods, following the beam of my headlamp, and stumbled in circles for a half an hour. God must have been looking out for us, because we never found the trail down to the creek. We also lost the trail back to the cabin, and after fifteen frigid minutes of trying to get our bearings, we finally spotted the glowing campfire off through the trees and navigated our way back home.

Within five minutes, I was in the tent with Challen. The next thing I remember, the sun was streaming into the tent and I could swear I heard Ed's chipper voice coming from the deck.

"Amazing recovery," I muttered to myself, and drifted back to sleep.

TWENTY-EIGHT

I Didn't Choose to Feel This Way

I find the great thing in this world is not so much where we stand, as in what direction we are moving: To reach the port of heaven, we must sail sometimes with the wind and sometimes against it—but we must sail, and not drift, nor lie at anchor.
—Oliver Wendell Holmes,
The Autocrat of the Breakfast Table

Though I felt a little shaky on New Year's Day, I cooked omelettes for our guests, and by 11 A.M., everyone had departed except Kit and Candy, Susan, and the girls. I figured a little motion might do Kit and me some good, so we loaded our day packs, helped the girls don hats and gloves, and set off in the car for a hike in Frozen Head State Park, about fifteen minutes away. After about a mile of hiking, Kit and I settled onto a rock for lunch. Our progress up the mountain stopped there, and we soon retreated to the car.

Back at the cabin, we all felt beleaguered, and by 8:30, the lights were out. I asked Susan if she wanted to make love.

"No, not really," she said. "But if you want to, I will."

Minor variations on that conversation had come to define our sex life over the past two years. Though she never initiated intimacy, she seemed inclined to tolerate my need for physical closeness. On New Year's Day, 1999, I realized that we had made love for the very last time.

Kit and Candy departed at 10:30 the next morning, and Susan started packing for her and the girls' trip back home. Just before she left, she deposited the girls in the minivan with its engine idling. When she came back inside, I hoped she would offer me any hope of reconciliation. Instead, she was as cold as stone.

"Susan, are we through?" I asked.

"I don't want to talk about it right now," she said.

"Just tell me, are you going to dump me?" I asked, never having been one to relish suspense.

"Now is not the time to talk about it," she said. "But I'll tell you this: I've been happy over the past few days while you've been gone, and I'm miserable when we're together. But I didn't choose to feel this way."

"No, but you chose to marry me," I said. "And what about the girls? Susan, if you and I get divorced, it will be a clean sweep for your family. Two parents and three siblings, all married and divorced. I think it's wrong to impose this on them. Their happiness is way more important than ours."

"I'm not sure of that," Susan said.

"I believe that divorce spawns divorce," I said, greatly oversimplifying a complex dynamic. "If you and I tank this relationship, then the girls will get married and divorced, and if they have two kids each, then that's four divorces that grow from our one, and it will go on like that forever."

I was voicing one of my principal fears: that our failed marriage would be perpetuated through time and over countless generations; that my great-great-great-grandchildren would, after several years of marriage, retain attorneys and divide up their assets as a direct result of what Susan and I were poised to do.

"Dave, I'm not happy," she concluded. "And I haven't been for a long, long time."

She turned and left, and suddenly, the 630-square-foot dwelling in which I had invested all my hopes for reconciliation and happiness felt like purgatory. I realized that Susan's heart was set, and our marriage was over. All that remained were the formalities: dividing up eighteen years' worth of shared possessions and hammering out how often and under what circumstances I'd get to see my girls.

I experienced a juggernaut of emotions, and I fought hard to keep from crying. If I started, I was afraid I'd never stop. I was angry that I was being forced to leave my home. I was sad because I realized I would be deprived of the right to walk into the next room and glimpse my sleeping daughters and plant a kiss on their foreheads. And I was frightened that the strain of my loss would pitch me into a bout of depression so deep that I'd never climb out.

On January second, after Susan had loaded the last of her belongings into the car, she started the hour drive toward Knoxville. As I watched her taillights fade away through the trees—and as I caught the last glimpse of the girls' blond heads above the backseat—I realized that the center of my universe—Challen and Logan—was shifting and I was moving into an outer orbit. I also realized that, while my family was heading home, I was already there, with Benton, and the trees, and the creek, and a gaping hole in my heart.

TWENTY-NINE

Destroyer of Worlds

I am become death, the destroyer of worlds.
—Vishnu, the *Bhagavad Gita*

I arrived in West Knoxville a couple of weeks later to pack a few things before heading to the cabin. Though I hadn't officially moved out, I was spending less and less time in our house in the city. Over the previous weeks, I had become an absentee husband and father, finding numerous excuses for delaying my arrival home. Often, I'd stop at a tavern en route and settle onto a bar stool to share the company of other displaced fathers and husbands, drinking beer and biding my time until everyone back home was in bed and it was safe to return.

I had grown up in Ohio, where eighteen-year-olds were then permitted to drink, and by the middle of my senior year in high school, a few friends and I started gathering at a small dark watering hole just off the main street, a place known for cheap pitchers and country classics on the jukebox. We were young, optimistic, at the threshold of life as adults, believing that anything was possible.

After a while, I began to notice that a group of middle-aged men whose sons and daughters attended school with us occupied the same seats at the bar every night. I regarded them from the perspective of an eighteen-year-old, and I remember thinking that they seemed hunched and bowed, and I noticed how little laughter passed among them.

These weren't the lovably maladjusted characters on *Cheers;*

rather, they represented men who exuded a sense of hopelessness and resignation, and each night they assumed their places at the bar, downing the same number of long necks, talking about football scores and discussing items in the news, anything to avoid articulating the emptiness that defined their lives.

Over the next few years, several of them divorced, abandoned their bar stools, and moved on to new relationships. Others languished and grew old, never moving too far from their assigned seats.

Now, as I sat on a stool at a sports bar, shoulders hunched, sipping a beer, and staring at old Super Bowl reruns on a muted TV, I glimpsed my reflection in the mirror over the bar, and I realized that I had become just another sad, middle-aged man avoiding home. Though I knew that Susan was happier with me gone, I also had begun to recognize how my absence was affecting the girls. When I did return home, their hugs lasted longer, and when they asked me, "Daddy, where were you?" I found myself telling them half-truths.

"I had a few errands to run," or "I had to work late."

The message was clear: My attachment to them wasn't as strong as my need to avoid the pain of being near a wife who seemed very much to want me gone.

That evening, as I gathered a change of clothes and grabbed my laptop computer, it occurred to me that Susan and I had left the girls in the dark in terms of where we stood with the relationship. We had been speaking frankly to each other about divorce—who would get what, what each of us would expect of the other, how we would arrange our time with the kids—but we had hesitated to share any of these developments with Challen and Logan.

The prospect of divorce terrified me—it represented a headlong plunge into the unknown—and I could only imagine the level of fear the girls were experiencing as they witnessed a complete disconnect between Susan and me but without any attendant information to help them interpret things.

As I laid my bags near the front door, I made a unilateral decision, which, in retrospect, was unwise and may, in fact, have increased the girls' level of hurt. I decided to lay things out for them, to tell them the truth about what was going on with their folks, who clearly didn't love each other anymore—or at least didn't love each other enough.

At the time, I was angry at Susan for shoving me away, for treating me with hostility one minute and utter indifference the next. I had been spending more and more time at the cabin, and I very much wanted for the girls to know that their dad wasn't abandoning them. He was merely trying to ease his suffering, and that meant absence. I wanted them to know that Susan had asked me to leave and that leaving wasn't what I had really wanted—at least not in the beginning.

After I had packed the car, I called them into their bedroom and asked them to sit down. "You guys know how bad things are between Mom and me," I began, "and I just thought you could use a little honest information.

"The bottom line is that I don't think Mom and I are going to make it," I said.

Logan, who was clutching a worksheet from school, covered her face with it. I gently pulled it away and saw pain in her eyes I'd never detected before.

"Dad, I've got homework to do," she said. By delving into her homework, by denying that she had heard the words I had uttered, she believed that she could rewind the tape and erase them.

Challen, an odd smile on her face, stood and pretended that she was going to faint, her own preadolescent expression of complete denial, a stage in the grieving process I, myself, had just begun to punch through.

"Guys, I know that this has to feel awful and scary, and it's very, very sad," I said. "But your mom is miserable with me, and it may be time for me to leave. But one thing you have to remember is that this isn't happening because of anything you've done. In fact, it's happening despite the fact that Mom and I have the greatest kids in the world."

Challen sat down, and her tears started to come. Logan insisted again that she had homework to do and left the room. I stayed with Challen, hugging her and feeling her sobs against my chest. The truth was working itself down deep now, and she was registering the fear and pain that had settled over me on Christmas Eve.

"Challen, I know this is horrible, but you have to have faith that things are going to work out, that things can actually be better for all of us," I said.

"Oh, Daddy," she said, crying.

I found Logan clinging to Susan in the kitchen; that pained look was still on her face, but she wasn't crying, something that troubled me more deeply than Challen's free-flowing tears.

I stayed with the girls until it was near their bedtime and considered staying through the night and leaving for the cabin the next morning, but I couldn't do it. I had to leave and shed my own tears, and I wanted to do it in a place that felt safe. Besides, I wasn't sure I could attend to my own grief while shepherding the girls through theirs. I also knew that once I was gone, Susan would offer the girls her perspective on things. I knew that as long as they were with Susan, the girls would be in capable hands. Susan possesses an amazing ability to function through crisis.

I had seen evidence of that several times before, and I suspect that much of it derived from her having lived through her parents' painful divorce when she was a teenager. After that, there were only minor crises.

I had fully grasped Susan emotional toughness one night when Challen was just shy of two and Logan was on the way. Challen had been running a high fever, and Susan and I were in the family room watching a movie. After the movie ended, Susan went back to check on Challen and called out to me in a firm but controlled voice.

"Dave, call 911; Challen's not breathing," she said.

I ran back to Challen's room. Her eyes were rolled back in her head, her face was ashen, her lips were purple, her body was rigid. She looked dead.

"Dave, call the life squad," Susan repeated.

My hands were quaking so much that I was relieved that I had to press only three numbers. I dialed 911 and tried to compose myself and provide the dispatcher with what few details I had, including the fact that Challen had been running a high fever.

The dispatcher urged me to calm down but I was well beyond that. As far as I knew, my daughter was dead or dying, and I was helpless to save her.

Eventually, the dispatcher said that she suspected that Challen was having a febrile seizure brought on by an extremely high fever, that as frightful as her condition appeared, she would probably be okay, and that the life squad was on the way.

A fire truck—the closest available emergency-response vehicle—pulled into our driveway a few minutes later, and two fire fighters clad in protective gear rushed into Challen's room just as she began to emerge from the seizure and some level of awareness returned to her eyes. Though Challen was less than two, to this day, she recalls awakening and seeing the two fire fighters leaning over her crib. The men confirmed that Challen had had a febrile seizure, but they urged us to take her to Children's Hospital just to have things checked out. As it turned out, there were no lasting effects; she was fine.

Through the crisis, Susan had remained composed, focused, completely functional, and it wasn't until the rescue workers left that she collapsed, sobbing, in my arms.

I knew that Susan's emotional toughness would steel her through the dissolution of our marriage. It would also allow her to respond to the girls' emotional needs in a controlled and capable way.

Much as Challen recalls the two fire fighters leaning over her, I will forever recall the memory of Challen standing in the driveway the night I shared the sad news with her and Logan about her mom and me. She stood with head bowed, watching me drive off, wondering what would come next.

The image stayed with me all the way to the cabin, and I drove the familiar route through a haze of tears, hoping to find solace in the depths of the forest. I coursed down the gravel road, pulled up in front of the cabin, opened the front door, and felt my way through the cold darkness. Instead of flicking on a light, I lit an oil lamp, recalling the comfort the lamps had provided through the days of the power outage after the ice storm. Within a half hour, I had the woodstove stoked, and I sat on the couch trying to convince myself that my life was at low ebb, that things had gotten as bad as they were ever going to get, and that everything was up from here. Then I realized that ending an eighteen-year relationship was going to take time, months to sort out the logistics and terms for the settlement. The emotional aspects would likely take years. I sat up until 2 A.M., staring at the fire and wondering what kind of a night the girls were having.

As it turned out, Susan and the girls stayed up till midnight, talking and crying.

Just after 2 A.M., I climbed into bed and tried to sleep, but I couldn't shake the image of Challen standing in the driveway, crying, watching me leave.

I called the girls the next morning and the next evening, and we talked about school and friends and Girl Scouts—about everything but separation and divorce. They didn't ask me when I would return home, but they did ask when they were going to see me. I asked them to spend the weekend with me at the cabin. It would be our first gathering as a fragmented family.

I returned to Knoxville two days later, my first visit since the disclosure. As soon as I walked through the door, Logan grabbed my hand and led me over to Susan, and drew our hands together.

"Now hold hands," she said. "You'll get back together, I just know it."

"Kid," I said, "this isn't *The Parent Trap;* this is real, and I don't want you to believe in things that probably aren't going to happen."

Within a few weeks, I had moved away from Knoxville for good, and the cabin became my home. But it would take weeks—and a disorienting foray out into darkened woods—before the trees and rocks, the dips and rises, became as familiar to me as the environs surrounding my former dwelling in the city.

VI

SPRING

THIRTY

Wild Embrace

The Promised Land always lies on the other side
of a wilderness.
　　　　　—Havelock Ellis, *The Dance of Life*

There were times when I forgot how complete the wilderness becomes a few hundred yards from the cabin toward the creek. One evening, eager to see if the lights from the cabin would penetrate the forest to the bluff, where the National Park Service planned to build a trail, I put on a headlamp and bushwhacked alone straight down the hill toward the sound of the seasonal creek that flows along the southwestern line of the property.

En route, the reconnaissance mission became something else—a late-night journey into the wilds, an adventure—and by the time I reached the bluff, I had forgotten the purpose of the trek. Beyond the bluff and several hundred feet below, Clear Creek, swollen from several days of rain, thrashed against the boulders of the streambed, and a sliver of moon peaked below the clouds just above the rim of the bluff on the other side of the gorge. I stepped over blowdowns and limboed under low-hanging branches, following the line of the bluff until I reached the pink tape marking my shared border with the National Park Service.

I switched off the headlamp and settled onto the ground, listening. Within a few minutes, I began to hear wild creatures scuttling through downed, dead leaves. I thought of the eerie baying of coyotes I had heard over successive nights just beyond my bedroom window and wondered if I'd ever see one of them. To my right, a large animal, probably a deer, rustled the leaves, moving toward me, but I determined to sit still until it had drawn to within a few yards.

As I waited, old fears surfaced of being alone in dark woods. The blackness was so immense, so complete, and the sliver of moon cast scant little light on the surrounding forest. I was enveloped by darkness and towering hemlocks, their graceful branches sweeping the ground. The seven-tenths of a mile that lay between my front door and the road provided for my privacy and positioned the cabin in a way that ensured that the woods, and not human development, would establish the tenor of the setting. Yet it struck me as ironic that a few hundred yards away from where I sat, my table lamps burned. But for the moment, the world was dominated by trees and rock and wild critters pawing the earth for food, a primordial forest that had changed little over the eons it took Clear Creek to carve its way down through the rock. Though the land had been logged decades earlier, the steep terrain along the bluff posed both risk and inconvenience for timber companies, so many of the hemlocks had survived the clear-cut and rose to heights of seventy feet or more.

I had experienced a similar feeling of wild embrace in the early fall, with J.J., when Clear Creek's warm waters still invited swimming and a full moon posed an irresistible temptation. We grabbed a couple of beers and donned headlamps. Within ten minutes, we were perched on the Rock, clad in our birthday suits and dripping from a dip in the creek. We watched the moon arc over the trees and come into view. Benton, his wet back glistening in the moonlight, explored the pool from edge to edge.

It was the first time I had experienced the creek at night, and though the features of the surroundings hadn't changed, I felt as if I were visiting the pool for the first time. The branches of hardwoods and hemlocks were edged in silver light. The ripples spreading away from Benton's darkened form caught the moonglow. Whippoorwills, owls, crickets, and cicadas filled the forest with sounds that merged into an enveloping drone. Coyotes bayed from the top of the bluff.

J.J. and I were visitors to a nocturnal world thoroughly alive and completely indifferent to our presence. Despite all of humankind's insults against nature, the creek, sheltered from loggers and homesteaders by sheer rock walls and steep pitched hillsides, had remained pure. Save for the Heinekens and headlamps, we might have been perched on the Rock in any year among millions.

Now, seated on the edge of the bluff one hundred feet above the creek, I felt light rain against my skin, and the patter of drops on leaves and branches drowned out the sound of the rushing water, the auditory compass needle that would lead me home. For an instant, I felt disoriented, knowing that the cabin lay close by but not remembering in which direction. I rose and switched on the headlamp. The trees, in the darkened woods, looked unfamiliar, even though I had trod through the very spot countless times in the daylight on my way to the creek. There were no landmarks, no familiar undulations on the terrain, no path, no lights.

I pushed off in a direction that felt right, but soon I entered a grove of fledgling white pines, not familiar hemlocks, and knew I was exploring new ground. After stumbling around in the woods for five minutes, I switched off the headlamp to see if I could glimpse the glow of lights from the cabin. Through the trees, I discerned a subtle brightening reflected on the clouds, and I walked toward it. Eventually, the forest ended and I entered a field and noted the silhouette of a lone oak and realized that I had looped around my cabin and arrived at Walczak's "food lot," as he called his favored hunting grounds. The oak had survived the clear-cutting of the field because Walczak envisioned it as a perfect perch for a tree stand.

As I walked across the open field, my face peppered by a soft rain, I glimpsed my cabin lights winking through the trees and set my course for home.

I realized that in time, the trackless forest behind the cabin would become as familiar to me as my backyard in the city, though I would have to give the process time. In many ways, I still felt like a visitor to these woods, in part because I still spent one or two nights per week on the couch in the city and logged the majority of my work week in my office at the university.

I was beginning to experience the difficulty of reconciling those two vastly different worlds. One was defined by a metal-edged cubicle in a climate-controlled office building largely bereft of windows. An umbilical tangle of wires under my desk served as a lifeline to the high-tech world and the information that was vital to my job. Around me, I heard the ordered sounds of clacking keyboards, whirring laser printers, the thud of the copying machine.

The other world was defined by an equally ordered cadence, by natural light throwing long shadows at sunrise and sunset; by the banshee call of pileated woodpeckers, the caw of crows, light breezes stirring wind chimes; by intervals of stillness so profound that I could hear pine needles dropping on dead leaves.

My spirit drew me so completely to the latter world while the former began to feel like penance. I sensed that in a couple of weeks, when I would begin a six-month leave of absence from the university, my one-day-per-week journey into Knoxville would be jarring, disorienting, and that a corner of my mind would dwell on what I might be missing moment to moment in woods awakening to the arrival of spring.

My hopes and expectations for the coming months in retreat reminded me of my days on the Appalachian Trail and the subtle transitioning that led me from visitor to resident of the woods. Early on in my journey, I couldn't wait to arrive in town, to savor hot showers and prepared food, to sleep on hotel beds, to read newspapers and call friends, to launder clothes caked in grit and reeking of wood smoke. But after several months on the trail, my stopovers in town grew progressively shorter, and it pained me to be shut up in a hotel room, cut off from the stirring of the woods and forced to endure the unnatural stillness created by Sheetrock walls.

I realized that it would take days of complete immersion in the cabin environment to repeat that transition, but logistically, there were a few things I could do to establish residency in Morgan County.

A few days earlier, I had visited the post office in Lancing and purchased a year's lease for a post-office box for fourteen dollars and driven to the courthouse in Wartburg and asked the attendant at the license bureau for a Morgan County sticker for my car plates. Henceforth, if my new neighbors were going to identify me as "other," it wouldn't be because of my mailing address and license tags.

THIRTY-ONE

A Separate Place

All paths lead to the same goal: to convey to oth-
ers what we are. And we must pass through soli-
tude and difficulty, isolation and silence, in order
to reach forth to the enchanted place where we
can dance our clumsy dance and sing our sorrow-
ful song.
—Pablo Neruda, "Toward the Splendid City," upon
receiving the Nobel Prize for literature in 1971

I circulated a memo around the office explaining that I
would be taking a six-month leave of absence. I was inten-
tionally vague regarding *all* the reasons for the leave. While the
memo hinted at such issues as passage through midlife and efforts to reconnect with nature, it said nothing of the problems
Susan and I were having.

Those who knew that the leave, in part, grew from marital
discord, expressed their condolences. Those who didn't, expressed congratulations. Friends who shared my love of the
wilderness and who recognized how deeply my Appalachian
Trail experience had affected me seemed to understand that I
was poised to begin a new journey. While the AT route had been
clearly defined by a well-worn trail and two-by-six-inch white
blazes painted on trees, my new path was largely uncharted.

As I drafted the memo, it occurred to me that the duration of
my leave was exactly the same period of time I had spent on the
Appalachian Trail. The AT experience endured as a major life-
shaping event in my life, an experience that completely shifted
my values and priorities.

When I regarded the leave in terms of its parallel with the AT
experience, I felt heartened and hopeful that the ensuing six
months would lead through pain and sadness to a place of heal-

ing and acceptance. I had fully engaged in the denial that is said to be part of the grieving process; I was ready to mourn and eventually to move on to the peace I believed lay somewhere out there, perhaps in the forest.

During my months in the cabin, I would witness the arrival of spring much as I had while hiking the AT. On the trail, I had experienced the awakening of spring moment to moment rather than through occasional and often distracted glimpses through the car window on my way to work or from the confines of my office building, where the few windows looked out over asphalt and concrete. Each day brought new discoveries, new plants probing through the dead leaves layering the forest floor, new buds on trees opening to the warmth and light of spring.

Though there were clear parallels between the AT experience and my months in seclusion at the cabin, I wondered if the leave from work would have a similar impact. I realized that to some extent the answer hung on how I used my time in retreat. There were occasions when I feared that my sojourn in the wilds of Morgan County might lead to madness and neglect of requisite responsibilities of a civilized world. Would I stop bathing and wear the same pair of shorts till they fell from my body in shreds? I feared that the experience of the ensuing months would reconfigure my thinking so thoroughly that reentry would be impossible.

While the AT experience was largely predicated on motion—moving each day twelve to fifteen miles north along the trail route—retreat to the cabin could inspire passivity, holing up in one place and disconnecting from the world that lay beyond the cabin's four walls and the surrounding forest. I recognized the risk of becoming a shut-in, a hermit whose reluctance to venture forth began with mild aversion and evolved into fear.

My friends at Wednesday Night Prayer Meeting, aware of the risk that I would become a recluse, had begun calling me "Ted" and joked about my skills at building letter bombs. But I recognized the fundamental difference between fleeing from the world—and the problems associated with it—and the decision to depart the world for a while to better understand one's place in it.

Though previously, my time at the cabin had been largely un-structured, I recognized the importance of ritual and routine. I determined to reestablish the twice-daily meditation sessions that had been an essential part of my routine through high school and college and while I was on the trail. I also decided that each evening, I'd power down the cabin, take my plate out onto the small table on the deck, light an oil lamp, and consume my meal of pasta or rice slowly as I watched the sun set beyond the bluff.

By dark, the finches and hummingbirds, active through the day, had disappeared, and the nocturnal soundmeisters—barred owls, whippoorwills, bobwhites, coyotes—would begin their evening shifts. Though they never made a visual appearance, they seemed to occupy the same corners of the darkened woods, and I began to recognize them by their positions and wondered on occasion what had become of them when familiar voices were absent.

On nights when the full moon rose above me, and my form cast a long shadow across the planking of the deck, I often felt sad that no one was there beside me to share in the amazing tran-quillity and beauty.

THIRTY-TWO

Witness to a Resurrection

The reports of my death are greatly exaggerated.
—Mark Twain, cable from London to the
Associated Press

I was reminded through the spring not to dispatch to the grave people and things that appeared moribund but that were, in fact, very much alive. It started with the expanse of barren soil behind the cabin, which had been scarred by the backhoe blade. The clearing shrank a bit more each day, and by summer's end had evolved into a verdant thicket of blackberry bushes, grasses, and saplings that revealed not a square foot of brown dirt.

But before I had taken the lesson fully to heart, it would involve two people I love deeply—a dear old friend and my father.

On a Saturday morning, Challen, Logan, and I met Susan in Oak Ridge—the halfway point where we would exchange the kids—and Susan took the girls back to Knoxville. I would hook up with them later for the annual father-daughter sock-hop sponsored by their Girl Scout troop. I lingered in Oak Ridge because a friend of mine, a former student who became an adopted grandmother, was in the hospital. Word from her daughter was that she was dying.

I had met Marshall Lockhart in 1987 while I conducted a writing workshop in Oak Ridge. She was seventy-six at the time, but, as she put it, she didn't "look a day over seventy-five."

She buttonholed me one day during a break and told me

about her days in the theater, her pursuits as an essayist, and an encounter she had had with Thomas Wolfe decades earlier.

"He was in sad shape," she said. "He wound up crying on my shoulder."

I was incredulous at the moment, but over time I came to realize that Marshall was always honest, sometimes painfully so, as I found out when she turned her attention to my teaching style and offered a blunt critique.

"Do you realize that you said 'ah' twenty-five times in the first half hour of your presentation? I know because I was counting."

"Ah, no," I said.

"There! You just did it again," she said, pointing an accusing finger at me.

I suddenly felt both irritation and extreme self-consciousness and sought some semblance of affirmation. "Well, did I offer you anything useful?"

"Oh, yes, you are a very effective teacher."

"Thanks."

"But you need to work on 'ah'."

With that, she spun on her heels and started *skipping* like a schoolgirl back toward class.

As I watched her disappear around the corner, I realized that I had just met a true one-of-a-kind, something abundantly apparent both in Marshall's manner and her dress.

Marshall wore her thinning white hair cut short, carried thirty extra pounds on her five-foot frame, and sported sneakers and brightly colored shirts she ordered from a men's catalog that caters to the surfer crowd.

On the last day of the workshop, Marshall invited me to lunch at her house, one of the original houses built to accommodate the scientists and other workers who descended on Oak Ridge in the early 1940s to work on the Manhattan Project. Marshall's deceased husband, George, had played a role in developing the world's first atomic bomb. I accepted Marshall's invitation and in so doing launched a decade-long friendship.

Through the years, I'd frequently visited Marshall in her home, a single-story rancher cluttered with enough books to stock a small college library. Her artwork, mostly landscape watercolors, adorned walls, and a life-size stuffed doll—a 1920s-era flapper—occupied a permanent seat in one of the chairs in her living room. A craft room off the dining room traced Marshall's evolution as artist, beader, sculptor, and dried-flower arranger.

A large pantry opened off the kitchen and boasted floor-to-ceiling stacks of canned goods. Having lived through the want that attended the Great Depression and World War II, Marshall wasn't about to risk having to do without, and over time, the cache of food grew to the extent that navigating through the room became impossible, as she continued to stockpile pallets of canned goods.

Our visits often began with lunch, elaborate offerings of pork roast, potatoes, asparagus, rolls, salad, and a pan of cake or brownies for dessert. Though I was constantly astounded by her generosity, Marshall thanked *me* every time I arrived for giving her a reason to cook.

After lunch, we'd settle into overstuffed chairs in her living room, and she'd query me about my family, my writing, and my plans for the future.

A few years into our relationship, I accepted a teaching position at a community college in Oak Ridge and worked for modest wages. Though she knew the job would plant me right in her backyard and we'd be able to spend more time together, she was concerned that the job might rob me of my passion to write.

"Don't let those people push you around," she admonished me often. "And don't you ever let go of your dreams."

Over the years, Marshall and I spent countless afternoons together in her den, and when, in the early 1990s, her son, George Jr., was diagnosed with brain cancer, she turned to me frequently for support. Several months later, when George died, she called me at 3 A.M. to come sit with her. After I arrived, we talked through the night and paged through photo albums that traced George's life from boyhood to fatherhood. And though Marshall was clearly pained by George's loss, she revealed a level of acceptance and strength that I'm certain had buoyed her through the loss of her husband a decade or so earlier and helped her confront a lifetime worth of disappointment.

"Yes, he was a sweet little boy," she said, peering at pictures of a small kid clad in T-shirt, shorts, and sneakers. "And a damned good father."

Though Marshall possessed a gift for accepting the inevitable with grace, she could also fight fiercely when she thought it might do some good. Some years earlier, she had suffered a stroke and after hours of struggling, managed to drag herself through the house to the telephone to call for help. Her doctors at the hospital advised her that she'd probably never walk again and would have to move into a nursing home. They clearly had underestimated their patient. Primed for a fight, Marshall dug in her heels, even if those heels and the legs that connected to them were numb and unresponsive.

"The hell with that!" she said to me over the phone. "I'll be damned if I'm going to live with a bunch of helpless old people!"

In the battle between Marshall's will and the wisdom of modern health care, Marshall prevailed and within a couple of weeks was back at home, maneuvering through her cluttered house with the aid of a walker. That was eight years ago.

Over the years, I had neglected my relationship with Marshall, investing my energy instead in trying to manage my life at home. I had foolishly believed that Marshall would go on forever, that there would be ample time to rekindle our relationship. I hadn't seen her for nearly a year, though she had called me often at the office, always closing the conversation by telling me that she loved me and appealing to me to, please, please, call her sometime.

After dropping the girls off with Susan, as I approached Marshall's room at the hospital, I was unsure of what to expect. Her daughter, Rosemary, had told me on the phone that her mother had suffered another stoke and had slipped into a coma. Though Marshall had emerged from the coma, Rosemary told me that her mother was probably not going to live much longer.

"The doctors say she's exhibiting all the signs that her body is failing, that she's dying," Rosemary had told me. How long and how steep her decline would be was anybody's guess.

As I entered the room, I felt as though I had witnessed a resurrection.

"These nurses are bitches!" Marshall shouted, brandishing a clenched fist. "I think I got one of them fired!"

A tangle of tubes coiled around her on the bed and infused her with oxygen and fluids. After she had recognized me as an ally, not a needle-bearer, her tone softened.

"Come give me a kiss, old friend," she said, holding out her hand to me. "It's been a long time."

I bent down and kissed her.

"Did you bring pictures of the girls?" she asked. For Marshall, photographs assisted a failing memory and kept images of those she cared about close and familiar. She had been collecting photos of my family—including our black Labrador, Morpheus—since I'd met her.

She peered at the school photos I'd brought of Challen and Logan and smiled. "Do they remember me?"

"Yes, of course they do."

"Please don't let them forget me."

She gripped my hand, and I noticed that she wore the woven surfer bracelets that I had given her ten years earlier.

"Do you know I've never taken these off since you gave them to me?" she said.

The stroke had robbed Marshall of her hearing, and through the afternoon, she talked and I listened. The stories were from her past, stories she had told me many times before, and she was as clear as ever on the details. But between the scripted stories, Marshall's mind drifted to other places, places none of the rest of us could see. As it did, she wavered between being lucid and being fanciful, between being anchored in the present and borne back into her past or peering ahead into the future.

"I'm now part of a great mystery," she said at one point, looking directly into my eyes. "They say I'm dead. Am I dead?"

"You don't look dead to me."

"Are we still at war with Japan?"

"What?"

"Aren't we at war with Japan and China?"

"No, we were able to avoid that," I said, not knowing quite how to deal with a confused mind.

"Did you know that he who lifts the smallest creature from the dust is greater than he who rules the world?"

"Yes, yes, that's true."

"The angel came to see me and showed me a world that's perfectly efficient and organized. Everybody there knows what he's doing."

"Yes."

"The doctors say I'm dying. Did you know I'm writing a book?"

At one point her daughter, Rosemary, entered the room.

"Who are *you*?" Marshall asked.

"I'm your daughter."

"You're who?"

"I'm your daughter."

"It's amazing; you look identical to my daughter. You could be her twin." I had to smile, though I realized that Marshall's inability to recognize Rosemary hurt her daughter deeply. It was just the kind of thing Marshall, the consummate joker, would have said had she been fully in command of her senses.

And so it went through the afternoon. Moments of frightening clarity. Lapses. Disconnected snippets. Scenes from decades past. Fragments from a mind struggling to remain with us while working to process *the* great mystery.

Once again, Marshall had proved a capable mentor as I watched her face her own journey into death. No fear, no regret. Just a mind active in two realms, floating somewhere in between, concerned about those she'd leave behind but fascinated by a world of perfect order, one bereft of incompetent nurses and failing limbs.

In her moments of clarity, she asked repeatedly about Susan and the family, and I wanted so much to reach out to an old friend and share with her details of my tattered life, about my cabin, about my loneliness. But I realized that the time for such discussion had long since lapsed.

Though we weren't blood relatives, Marshall would have mourned with me, as if part of her own family were coming apart, and I didn't want to distract her with details from a temporal world. Marshall and I had both embarked on solitary journeys that would lead us to new places, though neither of us had any assurance of the outcome.

The next weekend, Mom and Dad called. They were back from Florida, and Dad had gone to visit his urologist to get a fix on what had been happening in his cancerous prostate over the previous three months. After diagnosing the likely recurrence of his cancer in December, the doctors had urged Dad to follow through with his plans to head south to Vero Beach for the winter. The tumor seemed to be slow growing, and their treatment options, at that point, were limited. He could have cancer while freezing and slipping on the ice in Cincinnati, or he could have cancer while golfing and walking on the beach.

"We'll work you up when you get back," his doctor had said. "Go have fun, and try not to worry."

Now he was back, and the information was starting to trickle in.

"Dave, I've gotten some tests back," Dad began, and I braced for the worst.

"My PSA numbers are up, which means that the tumor is probably active," he continued. "But the increase is modest, and the bone scan and CAT scan came back clean. That's good news. It means that the cancer hasn't spread."

"What about treatment?"

"Well, we're probably just going to wait and see. The doctor says I may have two more years or ten, and I still may eventually die *with* prostate cancer, not *of* it. The next step is hormone therapy, but that's kind of a last-ditch measure."

"How you doing with this, Mom?"

"We had fun in Florida, and I'm grateful for that," she said on the other extension. "And I have a feeling I'm going to be putting up with your father's sloppy living habits for a long time."

THIRTY-THREE

Disposable Dad

Fathers are a biological necessity but a social accident.   —Margaret Mead

The night of the father-daughter sock-hop represented the first time I'd felt like a disposable dad, an add-on, a second-class parent. The girls donned "poodle skirts" Susan had made for them, and I dressed up like a college frat boy, circa 1955, for the dance organized by the girls' Scout troop. The year before, when I was still living in West Knoxville and was a constant in the girls' day-to-day lives, we had arrived at the dance and were inseparable through an evening spent dancing, slurping Coke floats, and playing hula hoop. The girls clung to my hands and seemed loath to let me out of their sight.

This year things were different. Shortly after we arrived, the girls scattered off with friends, and I spent much of the evening searching for them through the darkened gymnasium at the middle-school.

At one point, I found Logan and asked her to dance.

"Sure, in a minute, Dad," she said. "I want to go find Pauli and tell her something."

And with that she was gone, and again, I was alone. At that moment, I felt like the character in the Harry Chapin song "Cat's in the Cradle" who neglects his son through his childhood then, late in life, discovers that the tables have been turned and the son is emotionally distant from his aging father.

As I watched Logan walk away, I stood leaning against the back wall of the gym, envying the fathers on the dance floor whose daughters wanted, more than anything else, to be close to them. These were middle-aged men with hair slicked back and clad in penny loafers and decades-old letter jackets, twisting shamelessly and twirling daughters who beamed back at them. These were the dads whose wives had forgiven them their transgressions, whose daughters always ended their days with a good-night kiss from Dad. These were fathers who felt welcome—and even essential—in their own homes. These were the lucky dads, and I wondered if they realized how truly fortunate they were.

I recognized that I was idealizing these men's lives, but they all seemed so happy, so connected to their kids. Later, as I walked through the cafeteria, where the dance sponsors were serving soda floats, I glimpsed the darker side of the father-daughter dynamic. I noticed a number of men sitting silently at lunch tables beside their daughters but not connected with them; fathers and children staring blankly past each other in uncomfortable silence. Were these the neglectful dads I'd heard about who spent weekends away from home, golfing or fishing or playing cards with their friends? Were these the dads who logged too much time at work and not enough at home? Were these the dads of divorce? Were these the dads who had already, unwittingly, sacrificed what should have been the most important relationships of their lives?

As I mulled these questions, I wondered which groups of dads I rightfully belonged to. I didn't know, but the widening emotional gulf between my daughters and me had become painfully apparent. Whatever they had once needed from me, they seemed to be learning to do without.

I determined to search one last time for the girls, and I found them in the gym, dancing with their friends.

Disinclined to separate them from their buddies, I decided to join them. I squeezed into the circle, and started to twist and twirl to the music, aware that I looked ridiculous but suddenly very content. The girls responded, gripped my hands, and soon I was part of a conga line of eight- and ten-year-olds snaking through the gym, adding new fathers and daughters as we went.

The girls and I remained together through the rest of the evening, and later that night I realized that I had turned an important corner. While I initially wanted the girls to break from their friends to join me, I had come to realize that that approach was flawed, destined to fail, and even selfish. Instead, I realized that I needed to pursue them, to become part of what they were doing, to connect with them through activities that they loved. I realized, too, that the cabin was my thing, my space, and that I couldn't expect them to love it as much as I or to follow me there every time they needed me. I determined to spend more time with them on their terms, on their turf.

Spring break was a week away, and the girls and I planned to spend most of the break together. I began to think about what they wanted to do, about how to make it *their* week. Camping had been a part of their lives since Logan was one, and it quickly rose to the top of our list of vacation options. In terms of destinations, we agreed that it was time to explore the forests of the Cumberland Mountains and to trace some of its blue highways.

But I had broader goals in mind, goals that had little to do with maps and mileposts. Maybe the girls had begun to drift from me, but I was determined to align my course with theirs and intersect their path before they had passed out of sight.

THIRTY-FOUR

A Family of Three

The soul of a journey is liberty, perfect liberty, to think, feel, and do just as one pleases.
—William Hazlitt, *Table Talk*

Girls, you may each take one stuffed animal on the trip, but the rest are going to have to stay behind," I said, shifting my glance between a heap of stuffed bears, rabbits, racoons, and dogs in the middle of the great room floor and a burgeoning pile of camping gear that would have to fit inside the Jeep—along with three human occupants and an 80-pound retriever.

"Ah, Dad, that's not fair," Challen protested.

"Yeah, it's like someone asking you to choose between Challen and me," Logan added. "No parent should have to make a decision like that. How about letting us take three?"

"Okay, we'll compromise," I said. "Two stuffed friends, but they have to be *small*. And if it comes down to a choice between essential survival gear and a stuffed moose named B.J., I'm making the call. *Capisce?*"

"*Capisce,*" the girls chimed in unison before returning to their game of double solitaire. I gathered up tent, sleeping bags, sleeping pads, camp stove, cooler, and clothes and loaded them into the Jeep as a spring rain dampened the woods. Once I had stowed all the gear, the Jeep began to resemble the interior of an Apollo space capsule.

Before we wedged ourselves into the Jeep, I pulled out the

map of Tennessee and discussed with the girls our general plan of attack. We would head off and explore the Cumberland Plateau, stopping to take in mutually agreed upon points of interest, keeping things loose and relatively unstructured.

As the girls loaded in their menagerie of stuffed animals and we prepared to leave the cabin, I realized that my reluctance to fix on a strict schedule for vacations resulted in part from my father's penchant for overplanning.

Each year, as our annual two-week summer vacation approached, Dad would amass a mountain of brochures, pamphlets, AAA Triptiks, maps, and destination guides. Each evening, he'd sip a Manhattan and study his assembled materials, pausing frequently to read a passage that described one tourist attraction or another.

Departure days began early, often before dawn, and Mom and Dad would carry Steve and me, still in our pajamas, to the back of our vessel of discovery, a tan Chevy Nova station wagon, which Dad would have packed the night before.

Once on the road, making time became a mission, and I recall one trip when Steve had drunk one too many Cokes at our scheduled lunch stop and needed to use the bathroom, as the car streaked along a Georgia two-lane.

"Here, use this," Dad said, impatience rising in his voice as he handed Steve an empty sixteen-ounce soda bottle with a mouth that measured less than an inch across.

Through his life, Steve will never face a challenge more daunting than pissing into that tiny opening as the Nova bucked and swayed along the pitted roadway. At one point, the spray deflected off the bottle rim and hit Dad square in the back of the neck. From then on, Dad grudgingly accommodated our requests for potty breaks, but he also closely monitored our fluid intake while en route.

While making good time seemed to put Dad in a state of euphoria, the traffic snarls that were an inevitable part of travel in the early days of the interstate highway system pitched him into a funk. Steve and I came to recognize the signals of Dad's imminent meltdown—a death grip on the steering wheel, a forward-leaning posture that placed his nose inches from the windshield, and a color rising in his cheeks and forehead that was more purple than red. The only time I recall hearing my father swear was when the Nova was immobilized by gridlock on some congested road and his itinerary was being shot all to hell by unscheduled delays.

"Son of a bitch!"

"Ron!" Mom would chide, reminding Dad to watch his mouth. Meanwhile Steve and I sat trancelike in the backseat, sweat streaming down our faces in the un–air-conditioned car, just wanting to be there, wherever there was.

By the time Steve and I were in high school, we had prevailed on Dad to drive leisurely to the beach and let us ride the waves while he and Mom were off seeing the sights. And though I could tell it pained him to drive past signs that read SEE THE WORLD'S LARGEST FRYING PAN or STAND ATOP THE STATE'S TALLEST OBSERVATION TOWER, I like to believe he was relieved not to have to cling to his own impossibly ambitious itineraries.

Though my fully loaded Jeep brought back memories of the pinched space of the Nova—as did the vehicle's lack of air-conditioning—I realized that my approach to travel was the antithesis of my father's. The girls and I would drive until we felt like stopping. If we tried one place and weren't having fun, we'd find another. And the girls would be equal partners in deciding the places we'd visit.

As we bounced along the gravel road from the cabin to the road and rain splattered the windshield, Logan asked the question that's on the lips of every child embarking on a family vacation: "How long till we get there?"

"Can you handle a half hour?" I asked, setting my sights on Crossville. I knew we could get a cheap motel room there; even I didn't relish the notion of setting up a tent in the rain.

A Motel 6 offered us a good rate on a room and for five extra dollars gave us permission to let Benton sleep indoors. It was early afternoon, and I noticed that the girls had already turned on the TV as I began to unload our gear.

"Girls, we're not on vacation to watch TV," I said. "Let's get in the car, have some lunch, and go exploring." I knew there was a Mexican restaurant down the road, and a couple of miles beyond that, an old country store. If those diversions failed to chew up the afternoon, I figured we could go bowling. Any sport that required its participant to wear *those* shoes had to be fun, particularly for children who had never beheld the garish ambience of a bowling alley.

Through the afternoon, I was reminded of how much fun my daughters can be and how effortless it is to be with them. Once at the bowling alley, Challen and I howled as we watched Logan waddle, Chaplinesque, to the head of the lane bent forward under the weight of the ball. She would launch the ball with both hands then tumble onto her back, her legs splayed in the air. Hardly classic style, but she did manage to avoid the gutters on occasion. When she didn't, she insisted that the ball wasn't round or that the lane was banked.

"The ball is defective!" she shrieked after a string of gutter balls.

Weather predictions for the following day called for clearing skies, which meant, come tomorrow, we'd be happily ensconced in the Taj MaBrill, our family-size dome tent, not a motel, and we set out the next morning just after breakfast. Our first destination was historic Rugby, one of several ill-fated utopian settlements established on the Cumberland Plateau over the previous century.

In the 1870s, English author and reformer Thomas Hughes selected the plateau as a place to build a society to benefit what he termed the "Will Wimbles," the younger sons of British aristocracy. These young men were, because of the established tradition of primogeniture, deprived of their families' inheritances, which went almost entirely to firstborn sons.

Meanwhile, they were slaves to the custom that forced them to pursue "respectable" careers as doctors, lawyers, clergymen, or politicians. Occupations in manual trades were regarded as beneath them, and those who pursued such careers risked losing their social standing.

After a visit to the United States, Hughes sought to establish a colony where these men and their families could live in close communion with nature and work as craftsmen, farmers, and carpenters, using their hands as well as their minds. By the mid-

1880s, the colony, named Rugby in tribute to the famous British school where Hughes had studied as a boy, boasted more than four hundred residents and a collection of sixty-five buildings, including a three-story inn, a schoolhouse, an Episcopal church, and a library with more than seven thousand volumes. The original collection of books still lines the library's floor-to-ceiling shelves.

While the British settlers were richly endowed with ambition, they proved poorly suited to life in the wilderness. And by 1890, the colony was in deep decline, having suffered an outbreak of typhoid fever, a series of brutal winters, and a canning enterprise that failed because residents had neglected to plant enough tomatoes.

As the girls and I walked along the well-worn paths through the settlement and entered dark, century-old buildings that smelled of dust and aged wood, I couldn't help but reflect on the parallels between Hughes's enterprise and my own.

Both of us had sought fresh firmaments for beginning new lives beyond the reach of constricting traditions and customs. Both of us had sought the abiding goodness of a life in nature. Both of us had arrived full of hope.

But in the end, Rugby's residents carried within themselves the seeds of failure. When their efforts foundered, many returned to England overwhelmed by discouragement. I had been troubled often over the past few days by the notion that my retreat to Morgan County might, like Rugby, prove to be more of a folly than a journey of faith and that I, too, would return to the suburbs with broken spirit and shredded hopes.

With the broad expanse of America spread before Hughes and his followers, what was it that drew them here, to this region, to this high, wide plateau contained between deep river gorges? Perhaps it was the same things that had drawn me to the region more than a century later: a chance to start fresh.

As we left, the girls and I piled in the Jeep and drove past carefully preserved buildings whose elaborate architecture stood in stark contrast to the board-and-batten cabins and mobile homes that line Tennessee's back roads. And I couldn't help but regard those buildings as the gravestones marking dead dreams.

By midafternoon, we arrived at Big South Fork National River and Recreation Area, a 106,000-acre tract of forest that straddles the Tennessee-Kentucky border. The area's defining feature is the Big South Fork of the Cumberland River, which flows north between sheer bluffs that rise as high as six hundred feet above the streambed.

On the way to the campground, we descended along hairpin turns lined with flowering redbuds and towering hemlocks to where the road crossed the river. Challen, who, by virtue of a coin toss, had been assigned the backseat, insisted that she was going to "gack" if we didn't stop. The greenish hue in her cheeks suggested that she wasn't bluffing, so I pulled into the parking area beside the river. The girls spilled out and sprinted toward the water as I hooked Benton to his lead.

A group of people labored to drag several six-person rafts back up from the river to a waiting church bus, and four kayakers sliced the water with their paddles, angling toward the take-out ramp. All had red cheeks and forearms from an early spring day spent in sunshine.

The girls had stripped off their sneakers and were knee-deep in the river by the time Benton and I arrived. They giggled as the chill water lapped against their thighs, and they probed the water with their hands looking for interesting rocks.

Challen, in keeping with her gentle nature, daintily skipped small flat stones toward the center of the river. Meanwhile, Logan hefted cannon-ball-size boulders, pressed them to her cheek, and launched them shot-put style into the water, laughing maniacally when they exploded the river's surface and showered her with droplets.

Benton whimpered and tugged at the leash, and I realized I was torturing a water dog by leading him to the river's edge without releasing him to swim. I looked up toward the parking area and noticed that the Baptists were about to sit down to dinner at a picnic table. Hoping that the lure of the water would outcompete the aroma of food, I clipped Benton off the lead, and he plunged into the water and swam toward the center, snorting rhythmically as he purged water from his nostrils.

Logan picked up a stick on the bank and hurled it into the

river. It caught in the current and shot downstream, with Benton in hot pursuit. A couple of hikers cleared the woods and walked past me, stopping to watch Benton stroke toward the stick.

"Those dogs are amazing," one of them said. "They just live to bring things back to you."

"Not this dog. He *almost* brings things back," I said. "He's a sweet boy but a total flunky as a retriever."

As we watched, Benton, now a distant spot of golden fur floating on green water, snatched the stick and began his long slow turn into the current and back toward us. When he reached to within ten feet of the shore, he dropped the stick, as he always does.

I've had two black Labradors who were compulsive retrievers, and they had exhibited the trait from the time they were eight weeks old. On one camping trip, Smudge had tirelessly chased a Frisbee until we noticed that she was limping and discovered that her paws were bleeding. And one evening some years later, while we lived in the farmhouse, I had thrown a tennis ball off into the woods for Morpheus. She searched dutifully until it got dark and I called her in. The next morning, as soon as I let her out of the house, she charged off into the same sector of woods, picking up right where she had left off the night before.

It was as if a toggle switch in her head had been turned on, and she couldn't rest until it had been switched off. Morpheus was so intent on retrieving that she'd often scarf up anything that happened to be laying around, approach you, and lay her head on your knee, whimpering softly and wagging her tail. Her motto might well have been, with apologies to Descartes, *Fetchito, ergo sum.*

One Christmas morning, Morph pranced around a living room full of torn wrapping paper and open boxes wearing *that* look: "I've got something in my mouth. Care to see what it is?" When I commanded her to "drop," she deposited at my feet my cousin's dental retainer, which had been left on the coffee table. On another occasion, also during the winter just after a trip outside, she approached Dad, laid her head on his knee, and whimpered. When he said, "Well, Morph, what have you brought me this time?" she deposited a frozen turd into his palm.

At some point in his development, Benton's neural network had gone awry, and he had grown into an adult with a burning urge to "go get" but complete indifference to the task of "bringing back." The gene that for centuries has compelled golden retrievers to fetch fallen birds and drop them at their masters' feet was clearly recessive in Benton, if it was present at all.

"Benton, go get the stick!" Logan shouted. Benton looked back at the stick bobbing in the water then at Logan and continued on his way, drawing within two feet of us before pausing to shake the water from his fur.

"He's gonna blow!" Challen cautioned, her phrasing for when Benton showered those around him with cold creek water.

Benton may have been a half-assed retriever, but he boasted a fully evolved sense of smell and a healthy appetite, and once he was beyond my reach, he charged toward the Baptists, with water still dripping from his coat.

The congregation was somewhere between the prayer and the first course when Benton arrived. He announced his presence by baptizing the assembly with river water then, using a ploy that at some point in his life had earned him a food treat, tried to look adorable by laying his nose on the edge of the table while wagging his tail. The Baptists had scattered and Benton was moving toward the potato salad when I arrived.

Forgiveness for my dog's transgressions was not forthcoming, and impatient scowls greeted my apologies. As I led the sinner away, I overheard a middle-aged man and his wife arguing over the responsibilities of dog owners and the nature of pets.

"That animal is a menace!" the woman said, looking directly at me. "He should have been on a leash."

"Honey, it's not right to keep pure-bred dogs like that tied up all the time," the man countered. "Sometimes you just have to let a dog be a dog."

"Amen, brother," I said.

We combed the campground searching for the perfect site to erect the Taj MaBrill, and I scanned the occupied sites, secretly hoping to see other single parents with their kids. Instead, I glimpsed families of moms and dads and kids happily gathered around fire rings or pedaling bicycles in formation through the campground.

Since the separation, I had begun to feel like I wore a scarlet *D* pinned to my chest proclaiming to all that I was a matrimonial failure. Benton couldn't retrieve, and I couldn't sustain a marriage. Beyond that, I couldn't shake the feeling that, when the girls and I were together, we might have been a majority but were somehow still short of a quorum. To me, our abbreviated family unit felt incomplete, diminished, compromised, like we were pieces of something not quite whole.

To Susan, a child of divorce, a family might have been a single parent and kids; to me it felt lacking. I could only imagine how it felt to two young girls who loved Susan and me dearly and unconditionally and couldn't understand why we couldn't love each other.

After dinner, I lay on a sleeping pad and paged through a book in the waning daylight. The girls asked if they could play hide and seek, and I told them they could, as long as they stayed in sight of the camp. They soon tired of the game and started challenging each other to footraces along the paved road through the campground.

I should have anticipated what would result when two competitive siblings tore off helter-skelter along darkening pavement. While en route back to the tent from the junction that connected with the adjoining loop, Logan pulled ahead of Challen and tripped. Challen leaped clear, but Logan skidded to a stop on her hands and knees.

First I heard her tumble, then the crying started. Before I could climb to my feet and respond, mothers from the three campsites closest to ours rushed to assist.

One of the women arrived with a dampened paper towel and a tube of first-aid cream. In the time it had taken me just to arrive at the scene, she had somehow managed to gather up first-aid supplies.

"Here," she said proffering the paper towel. "You can use this to clean the wound."

"No, thanks, really, we're fine," I said. I'm sure my response sounded defensive, and I suppose it was. For some reason, I needed to handle this on my own. I wrapped my arm around Logan and we limped back to the campsite. As the tears streamed down her cheeks, I braced for the words I knew were on her lips but that I really didn't want to hear. Whenever either of the girls was hurt, even if I happened to be standing right beside her, she would rush past me and into Susan's arms, sobbing "I want Mommy."

This time, Logan contented herself with nurturing from Dad, and it occurred to me that perhaps her composure resulted from the fact that Mommy was three hours away back in Knoxville. For whatever reason, Logan let me doctor her wounds, and I gained as much from the treatment as she. A few minutes later, she brightened when I suggested that we take a night hike, a ritual that has been part of our camping routine since the girls were old enough to walk.

Together, we'd wandered off countless times, hand in hand, into darkened woods and sat stone still, listening to the sounds stirring around us. The girls had taken special delight in calling out to barred owls after a night in the Smokies when a particularly vocal raptor roosted in the tree above our tent and serenaded the girls through the night with its resonant call.

After a short walk, we settled onto the ground, and I felt the girls press close to me. We nestled together and welcomed the night as an abbreviated family that, at least for the moment, was sufficient, if not complete.

THIRTY-FIVE

Daddy Doesn't Live Here Anymore

If to be absent were to be
Away from thee;
Or that when I am gone,
You and I were alone;
Then, my Lucasta, might I crave
Pity from blust'ring wind, or swallowing wave.
                              —Richard Lovelace, *Lucasta*

I dropped the girls off in West Knoxville midafternoon and unloaded four days' worth of muddy shorts and sodden sneakers. Before I left, the girls clustered around me and made their best case for my remaining with them for the night.

"Please, please, please stay, Daddy," Challen pleaded.

"Why can't you leave tomorrow so we can have a movie-and-pizza night?" Logan asked. Over the previous five years, we had celebrated the end of the workweek with a video and pizza on Friday nights. It was an inviolate tradition, and our friends knew that there was no use in asking us to plan any activities on Friday nights. We'd rent a family movie for the four of us and a new release for Susan and me after the girls had gone to bed.

I had introduced the Friday night ritual at the cabin, trying to ease the transition for the girls. I bought a small TV with built-in VCR. It was no small irony that fifteen minutes after I had plugged in the unit for the first time, the phone rang. It was the Nielsen people, asking if they could monitor my family's TV viewing patterns over the following week.

"You picked the wrong residence," I said, laughing. "We live out in the woods beyond the reach of TV signals. We have ninety-nine channels of static."

There was a long pause.

"Are you serious?" the man asked, stunned that, in the waning years of the twentieth century, network programming hadn't penetrated every household in America.

"Completely."

"Okay, well, thank you anyway."

While our decision to do without TV perplexed Mr. Nielsen, my reluctance to spend the night in the city was equally confusing to my daughters.

My investment of special time with them over the previous four days had drawn us close. We had connected in a significant way—it represented the longest span of days and nights they had been with me and away from Susan—but I began to sense that my profit might have been their emotional loss. Growing close to me during extended periods together meant more hurt for them when I left. It was a cruel trade-off.

Though I had, on occasion, spent the night with them at home, mainly out of necessity when obligations required me to be in Knoxville, my evenings there had grown increasingly tense, not to mention uncomfortable. I slept on the couch in a room with Clarence the hamster, whose nocturnal activities chiefly involved gnawing on things and sprinting on a squeaky metal wheel.

"Girls, I can't stay," I said. "I don't live here anymore. Besides, Mom and I need some space, some time apart."

"Daddy, this isn't fair," Challen protested. "Why can't we be like a real family?"

"Challen, this feels as strange to me as it does to you, but this is the situation we have to work with," I said. "We're still a family, and we'll always be a family, but our family is going to take a different form. Besides, I think Mom is a lot happier when I'm not around."

"Yeah, maybe she is, but Logan and I aren't," Challen said.

"Challen, just know that I didn't choose this; this isn't what I wanted either," I said, attempting to skirt a minefield. Susan had

asked that I not share with the girls or any of our friends the particulars of who had initiated the separation.

She also asked that I not talk to the girls about the separation
without her being present. That had already proven impossible.
If the girls hit me with a tough question while they were with me,
I wasn't about to defer the answer until Susan showed up. Besides, Susan and I had different takes on what the truth was, and
I didn't want to offer the girls a sanitized explanation that left
them with the impression that their dad had bailed out on them.

Before I left to return to the cabin, after Challen had asked me
to stay the night, I prevailed on her once again to trust in God to
guide her and the rest of our family. It had taken me most of my
life to begin to trust, truly trust, in God's wisdom. During my
time at the cabin, both alone and in the company of friends and
family, I'd felt my faith growing deeper and a sense of peace settling over me at a time that, by all rights, should have been
marred by stress and fear. My marriage was coming apart, but
somehow, I was okay, my heart and mind were becoming still.

But how to impart this belief to my girls, how to persuade
them to surrender and trust, when their Mom and Dad were
drifting apart? I knew enough from my own search to realize
that each person's spiritual path is a singular one and that no
prodding can compel someone to make a journey she's not ready
to take.

But I could, as my Christian friends have taught me, live a life
in faith and shine whatever measure of light is inside me outward
into the world and onto my children and hope that the small
glimmer of the divine they might see in me will incline them,
when they're ready, to trust and yield, as I have.

"Ye are the light of the world . . . ," Matthew writes in the
New Testament. "Let your light so shine before men, that they
may see your good works, and glorify your Father which is in
heaven."

I hoped Challen would surrender to God's will sooner rather
than later. Such faith has buoyed believers through trials much,
much worse than anything we were contending with.

"Even though it might not feel like it right now, God is taking
care of us," I said. "We just need to trust that everything is going

to work out. Besides, aren't you happier not seeing Mom and me fight all the time?"

As soon as I said it, I realized that I had posed a question that no ten-year-old is equipped to answer.

"I don't know," she said. She hugged me, and I could feel her shoulders shaking. I tried to keep my composure but failed and surrendered to the moment's emotional tug. For a few minutes, we gripped each other and cried.

I arrived at the cabin at 7 P.M., and the setting sun glinted through leaves of frail, new green. The azalea bushes I had planted two weeks before were in full flower. Tiny bluets, spring's earliest messengers, trembled in the breeze and added dashes of color through the awakening forest. I settled into a chair on the deck, opened a beer, and watched the sun drop below the bluff.

The solitude felt soothing, and when the phone rang, I was tempted to ignore it, but I thought it might be one of the girls calling for their nightly "Daddy-fix." Instead, it was J.J. He had set off toward Big South Fork with Jasper, his lean leggy hound, to camp for the night. When he tried to erect his tent, he noticed one of the poles was broken. He was preparing to mend it when a microburst pummeled him with rain and hail. He ducked into his Land Cruiser and dialed me on his cell phone.

"Whacha doing, guy?" J.J. asked, and I immediately recognized an increasingly familiar tone of someone who was about to invite himself to the cabin.

"Not much, just chillin' out in the Garden of Eden. What about you?"

J.J. explained his predicament with the tent, and I extended an invitation to join me for a pasta dinner. Over the previous months, J.J. had grown to be a dear and loyal friend who frequently called to check on me and had listened patiently as I discussed my difficulties at home. Though I considered the relationship reciprocal in that regard, J.J. seemed to value his privacy and only on rare occasion had delved into his own problems at work or home.

But if there ever was a time for him to value a good friend with a welcome ear, it was now. Two weeks earlier, his mother had died after a long illness that had forced her to endure twice-weekly dialysis treatments. A virus had attacked her already weakened immune system, and she returned home after a week-long hospital stay and died less than twenty-four hours later.

J.J. had left a short message on my answering machine. He was sorry, but he would have to miss Wednesday Night Prayer Meeting.

"Mom died last night," he said, then ended the message. Though the message was terse, the quaver in J.J.'s voice, and not his choice of words, communicated how much he was hurting. I called him frequently over the next few days, just so he'd know I was thinking about him.

At one point, he told me that he could use a weekend at the cabin to mourn the loss, and I was gratified to know that he, too, looked to Benton's Run as a place to heal and reflect. When I got J.J.'s call from Big South Fork, it occurred to me that this might be his weekend.

He arrived an hour later. We ate dinner on the deck by lamp-light, and afterward, we sat with our legs propped up on the deck railing and talked until after 2 A.M. This time, it was my turn to listen. J.J. discussed his frustrations with the hospice program, which, he felt, had complicated his mother's final hours rather than facilitating a gentle transition into death. He spoke about his father's selfless devotion to his wife through all those years of illness.

He talked about a doctor who had rallied after hospice had faltered and went to extraordinary lengths to make sure J.J.'s mother received the pain medication she needed. He described his mother's final hours and the peace that seemed to attend her passing, how his father had climbed in bed to lie next to her in the moments after her death, how J.J. had held his mother's hand until he felt the warmth leave her body.

Then, he fell silent, and we sat together in stillness, and I hoped the embrace of the forest would sustain him the way it had comforted and sustained me.

THIRTY-SIX

Marshall Fights Back

Do not go gentle into that good night, old age
should burn and rave at close of day; rage, rage
against the dying of the light.
  —Dylan Thomas, "Do Not Go Gentle into that
    Good Night"

I made a trip in to Oak Ridge one afternoon to visit Marshall, who had been moved from the hospital into a nursing home. Though her physical condition had steadily improved to
the point that she was somewhat mobile, she had experienced a
steep emotional decline, which she communicated in her tone and
through the look in her eyes. I had had a conversation earlier in the
week with Emily, a mutual friend who had taken it upon herself to
serve as Marshall's primary caregiver, a role Marshall's daughter,
Rosemary, surely would have filled had she lived in town.

Emily described Marshall, plagued by painful and frustrating
symptoms of a failing body, hugging Emily and trying her best
to cry.

"It was very difficult for her," Emily said. "It seems like she's
lived her entire life without learning how to grieve or cry. She
sobbed and sobbed, but there were no tears."

I had sat with Marshall the night her son died, and though she
was clearly pained by his loss, she never cried. If she had endured
that night without tears, it occurred to me how profound her
current suffering must have been to bring on such an unpharac-
teristic outpouring of emotion.

As I coursed down a long hallway, I tried to smile at cadav-
eresque octogenarians who sat babbling senselessly in wheel-

chairs. An Asian woman stared blankly at the floor, shrieking nonsense syllables, and rotating her wheelchair in tight, compulsive circles. A white-haired woman walking purposefully down the hall looked at me with alert eyes and asked if the boy had arrived with his lawnmower to cut her grass. The smell of feces and urine and the disinfectant used to mask their scent was reminiscent of a day-care center, but the nursing home was absent the smiling, cherubic faces and babbling that would evolve into patterned speech. This was the last stop for most of Marshall's housemates who existed like zombies bereft of sanity and trapped in bodies that refused to yield to death.

I reached Marshall's door, not knowing what to expect, and I was relieved to see her sitting in a chair clad in a short-sleeved shirt with vertical turquoise and white stripes, like the ones sported by the Beach Boys in their early performing days. I'm certain she had ordered the shirt from her favorite "surfer" mail-order catalog.

"These people are trying to train me to use *that* thing," she said, pointing disdainfully a few feet away at a portable toilet mounted on wheels. Someone had attempted to disguise the appliance by draping a towel over its top.

Marshall didn't detail how her training had been progressing, but she described orderlies entering her room one night after midnight, stripping off her clothes, and leaving her to spend the rest of the night cold and naked. It occurred to me that the story might have been more metaphoric—in essence, being stripped of her dignity—than literal, though I was inclined to believe her account. I was also certain that the orderlies had arrived with a purpose beyond harassing her.

After a time, she looked at me with sad eyes. "If my doctor won't let me go home, I'm going to fire him," she said, and I was encouraged to see that her fighting spirit was, at least, partially intact.

"Why do you need his permission?" I asked, not so much out of naivete as irritation. What law barred an eighty-nine-year-old woman from deciding her own fate, even if going home meant hastening her own death? Which was more cruel, withering to nothing in a place full of people who had lost control of their minds and bowels, or spending one's final days in solitude surrounded by familiar things that offered comfort and prompted memories of happier times?

"You're not crazy," I said. "So why can't you just check yourself out of this place?"

"I can't get around very well, and I'll need someone to take care of me, but then I don't want a home-health nurse living with me all the time."

"So don't hire one."

An orderly arrived at the door with Marshall's dinner—barbequed beef and scalloped potatoes—and I helped maneuver the tray table in front of her. She had graduated back to solid food from the pureed slop they had been feeding her in the hospital—a good sign, I thought.

A couple of weeks later, after the girls had spent the weekend with me at the cabin, I drove them to Oak Ridge to visit Marshall. She hadn't seen them for over a year, and I hoped their visit would buoy her spirits; I also hoped the girls would gain perspective on what life is like in the building that adjoins the boneyard.

"Okay, girls, what you're about to see can be scary and sad," I said, as we turned down the road to the nursing home. "You're going to see old people who have lost their minds, and the place smells really, really bad. If you get uncomfortable, let me know and we'll leave."

"Will Marshall recognize us?" Challen asked, as we pulled into the parking lot.

"Yes, I think she will, but it might take her awhile." As usual, I was guilty of underestimating Marshall and her affection for the girls.

After punching a series of numbers into the electronic key pad at the door, we heard the lock click open.

"Why do they lock the doors here?" Logan asked.

"Because some of these people might wander off and get into trouble."

"You mean they'd rob banks and stuff?"

"No, they might stray into traffic or just walk off to where no one could find them. These folks are a lot like little kids; some of them aren't able to take care of themselves."

We walked down the long entry hallway, and the girls were wide-eyed and silent. The white-haired woman, as always, asked me if the man had come to mow her grass.

"He should be here any minute," I said. She looked at the girls, and her face softened into a smile. She extended her hands.

"Hello, you sweet little things," she said.

The girls tentatively took her hands but didn't return the greeting. Even kids have a way of recognizing the non sequiturs of dementia.

Eventually, we navigated the labyrinth of long hallways and connecting wings to Marshall's room. Inside, Marshall sat slumped forward in her wheelchair, and the sight initially unnerved me. She looked dead, and I feared that I had exposed my children to a scene they weren't quite ready to confront.

As we gazed on Marshall, propped lifelessly in her chair, I experienced a moment of panic. Then I noticed her chest was moving; she was just catching a nap.

I walked over to her and whispered in her ear, "Marshall, you've got visitors," but there was no response. I had forgotten that she had lost most of her hearing. I tapped her lightly on the shoulder, and she slowly rose up and opened her eyes.

"Challen and Logan!" she said, recognizing the girls the instant her eyes opened. "Come give me a kiss."

They looked at Marshall, then at me, as if to ask, "Is it okay to kiss someone who looks so fragile that she might fall to dust at the slightest touch?"

"It's okay, girls," I said. They slowly edged close, kissed her cheek quickly, then returned to my side on the bed. I recalled the unsettling experience as a kid of drawing close to an ancient face covered in what looked like white tissue paper and feeling like you were pressing your lips against something more dead than alive.

I looked over at the girls, as they sat with hands folded, the color of sun on their cheeks, the first blond streaks of summer in their hair, their blue eyes so bright and attentive. Then I looked at Marshall and gazed at the ravages of age and failing health. I wanted to say, "Girls, this is where we're all heading; celebrate your youth, live large, drink deep, make it count—but be home by eleven."

I scanned the room and noticed that the drawings the girls had composed for Marshall hung from the wall.

"Look, girls, it's the Brill Gallery," I said, pointing out their artwork.

"Thank you for my pictures," Marshall said.

"You're welcome," they said in unison, their hands still folded on their laps, the universal signal to parents that their children are either straining to be polite or feeling downright uncomfortable.

Then Marshall started to bitch, something she does exceedingly well. "Did you know they tried to stick me with a roommate?" she asked. I knew that her daughter was fighting hard to get her a single room, but the long waiting list made it unlikely that Marshall would survive long enough to get one. The incompatible temperaments—and Marshall's willfulness—had forced the nursing home staff to move the woman down the hall after a few tense days of cohabitation.

"We had absolutely nothing in common. I was sweltering; she was freezing," she said. "If they don't let me go home, I'm going to sleep out in the courtyard!"

I laughed. The girls laughed. And as they did, I suspect that they started to grasp that a ragged body can house an active mind. They were learning not to be deceived by these sometimes unsightly containers that house our spirits.

We sat with Marshall for a half hour and left when the orderly arrived to clean and change her. The girls had seen enough for one day.

"I love you and your whole family, and tell Susan to come see me," Marshall said, as we left. "Please, please don't forget me."

Along the road home, the girls didn't say much, and I knew they were processing things. Marshall was propped up in a wheelchair, about to begin a new journey. Meanwhile, they were healthy and alive, with years and years and years to sprint on strong young legs.

THIRTY-SEVEN

Journey to Genesis

In God's wilderness lies the hope of the world—
the great fresh unblighted, unredeemed wilderness.
—John Muir, *Alaska Fragment*

When I describe the cabin's setting as "wilderness," I'm guilty of hyperbole. True wilderness does not include roads and power lines and third- or fourth-growth forests. It exists as a pure thing that doesn't reflect back at man a single element of his efforts to tame or to alter or to change the natural environment. It's the place we must visit if we want to return to the genesis, to the way things were before human clusters evolved into settlements, and from there into communities, and from there into cities.

Wilderness is still out there, even in the fragmented Southeast, and pockets of it lie less than forty miles from my cabin. To get there you have to follow roads that grow progressively smaller and less defined to places where your Jeep bucks and groans over boulders, snaps through tight tangles of branches, and plunges down to the wheel wells in fast-moving creeks before stopping dead before an unyielding threshold of trees and vines and rock. From there, the journey, rightfully, continues on foot, into the heart of the Cumberlands.

My neighbor, Bob Reed, and I set out in the Jeep before dawn one morning to explore one such parcel of wilderness two hours north of the cabin. Our mission, in part, involved scoping out possible routes for the Cumberland Trail. Once complete, the

Cumberland Trail will extend more than two hundred miles from just north of Chattanooga to Cumberland Gap on the Kentucky border. Only about sixty-five miles of the route had been completed, and though the remainder had been roughly plotted, the fine-tuning required field work involving small maps, large watersheds, and repeated compass bearings.

Bob and I had offered our services as trailblazers. I can't speak for Bob, but I had spent the past twenty years benefitting from the tireless work of the volunteers who built and maintained mountain trails. The Cumberland Trail provided a way for me to clear the way for others, to give something back. It also provided an excuse, not that I needed one, for probing deep into the wilds of middle Tennessee.

The Cumberland Trail Conference had assembled teams that boasted complementary skills. So it was with ours. Bob, who holds a Ph.D. in botany, would identify plants and trees, looking for rare species and unique pockets of flowering plants. As a hiker, I would study the topography and scope out possible routes for the trail.

I had known Bob for years, though we had become better acquainted after he and Willow bought the property adjoining mine. They spent most weekends at their cabin, a ten-minute walk down the road from mine, and I saw them frequently. They took their two dogs for evening walks, and their turnaround was at my cabin.

The two-hour drive to and from the mountains would provide some solid male-bonding time for the two of us, and I welcomed the opportunity to capitalize on Bob's knowledge of our region's wild plants once we hit the trail.

Our mission took us deep into the wilds of Scott and Campbell counties, areas marked by three-thousand-foot peaks, high forested ridges, and remote hollows inhabited by the descendants of the Cumberland Plateau's original families.

We coursed north along Route 116 past Brushy Mountain State Penitentiary, a hulking brown fortress tucked into a crease in the mountains and encircled by high fences topped with concertina wire. The guard towers disappeared into the fog, and floodlights created eerie halos in the dank predawn air.

We continued north an hour farther to where the pavement ended and the gravel road snaked through tiny hamlets with names like Stainville, Smoky Junction, and Hembree. After we'd driven past miles of unbroken forest and sensed that we had left civilization far behind, we'd round a bend and glimpse settlements of cabins clustered around ma-and-pa grocery stores and Baptist churches. Well-worn paths marked the way from the chapels up the hill to his-and-her outhouses. At one point, we passed a dead oak tree with a brotherhood of black vultures roosting on its craggy limbs.

Roadside vegetation ensnarled rusting hulks of cars and trucks whose soft, rounded lines traced back to Detroit of the 1940s and '50s. One tiny cinder-block dwelling coated in salmon-colored paint was dwarfed by a satellite dish. These hollows were among the early beneficiaries of the Tennessee Valley Authority, which snaked wires over the mountains back in the 1930s, bringing power and paving the way for TV and other modern conveniences. I couldn't help but wonder how the residents of these settlements reconciled the discrepancies they noticed between the world they viewed out their windows and the one featured on their TV screens.

A sign advised us to yield to coal trucks, and soon we encountered the first of several massive vehicles, heaped with coal and lumbering down narrow, serpentine roads. An orange DE- TOUR sign posted on a tree caused us to slow and look for the alternate route in a valley barely wide enough to accommodate a single two-lane road, but we then encountered an interstate sign for I-71, which runs from Louisville, Kentucky, north through Ohio, and realized that both signs had been hung in jest.

Eventually, we drove along the vibrant green bottomland lining Smoky Creek and located a narrow break in the vegetation marking the old road that, on the map, paralleled Cave Branch. I shifted the Jeep into four-wheel drive and entered the forest. For several hundred yards, we bounced down into deep ruts and splashed through the rushing creek. A tangle of blowdowns signaled the end of the road for the Jeep, and we shouldered our packs and continued on from there on foot.

The old roadbed narrowed and eventually disappeared altogether, and we stopped to study the topographic map and fix our location. Our destination, Gibson Knob, loomed 1,700 feet above us in the low-slung clouds.

Where the road ended, the verdant bounty of wild blooms and shoots began. The Cumberlands are known for their profusion of spring wildflowers, and we had arrived at the season's peak. White, yellow, and purple trilliums, their tri-lobed blossoms perfectly offset with three broad mottled leaves, covered entire hillsides. The dark green variegated leaves of bloodroot clustered around hooded jack-in-the-pulpits. The single yellow blossom of may apples cowered, shaded and dry, beneath broad green umbrellas. Thickets of wild ginger spread in the shade of buckeye trees.

Bob, a subdued man rarely given to emotional outbursts, soon found himself knee-deep in botanical utopia and couldn't contain his excitement.

"Look! It's foam flower! Here's a toad-shade trillium! Over there is wild geranium and phlox!" Every ten yards of trail brought new discoveries, and as we angled up away from the creek and bushwhacked toward the knob, we ascended through tier after tier of distinct floral offering. As we did, we witnessed succession in reverse, with higher elevations revealing species that had bloomed days or even weeks earlier down along the warmer clime of the creek.

Bob's botanical bent and my focus on topography complemented each other perfectly in terms of choosing a trail route that would conform to the contours of the mountain while coursing past unique pockets of vegetation. But on occasion I sensed that we might have been working at cross purposes. My focus reflected the macro perspective defined by an entire watershed; Bob's tightly trained perspective fell on the patch of green directly under his gaze.

"David, you just stepped on a jack-in-the-pulpit," Bob said at one point, lifting a fractured stem from the humus.

"Oh, sorry, didn't see that one," I said, wondering how a Zen master—who values all life—might have executed his duties at trailblazing in spring woods.

I tried to tread lightly on the fledgling plants, but they were too dense to avoid. Beside, I was engaged in a favorite pastime—exploring a tract of unbroken wilderness with nothing but a map and compass—and I found that my desire to reach the top soon supplanted my concern for the unfortunate sprigs I crunched under my boots.

Though the clouds never gave us a clear glimpse of the surrounding terrain, we moved steadily upward through dense brush under a towering canopy of tulip poplars, buckeye, and hickory, following the compass arm due west, cutting straight across the tight contour lines that led to Gibson Knob on the map.

When we reached near the top and the terrain began to soften, we encountered a Jeep road, and I realized that our wilderness sojourn was over. Though over the previous two hours I might have convinced myself that I was deep in uncharted forest, the smattering of trash along the Jeep road returned me to reality that I was home in the Tennessee backcountry. Dozens of blowdowns and a few sizable trees sprouting along the mound between two old wheel ruts indicated that the road hadn't been used for quite some time. But we could see the tread of all-terrain-vehicles stamped into the mud.

We followed the road for a few hundred yards to where it forked. While Bob remained at the junction, studying the plants, I reconnoitered, following the less-worn fork—recalling Frost's advice in "The Road Not Taken"—that coursed along a narrow spine at a right angle from Gibson Knob. The setting had the familiar look of an old homestead—a clearing, a pile of old glass bottles and metal cans that for some reason trouble me less than recent-issue twist-cap plastic containers and cans with born-on dates—and within a few hundred yards I confirmed my suspicion. A grave angled away from the trail. It was marked with a simple stone plucked from the earth. BOWLING had been painted on the rock in rough, white letters.

I stood for a few minutes at the grave and scanned the woods around me. The ridge spread seventy-yards wide then dropped away steeply. Native grasses grew where the trees had been cleared away and created a narrow linear meadow. I imagined that it might have been a fine homesite for the Bowling family.

The withered flowers set beside the makeshift headstone suggested that the family's descendants still lived nearby.

After a brief lunch atop a square, house-size boulder just below Gibson Knob, Bob and I followed the old logging road south and soon picked up a faint foot trail, which eventually headed toward the adjoining watershed. Its course made it obvious to both of us that the trail was not going to lead us back to the Jeep, so as a light rain began to fall, we took a bearing and dropped off the ridge and plunged back into the forest. Though neither of us was absolutely positive of our position, we surmised that if we traveled east-by-southeast, we'd intersect Cave Branch. Once we reached the creek, we could follow it downstream to the old road and on to the Jeep.

As we followed along the creek through dense woods, I peered ahead through the trees and saw the flash of red metal—the Jeep—and for a second the image didn't compute: "What the hell is that!?" Then I realized that our navigational hunch had paid off and we had completed the meandering six-mile loop.

We stowed our packs in the car just as the clouds opened, and the windshield wipers slapped time all the way home. As I drove, Bob flipped through a wildflower book and kept an alert eye for oncoming coal trucks.

I dropped Bob off at his cabin, and he invited me in for a beer. The rain had brought cooler temperatures, and Willow had stoked a fire. As we sipped our beers, we shared with her the day's discoveries—the wild birds and plants we had identified—and how the unwavering compass needle had led us to the mist-shrouded mountaintop and back home.

I emptied the beer and felt a longing to be home by my own fire, to reflect on a day spent in the wildness of my own mountains. As the Jeep crunched to a stop at the cabin, I saw Benton on the porch, his tail wagging, his nose pressed against the mesh of the screen door. It felt good to be missed, to be welcomed home.

THIRTY-EIGHT

Passage through the Doldrums

Day after day, day after day, we struck nor breath nor motion. As idle as a painted ship upon a painted ocean.
—Samuel Taylor Coleridge, *The Ancient Mariner*

L ike Coleridge's mariner, I arrived in the doldrums, and I pas-sively awaited the albatross, the harbinger of rebirth, though I began to fear that the species wasn't indigenous to my woods.

The girls and Susan had traveled to Amsterdam to visit Susan's dad and his wife, who spend several months there each year, and they'd been gone nearly a month. When the girls left, I asked them to give me a hug that would last a month; it lasted barely a week before I found myself peering at the pictures of them I kept at the cabin and feeling off balance, as if two of the legs of my three-legged stool had been temporarily removed.

Though the girls had called three times from Holland, and they'd detailed their bike rides to open-air markets and trips to ancient castles and assured me that they loved me, hearing their voices just made them seem that much farther away. I worried that they were missing me less and less each day and finding greater contentment in Susan's family of origin: mom and kids, with Dad a distant voice on the telephone.

I'd been pacing the pine floors through endless days, glancing out windows at motionless summer woods that had begun to feel more like a barrier than a protective buffer. My fingers hovered, tentative, over my computer keyboard. The creek seemed too far away to warrant the ten-minute hike to and from.

Though I sought the escape of sleep, Susan had begun to dominate my dreams, wounding me by turning the kids away from me, by continuing to reprove and chide me, by thriving as I slump into loneliness and sadness.

Even Benton seemed to have lost his energy. He lay on the floor motionless though the day, though his paws twitched occasionally as he chased rabbits through the fields of his dreams.

After Susan and the girls returned on the following Saturday, the day before Father's Day, she and I would schedule an appointment with a mediator and begin to formally—and legally—dismantle our family. I had meditated for days on the right course, vacillating between self-sacrifice and self-determination, between self-recrimination and anger, wondering always how best to tend to the girls' needs.

I broached the subject with a colleague and friend at the university who knew us both.

"I'm thinking about approaching Susan and pledging to change, promising to address her concerns—all of them—and to become the man she wants me to be," I said. "Maybe if I do, if I sacrifice myself, I can save our marriage."

"Let's say Susan has a list of five things you do that she can't tolerate," he said. "And let's say you resolve all five. The question is, will she just find five more?"

My fear was that she would, that this was less about me and my suitability as a mate and more about Susan's need for independence.

It occurred to me that my inkling the first time I saw her, that she was way, way too good for me, that she deserved someone more spirited than me, might have been right on target. Susan had aged gracefully and was as beautiful at thirty-eight as she was at twenty. I can't say the same for me. Meanwhile, my income never allowed me to pamper her, to buy her an upscale house and elegant car. My desire for entertainment typically led to the woods while hers increasingly involved restaurants with white-linen tablecloths.

Maybe she was beginning to realize how well she might have done—and might do, still—were she not tethered to me. Maybe, try as I might, I could never be enough for her. Maybe she had outgrown me.

In my dark fantasies, I saw her married to an Adonis whose good looks, self-confidence, and high earnings provided Susan the kind of life—and mate—she wanted. That much I could handle, but when I thought about another man sleeping with my wife in the bedroom down the hall from my kids' rooms, when I thought about another guy kissing my girls good night while I was off somewhere missing them, I got a little crazy.

I didn't deserve this, and neither did my girls.

I sometimes wondered what would happen if I showed up at the door in Knoxville and announced that I was moving back in. During a brief consultation, a lawyer told me that if I moved out, even if I was edged out, Susan had the right to bar me from reentering the house—my house. But would she?

My girls deserved—and needed—my physical presence in their lives every day, but at what cost? Could they grow up whole and well-adjusted with an ancillary dad? Could I adequately execute my duties as father from the isolation of the cabin? Could I survive without daily contact with them?

These were dark, doubtful days. I missed my girls.

The "black dog" of despondency decided to stay. Five days without seeing or speaking face-to-face with another person. Nearly a month without seeing my girls. Racing heart, racing thoughts. Wondering what would come next in my life, my marriage.

I decided to stir myself into action, to see if a little motion would help vanquish the blues. Late in the afternoon, I loaded my day pack and grabbed my fishing rod, and Benton and I hiked down to the creek. Temperatures in the mid-seventies, perfect blue sky, water in the creek so still and clear I could make out the rocks on the bottom, even twenty feet down. I stripped and waded into the warm water and swam out to the Rock and sat facing the sun, trying to quiet my mind. Benton sat beside me, alert, his ears cocked, his eyes scanning the woods for motion.

I removed his collar so he could be naked, too. We were, for the moment, two feral creatures perched on an ancient rock soothed by timeless still water.

Kingfishers coursed along the length of the creek, three feet above the surface. Swallows darted like winged electrons, snatching insects from the air. Buzzards circled above us on the thermals. The shrill *pweeee* of a broad-winged hawk issued from somewhere up in the trees. Perhaps it was the same one I'd seen twice flying from the field with snakes dangling limp from its talons.

The water surface mirrored the sky and tinged it emerald green, and hundreds of tiny hatchlings, silver-red and less than a half-inch long, glinted like sparklers when their scaled sides caught the sun. Young bullfrogs, which three weeks back wiggled through the pool like corpulent sperm cells, had sprouted legs, shed tails, and now bellowed from the margins of the creek. Cicadas that had emerged from years in earthen burrows scratched out their tunes.

We remained on the rock until the sun started to fade. Once back at the cabin, I ate dinner, as I always did, on the deck, with an oil lamp burning on my small table and the whippoorwills and bobwhites signaling the onset of night.

Willow called and seemed to sense my mood. "How are you doing, Dave?" Her tone suggested that she was worried about me.

"I guess I'm okay, but I miss my girls."

Bob came on the line. "We're thinking of you, David," he said. "Call if you need us; we're at the cabin tonight."

I appreciated their offer, but I was wrestling with fears that only I could resolve. I decided to grab a camp chair and headlamp and hike down to the bluff, a place I had come to call the "Rock of Decision-making."

I closed Benton in the cabin—I knew his crashing through darkened woods would distract me—and set out at about ten P.M. Within five minutes, I was seated on top of the bluff, with the river one hundred feet below me. I switched off the headlamp, and as my eyes adjusted to the darkness, I could see patches of sky—stars and a crescent moon—through the branches of the trees around and above me. I plucked a wintergreen leaf from a plant at my feet, crumpled it between my fingers, and held it to my nose.

Soon, creatures began to stir in the brush around me. Mostly field mice and chipmunks, but larger animals, too, probably deer.

As I sat, some things became clear to me: I was in love with the concept of family; I was no longer fully in love with Susan, as my friend Jim had suggested a few weeks earlier. I was being unfair to both of us by clinging to a relationship that was already dead. I realized that it was time for me to surrender and yield to the inevitable; it was time to let go.

Though I wasn't seeking distractions—in fact, I was inclined to turn away from them and remain focused on the process I was working through—troubling events on the other side of the bluff were about to capture my full attention.

VII

SUMMER

THIRTY-NINE

Space Invaders

> *Noise is the most impertinent of all forms of interruption. It is not only an interruption, but also a disruption of thought.*
>   —Arthur Schopenhauer, *Studies in Pessimism*

I am not an overprotective father. In fact, I've always sought ways to encourage the girls to take risks—calculated ones, mind you—that will bolster self-confidence and reward them with adventure. I allow them to plunge into the creek, even when the current's up, and swim from rock to rock or paddle the kayak under my watchful eye but without direct hands-on clinging.

I've led them up mountain trails through thunderstorms without experiencing a moment of parental angst. I know the woods pose a host of perils: poisonous snakes, ground bees, sheer cliffs, hypothermia, and numerous opportunities for becoming hopelessly lost, but I've never really worried much about those things during our outings. And when the girls aren't with me, I assume they're in good hands and don't fret about their welfare—just more occasions to trust in God.

But where the cabin was concerned, I had become the consummate hand-wringing, neurotic parent, determined to protect the sanctity of my forest and to thwart anyone intent on disturbing my peace or violating my space. I assumed the figurative role of the shotgun-toting landowner in the movies who confronts intruders by saying: "Git ye' offen my land 'fore I blast yer seat full o' buckshot!"

When the National Park Service announced plans to construct a trail along the bluff behind the cabin, for instance, I wrote impassioned letters, attended public meetings, called the superintendent and his subordinates directly to let them know that, while I embraced the notion of a foot trail, I had a *big* problem with their providing access to horses or ATVs. In the end, I prevailed.

When developers miles upstream hatched plans to dam Clear Creek to provide a community with drinking water, I wrote an angry letter to the state asking, in effect, "*How in the hell can you even think about damming a* Wild and Scenic River?!"

Beyond that, I fully supported erecting a gate at the entrance to the property and always kept it locked, lest anyone wander back to my place "just to check things out."

And during the construction process, I had felt my blood pressure spike as I watched backhoes and Bobcats damage perfectly healthy trees. Even though I had ten-acres' worth of oaks, maples, hemlocks, and pines, I was loath to sacrifice a single tree, and after the backhoes had left, I launched an elaborate—and to some extent futile—campaign to save some of the casualties by wrapping wounded trunks and using ropes to pull bent trees erect.

In all my neurotic ruminating on the threats—real and imagined—to the cabin and its environs, I had always focused my concerns on physical encroachment. I never, never, imagined that the impacts would assault my ears rather than my eyes.

One Friday night, J.J. and I sipped beers on the deck, watching goldfinches crowd the feeders and listening to the calls of mourning doves, hawks, and pileated woodpeckers. A breeze rustled the leaves. The sun sank toward the horizon.

Ahhh, solitude, I thought. A quiet summer evening in the woods. Life is good, damned good. The happy reflection was still lingering in my synapses when a shrill voice, amplified through a PA system, echoed up from the gorge. It was followed by the "Star Spangled Banner."

"What in the *hell* is that?" I said.

"Sounds like our national anthem to me."

"No shit, Sherlock, but why are we hearing it at seven P.M., from the direction of the creek—a *wild and scenic* creek?"

"Bound to be from the other side. God knows what's over there. Sounds like a festival of some kind. Could be a Klan rally."

"Yeah, right. Or a gathering of Tennessee Militia ramping up for Y2K and the End of the World as We Know It."

Then we heard the whine of engines—dozens of them—lawn-mower motors hopped up on steroids.

"It sounds like a friggin' NASCAR race—in the forest!" I said.

We sat stunned for a few minutes, waiting for the aural assault to end. It didn't. It only got worse. Within 15 minutes, we were in J.J.'s car on a recon mission.

Soon, we drove through a neighborhood of well-maintained farmhouses and horse stables. Stenciled signs that read STOP RACING IN OUR NEIGHBORHOOD hung from trees lining the road. One sign went on to intimate that old people were actually dying inside the farmhouse at the end of the gravel drive. Clearly, they would be deprived of a peaceful passage.

I could only imagine a fading octogenarian muttering his final words and his distraught family members, gathered close around his bedside, saying, "Yer gonna have to speak up, Pap; got a race going on over at the track."

Though the development scenario hadn't been played out to its conclusion, I could only imagine how it might go. There are no noise ordinances or zoning laws in the county, thus, no legal grounds on which to base a protest. These farm families—whose roots trace back generations—would tolerate the noise as long as they could and wage an honest grassroots fight to reclaim their peace and quiet. But after a time, resignation would supplant their zeal to resist, and they'd sell their land cheap, just to get the hell away from the racket. Businesses that didn't mind the commotion, or, more likely, would contribute to it, would snatch up the land. What began as a small dirt track with five-tiered bleachers and a small concession stand would gradually expand: bigger track, more stands, brighter lights, more noise. Voilà! An auto-racing mecca. And just one more piece of tranquil rural countryside lost.

As we approached the glow of lights from the track, I was angry.

"These people are violating natural law and disturbing the

peace, not just of the people who live in the area, but the animals, too," I said.

J.J., who's much more in tune with the temperament of my rural neighbors than I—and the risks associated with provoking their ire—urged caution and restraint.

"David, don't piss these people off," he said.

We pulled up to the booth at the entrance. A middle-aged woman in shorts and a T-shirt emerged.

"You fellows want to watch the races?" she said. Despite the enthusiasm in her voice, and absence of even the slightest hint of contrition, I kept my cool.

Thinking: Lady, I fully endorse legal efforts to shut you down. Saying: "Gee, you've got quite an interesting facility here."

"Yes, it is, we draw racers from all over the region," she announced proudly.

Thinking: These rasping little hell wagons are sins against nature! Saying: "What type of cars do you race?"

"These are go-carts." The question obviously pegged us as outsiders, if J.J.'s Acura with Anderson County plates hadn't already given us away. "Where are you fellas from?"

"Oak Ridge," said J.J., rubbing his beard, the signal that he, too, was repressing the urge to throttle somebody.

Thinking: Who are the people driving these clamorous contraptions? Saying: "Are those adults or kids behind the wheel?"

"Well, we've got both. Youngest is about sixteen."

Thinking: When do you begin disturbing the peace *of dying old people and little babies—for God knows how many square miles?* Saying: "What time do you start and end?"

"We start just after seven and run until eleven or so."

Thinking: Lights-out in rural America is about 9:30, so *you're subjecting dying old people and babies* to an hour-and-a-half of anxiety and insomnia. So exactly how many nights during the week do you *create complete chaos?* Saying: "Do you stage events through the week?"

"We race every Friday night."

Thinking: Yeah, but only until you've driven off your neighbors, expanded the size of your track, and decide it's profitable to add more events. Saying: nothing.

"How much to get in?" J.J. asked.

"That'll be ten dollars each."

For the average Morgan County resident, who shops at the Save-A-Lot grocery store, that's a six-month supply of pinto beans.

"I think we'll pass," J.J. said. "But can we pull up and watch for a minute?"

"Sure, but don't get near that break in the fence. The cars come flying through there after the race."

I considered positioning myself directly *in front* of the opening, letting one of the drivers mow me down, then suing the *bejesus* out of him.

"You'll be hearing from my attorney!" I'd yell from the stretcher, as they loaded me in the ambulance. "When I'm done with you, you won't have enough pocket change to afford a gallon of premium gas!"

I reflected on the pain of having a motorized vehicle, traveling at a high rate of speed, drive over my torso and decided the circumstance didn't yet call for martyrdom. Short of that, I wasn't sure which path to pursue.

We eased the car forward toward the fence. Beyond, men in jeans and T-shirts carried about a dozen tiny vehicles onto the packed dirt track. They arranged them in formation and climbed inside. With shoulders and helmeted heads emerging from cramped cockpits and hands gripping steering wheels the size of Play-Doh lids, the drivers had the comic look of portly Shriners mounted on miniature motorcycles at a July Fourth parade.

Meanwhile, fathers and sons, many wearing shirts boasting the numbers of their favorite NASCAR drivers, sipped from cups of iced Coke and munched hot dogs as they migrated back to their seats in the stands. Insects and bats circled in the halo of the light towers.

As the engines revved to life, it occurred to me that, if I had shut my eyes, I might have been at a rally of Weed-Eater enthusiasts. A now-familiar voice barked over the PA system, but the only word I could discern was "race"; the other syllables were garbled and distorted by overtaxed speakers.

Soon the twelve diminutive vehicles sped around the oval

track at speeds that must have approached fifty miles per hour. In five minutes, a man emerged from the cinder-block tower and waved the checkered flag as the winner crossed the finish line and for a blessed moment, the noise ended.

The woman from the entrance booth approached.

"You fellas can go on in if you want. No charge."

She was trying to be nice, and her gesture reminded me that here we had good people doing what I regarded as bad things— or if not bad, at least improper—probably just trying to make a living in a county devoid of many options.

"Thanks," I said, softening toward her. "Not tonight."

As J.J. and I left, the cars were stacked on the track, prepared for another race, and I knew we'd endure another couple of hours of ruckus before the track's lights went dim at eleven.

I contacted the National Park Service the next Monday to see if it had any legal grounds to close down the track because of its potential for compromising the experience of boaters camping along the river.

"No," said the ranger. "We really don't have a dog in this fight, but there are some folks who live near the track who are trying to shut it down." She gave me names and phone numbers. I called and talked to a woman who sounded a little beleaguered but encouraged that someone else, from outside her neighborhood, also found the noise disturbing. As it turned out, she and some of her neighbors had retained an attorney and were waging a legal battle against the track owners. They had achieved a partial victory by forcing the track owners to limit racing to one night per week—Friday.

As we drove from the track back to the cabin, the headlights illuminated a snake slithering toward the brush at the entrance to our gravel road. I found it significant that he was heading in the *opposite* direction of the race track.

As soon as I saw it, I recognized the markings. "You know what that is?" I asked.

We stepped out of the car for a closer look and drew to within three feet of the snake, which was beginning to coil into a defensive position. We studied the snake's brown, tan, and black skin and shiny, copper-colored head.

"*That* is a copperhead," I said.

"Yup," J.J. said. "It's a copperhead all right. Beautiful snake."

"Yeah. Too bad he's poisonous."

"You need to warn your girls about this."

Logan had already cultivated a disabling fear of insects; would I precipitate a full-blown case of agoraphobia if I shared with her the story of the snake? As it turned out, her fear was limited to bees. Several months later, we discovered a resident copperhead living in the wood pile in front of the cabin. We named him the "Window Viper," because the wood pile lay just beyond the window over the kitchen sink. Logan and Challen frequently leaned against the logs to get a closer look at the snake.

"Cool," was Logan's assessment.

"He's pretty," said Challen.

The first time I had encountered a copperhead I was in Hot Springs, North Carolina, staying at Randall's farm during a break along the Appalachian Trail. We had been sitting on the front porch of his cabin when Randall suggested we walk out into the open field and check out the stars. I was barefoot, and I remember that the damp grass felt so cool and good on my feet.

We stopped a hundred feet in front of the cabin and studied the stars, and Randall's dog, Amos, started barking and circling around us in the darkness.

"Don't move!" Randall said.

"Why?"

"Amos has spotted a copperhead somewhere around us. Just stand still; don't move."

We had no source of light, so we were left to rely on Amos's heightened senses of smell and hearing. I remember being torn between the urge to run like hell back to the safety of the front porch and being paralyzed by the fear that any step I might take would fall directly on the back of a venomous snake. Just another reason to wear shoes, I thought, as I waited for someone to make a command decision on how to proceed.

Eventually, we all broke and sprinted for the porch like men dashing across hot coals, intent on exposing as little surface area as possible. There were no casualties.

Over the two miles before J.J. and I had reached the turnoff to our gravel drive, the pavement was alive with leaping toads, a favored meal of copperheads. J.J., intent on keeping his karma intact, had swerved to avoid hitting them, although more than a few squished under his wheels.

"Don't feel too bad," I said. "You're actually improving the gene pool; the smart ones don't try to cross the road."

We surmised that the snake was out feasting on toads, taking advantage of the bounty.

I knew the woods around the cabin provided perfect habitat for copperheads and timber rattlers, and I realized that on our frequent forays to the creek after dark I had probably planted my feet—protected only by the straps of my Teva sandals—within inches of the snakes. But somehow they had remained an abstract threat until I glimpsed the snake in the middle of the road and pictured that triangular head, fangs bared, mouth agape, striking for my bare leg. When we reached the locked gate, I thoroughly scanned the gravel before I swung my leg out to go open the combination lock. Later, J.J. suggested we cancel our planned hike down to the bluff.

"Eeeks," he said. "Snakes!"

J.J. and I determined that the best antidote for the drone of go-cart engines was a day spent in the wilds, so we decided to run one of the area's creeks. The bounty of runable whitewater within a half hour of the cabin made the choice difficult. Three days of hard rain had made all of the area's waterways navigable after several weeks of drought.

To that point, J.J., the girls, and I had explored most of the back roads and visited most of the natural attractions, but our aquatic forays had been limited to the pool behind the cabin and the put-in point at Jett Bridge, a mile down the road.

I called the National Park Service office in Wartburg and talked to one of the rangers, hoping to get her recommendations on where to go. I described our boating proficiency (minimal) and our watercraft (a cumbersome seventeen-foot Coleman canoe designed for flatwater).

"Uh, that boat's going to give you problems," she said. "Clear Creek and the Emory, with the water as high as it is, might be a bit too challenging."

Finally, she suggested that we run White Creek, which runs from the north and connects to Clear Creek just above Barnett Bridge.

"How difficult?"

"Well, you're looking mostly at Class One, an occasional Class Two. But I'm not sure how you're going to do in that Coleman. It's a narrow creek."

J.J. and I huddled. I had purchased a sit-on-top kayak the week before, primarily to give the girls a boat to paddle around the pool. Problem was it accommodated one rower. I had also purchased two inflatable inner tubes protected by thick nylon sleeves. They were designed to be pulled behind ski boats, but we used them as floats in the creek. Together, the kayak and one of the tubes would make a suitable flotilla.

Our plan: We'd run White Creek four miles from the bridge on 62 down to Barnett Bridge. One of us would float the tube; the other would paddle the kayak, which J.J. had dubbed "Frau Sit-On-Top."

We left J.J.'s Acura at Barnett Bridge and parked the Jeep at the put-in point upriver. The nearest we could park was the edge of the bridge one hundred feet above the river, so we dragged the boats, paddles, dry bag, and life vests through waist high weeds and a thicket of willows down to the lip of the creek.

As I settled into the kayak, I was a little edgy. Partly because I had logged a total of about fifteen minutes in the boat, all of it on flatwater. But I was also unnerved because I had watched rescue workers pull a drowning victim out of the Ocoee River, near Chattanooga, a few years earlier.

As J.J. and I set out, and as I felt the boat buck through the first set of rapids—moderate though they were—I couldn't help but picture that bloated face. Within a river mile, I had tipped, plunged out of the kayak, and recovered at least a dozen times.

I realized that I'd have to actively work at drowning in the moderate current and began to relax and enjoy the float trip and the pristine forest lining the route.

The creek run was a four-mile continuum of wide flats and narrow, churning chutes. Hemlock groves, gray sandstone boulders, rhododendron, and late-blooming azaleas lined the route. Light-pink blossoms drifted with the current, and dragonflies provided a winged escort as we passed down the river. Until we approached the confluence of White and Clear creeks at the end of the trip, we didn't see a single marker of civilization. Just water, and rock, and dense forest. At the end of the run, two lawn chairs perched on a gray boulder suggested that we were about to reenter civilization.

For the first half of the four-hour trip, J.J. plied the double-bladed paddle, bouncing through most of the rapids on the inner-tube, while I navigated the kayak using a single-bladed canoe oar. We switched watercraft at the halfway point, and I took perverse delight in watching J.J. repeat my performance and swamp and tip in many of the rapids. On each tumble, the padded seat floated off in one direction, the paddle in another. J.J., his free arm hula-hooping through the air, struggled to maintain his balance, hanging onto the kayak with the other hand as his feet slipped on silt-covered rocks.

Clearly, navigating the kayak with grace and precision involved a steep learning curve. And I was relieved that we hadn't received our baptism on Clear Creek or the Obed, with rapids much more menacing than any we faced on White Creek.

Dark-gray cumulonimbus clouds drifted overhead and in the early afternoon disgorged their load. Hard rain pocked stretches of flatwater, and the forest hissed under the onslaught of millions of pea-size droplets.

"Damn," J.J. said, grinning from under his ball cap. "Now we're going to get wet."

"Gotta hate that," I said. "Every once in a while, we should cast a glance upstream, see if a tidal wave is coming. Perfect conditions for a flash flood: Grounds saturated from two days of hard rain. Creek's way up."

J.J. recalled the flash flood that killed several hikers passing through a narrow gorge in Arizona a couple of years earlier.

"Shitty way to go," he said. "Never knew what hit 'em. Sun was shining one minute; they were human flotsam the next."

The rain ended within a half hour, the sun emerged, and we soon tumbled into Clear Creek one hundred feet upriver from the take-out ramp at Barnett Bridge. We paddled across the current to the far side and pulled the boats out of the water.

We had christened Frau Sit-On-Top and the tube and had our first taste of Morgan County whitewater. We had run but four of the hundreds of miles of blueways lacing the hills and hollows around the cabin.

"We need to do more of this," J.J. said.

"But we need to learn how to control the kayak first. Not all water around here is as forgiving as White Creek."

"We need to drag the kayak down to the pool and practice rolling."

"Or at least learn to effect a more graceful exit after we tip."

The next week, I had to attend a meeting in Knoxville, and I spent the night on the couch in the family room at home, feeling like an alien in what used to be my house. Unable to sleep, I turned on the TV and watched the show *Cops*. Perspective seemed to come to me from the most unlikely sources.

On the program, a man—a custodial father of two young girls and who sold drugs and sex from his home—was busted. As he was being cuffed, his daughter—maybe five years old—was terrified. Her family unit, diseased though it was, was being dismantled.

"Please, please don't take my daddy away!" she screamed. She ran and threw her arms around her father's waist. "Please, please!"

The cops led him outside, and the little girl collapsed, sobbing, on the kitchen floor.

Perspective.

Kids have a remarkable ability to see past their parents' failings and love them unconditionally, or so I hoped.

So far, the girls had seemed okay, steady, though disinclined to talk about what was happening to their family. Had they accepted the inevitable, even as I had resisted? Were they ahead of me in terms of progressing through the stages of mourning and loss? Or had the seeds of dysfunction already begun to sprout in their hearts?

FORTY

Journey to Forgiveness

Children begin by loving their parents; as they grow older they judge them; sometimes they forgive them.
    —Oscar Wilde, *The Picture of Dorian Gray*

A friend of mine once said, "Suffering and pain will expand to fill whatever space is available to them, but God never imposes more hardship than you can contend with."

She added the corollary: "Human beings are amazingly resilient creatures."

Another friend said, "Suffering promotes change, and change promotes growth."

Raïssa Maritain wrote, "Suffering is an auxiliary of creation."

As I reflect back on my months in retreat—and back further still to the difficult years that preceded them—I recognize the truth in those words, all of them. The notion of pain as a promoter of growth resonates deeply. But I also realize that there is a threshold beyond which suffering engenders, not growth, but callousness and fear, an erosion of tenderness and compassion.

"Hot fire forges hard steel," yet another friend once offered. But hardness is exactly what I feared most through this process—for all four of us, but particularly for the girls. To love fully and unconditionally, to allow someone to infiltrate your molecules, requires an open and trusting heart. From the moments of their births, through the process of imprinting, through gazing on the faces of their parents united in their fields of view, the girls had invested their faith in us, that we would remain a constant in their lives, that the uncertainty of the world couldn't corrupt the harmony of their family. Instead, we were demonstrating to them the notion of impermanence.

During their visits with me through the spring and summer, I watched the girls' tears ebb and gradually give way to acceptance and even assertiveness in seeing that we stayed connected and insisting that I hear *all* about the events, both great and small, that filled their days away from me.

One night I was seated on the deck having dinner, and I heard the answering machine click on: "Dad, get off your rear and pick up the phone," Challen shouted. "I need to tell you about my day."

Logan called one night to tell me she had scraped her knee when she fell off her bicycle. "I have the *hugest* boo-boo on my leg," she said. Then came the non sequitur: "Dad, things just aren't the same with you gone," she said. "I even miss your little messes."

Then she laughed, and the laugh offered reassurance that she was adjusting to things. She seemed to have accepted the death of her parents' marriage and was now reflecting fondly on the way things had once been. There had been much humor and happiness—along with the strife and discord—in our lives together, and Logan had reached a place where she could begin to appreciate the good times we shared.

"The house is just, well, too neat and tidy," she continued. "I miss you, Dad."

I've come to realize that it wasn't concern for my own suffering that kept me stuck for so many years in a destructive marriage; it was concern for my children. As I had once told my father, I would slowly bleed for the rest of my life to prevent my daughters from suffering a single moment, but in the end I realized that their watching me bleed would only have increased their suffering. Susan once told me that, after her parents split, she worried constantly about whether her father was okay. Seeing me healthy and whole, if nothing else, inclined the girls to embrace the faith that things would, somehow, work out for me, for them, and for Susan.

In the months after my departure from my home, I found myself obsessed with watching them, straining to detect the slightest hint—a pained expression, an odd gesture, a numb affect, a neutral word tinged with anger—that might reveal the scars Susan and I had inflicted on them. I knew we had hurt them, though I couldn't fathom how deeply or how long-lasting the effects. I feared that the damage would extend through a lifetime of jaundiced expectations and an abiding belief that relationships really weren't meant to last. I hoped they would prove me wrong, but the outcome wouldn't be apparent for years, until they had entered their own relationships.

There was so much I wanted to explain to them, about how and why things came apart, about how yielding to Susan's will and leaving my home—their home—was the hardest decision I had ever faced, about how what their mom and I had done was an act of supreme mutual selfishness.

What worried me most was the fact that they weren't talking, with the exception of the occasional quip, like Logan's comment about missing my little messes. Even on those occasions when I asked them how they were doing with "things," they'd pretend as if they didn't know quite what I was talking about. Their responses to my queries—both direct and indirect—reminded me of the night in February when I had told them I was leaving, when Logan insisted she had homework to do and Challen feigned a fainting spell.

The most self-serving interpretation of their silence would have been to conclude that they were doing fine; that they had managed to process the trauma; that the black box containing their spirits would withstand the crash.

But I feared that wasn't the case. I knew they were viewing the world through smudged glass and surrendering some small measure of their faith in the world's inherent goodness, a faith that every child is born with and a fortunate few sustain through a lifetime.

During a visit to the cabin in the spring, Kent, my high-school friend and member of the Christian Brotherhood, sat with me by the fire into the early hours of the morning, listening to me babble on about anger and perceived injustice before I finally arrived at the essence of what I really wanted to say.

"Kent, I know that what Susan and I are doing is wrong; it's sinful," I said. "I can feel it in my heart, and the guilt is crushing me."

"Have you sought forgiveness?" he asked.

The fact was, I hadn't. To that point in my life, my gravest transgressions had involved thoughtlessness, discourtesy, indifference, pride, vanity, caprice, shortsightedness. I saw only minor blots on my cosmic panorama. But playing a role, even a reluctant one, in splintering my daughters' family of origin pitched me headlong into the high-stakes realm of sin. Even though I sought eventual release, I wanted to live with the sin for a while, to let it evolve into penitence that engendered suffering before it gave way to peace. I had condemned my daughters to suffer, and it was only fair that I suffer with them; I only wish I could have suffered *for* them.

"For the sins of your fathers you, though guiltless, must suffer," Horace wrote in *Odes*.

In the isolation of the cabin, I reflected often on the path of contrition, the power of forgiveness, and I realized that it was a multifaceted issue. It began with forgiveness of Susan for her determination to end our marriage.

I had felt that forgiveness come over the previous weeks as I began to regard Susan as a person who was doing the best she could with the spiritual and emotional tools she was equipped with. Susan had been "slowly dying" in our relationship, as she once told me, and her emotional death would have distorted the experience of family for all four of us. She had decided to end things as a way of saving herself, an act of marital triage that ensured she could continue to function as mother to Challen and Logan, a role she played exceedingly well.

The path to absolution also involved asking Susan to forgive me for all the things I had said and done that had hurt her over our eighteen years together. And I needed to ask the girls for their forgiveness. While asking for their forgiveness was something I could approach unilaterally, I realized that only they could grant it, and I was prepared to wait a lifetime for it if necessary.

But when I asked to be forgiven, I wanted to approach the girls with a pure heart. To do that, I had to find a way to forgive myself, and that, I realized, was something I couldn't do alone.

I recalled the prisoner I had interviewed while in graduate school who had been a triggerman in the murders of five people. I remembered how, as darkness had closed in around him in his prison cell, he had begged for God's forgiveness and how it had been granted—how the crushing guilt had been lifted from his shoulders. If God could forgive him his sin, I knew, he could also forgive me mine.

When it came time for me to seek redemption, I wanted to enter hallowed space and strip away anything that might have distracted me from my purpose. I wanted to experience fully the brunt of my transgression in a place of peace, hope, and steadfastness. I wanted to give full vent to my grief, and once I had purged it, to let the Holy Spirit fill the empty vessel.

Early one afternoon late in the summer, I felt that it was time for my pilgrimage. I called to Benton, and we began the trek down to the river. Once we reached the shoreline, we pushed downstream about a quarter mile through a tangle of laurel and rhododendron to a bend in the creek.

I settled onto the sandy shelf just above the water and positioned myself facing the creek and sat through the afternoon and evening, reflecting on all the wrongful things I had done and said to Susan, on my emotional withdrawal from her, on the ways I had failed her and my children during our lives together, on the ways I had turned away from God. When the feeling of remorse and sadness felt like it would consume me, I began to weep, and weeping, I asked God to forgive me.

I knew that forgiveness would arrive, but I also realized it would come to me in time. I had prayed for the experience of peace and grace on Christmas Eve—the darkest night of my life—and eventually it came, but only after months of doubt and struggle. I came to realize that those difficult months between the prayer and the deliverance were all part of the fulfillment of God's assurance. The anger, the longing for Susan, the desperate hope of saving something that was beyond redemption, had to die away before my heart could mend and awaken to the promise of hope.

FORTY-ONE

Deliverance

To where beyond these voices there is peace.
—Alfred, Lord Tennyson, *Idylls of the King*

Susan and I had our first meeting with Richard Kessler, a mediator and lawyer who would guide us through the process of ending our marriage and equitably dividing shared assets and debts.

If the copperhead coiled on the gravel road made the threat of poison serpents real, the meeting with the mediator made tangible the likely endpoint of my marriage to Susan, though in many ways, we were engaged in the formalities of a fait accompli.

At the end of our first two-hour session, Richard said he believed we could complete the agreement in two, maybe three, more meetings, because, as he put it, we seemed to be operating in a "cooperative spirit." It amazed me that it would take fewer than eight hours—the duration of a standard workday—to dismantle a relationship that spanned nearly two decades and directly entwined the lives of four people.

The session began with Richard asking each of us what we wanted out of the mediation process, and our responses were remarkably similar: we sought a fair and equitable settlement; we desired above all else the fewest disruptions to the lives of our children. The discussions were, for the most part, impassive and practical—sweeping up the pieces of the broken clay pot that had once contained our lives.

I showed up at Wednesday Night Prayer Meeting after the session with Richard, and J.J. and Sam were eager to hear details from the first round. But I told them little, saying only that "this is the beginning of the end, and it will be mercifully short."

Through the process of mediation, I began to grasp fully that my marriage was dead, that any hopes of reconciliation were foolish fantasies, that I would never again be a resident of—rather than a visitor to—our home in the city. I realized, too, that whatever perspective, life skills, and theology I would need to survive the process, either were already part of my operating system or I'd have to progress through the transition without them. I felt so blessed to have been granted the opportunity to retreat to the cabin as I struggled toward a point of acceptance and peace.

For the next few days, I slumped into a period of sadness, and the cabin's isolation only seemed to amplify my mood. I spent long hours sitting on the bluff or perched on the Rock of Contemplation, registering thoughts that were as achingly clear as they were undeniable. I had to resist the temptation to reach out to Susan for comfort and reassurance. This was a burden I needed to carry alone. The cabin's starkness provided few diversions to distract me from confronting the obvious endpoint of things. But then, slowly, the sadness began to lift, and I began to see things in a different way—as if through new eyes.

At a Fourth of July gathering, Susan spent the day at the cabin with the girls and me and our mutual friends, the Youngs, and as I watched her through the afternoon and evening, I realized that I was observing her in a new context. The physical longing for her was gone, the anger had all but ebbed, the feeling of intimacy had been supplanted by an odd detachment. I was seeing Susan the person, not Susan my wife.

It was time for me to let go, to let Susan create for herself the life she wanted. It was time to release my hold on our marriage, the one thing I had always believed would endure. It was time to float free for a while and trust. It was time to test my faith.

As I had struggled through the demise of my marriage, and as I had struggled to define for myself the meaning of spiritual faith, I had mistakenly regarded them as separate issues. I began to realize that they were entwined, always had been, and that mustering the trust to let go of Susan represented the essence of faith. I was at the brink, poised to take the great leap.

I had, through my months in isolation, asked God to guide me, but I had kept myself tethered by a lifeline to Susan and our shared past. It was time to clip off the rope and trust that God would arrest my fall as I began the long ascent from the shadows of the gorge into the sunlight.

Part of letting go was learning to connect with Susan in a new way and establish the context for a relationship that would extend through the rest of our lives and unite us forever through our daughters.

I hoped that we could reach a place from which to lovingly guide their paths, to watch them grow into women, with the shared joy that had attended their births. We needed to become partners, even friends, in an enterprise that would carry the imprint of our genes and our personalities forward through the generations.

Somewhere down in my belly, I feared being forgotten and no longer needed. Or that I would become the loathesome "ex" in Susan's anecdotes about our years together. I worried that my girls would gain a new dad through remarriage. When they faced problems at school or argued with their boyfriends, would they turn to the man who was physically present in their lives? Would I become a "second-place dad," as Challen and Logan termed J.J. and Sam?

I recalled Marshall's admonishment, as the girls and I left her room at the nursing home, to, please, remember her. It seems that we spend lifetimes amassing possessions and erecting houses and investing ourselves in careers, endeavoring always to leave our thumbprint on the world. But in the end, what really matters are our actions and interactions and the bits of us that stay lodged in the memories of those who survive us. Being remembered fondly by the people we've loved—and who have loved us—is the only genuine tribute.

I returned the girls to the city midweek after our Fourth-of-July party and discovered several home-maintenance chores begging attention. The battery on the riding lawnmower was dead, and the grass was knee high. The spigot on the front of the house had blown a washer, and Susan told me it had been running continuously for two weeks. Easy fix-it jobs, but whose?

"I've called repairmen," Susan said when I asked if she wanted help.

"But repairmen cost money; I can fix these things."

"No, really, that's okay. I'll handle it."

A repairman from the small-engine repair shop up the street knocked on the door a few minutes later, and Susan led him to the dead lawnmower. I tagged along behind, feeling like an interloper. She had sanitized her language to the extent that she referred to "her" mower, "her" yard, and "her" house.

"Your battery is dead," the repairman said, after hooking a handheld voltage meter to the terminals, while I hovered in the background, thinking, No shit! And how much is this inspired observation going to cost?

It occurred to me that, meanwhile, he was wondering about my status in the household. Was I boyfriend, brother, neighbor, or estranged husband?

"We can install a new battery for you, but it would cost a lot less if you put it in yourself."

"Yeah, I'll handle the installation," I said, stepping forward. As far as I was concerned, I still had a vested interest in the machine I had purchased new nine years earlier and lovingly tweaked and tuned and infused with fresh oil.

After he left, I pried loose the corroded bolts that attached the wires to the battery terminals. In her efforts to diagnose the problem before I had arrived, Susan had stripped the Phillips head screw—she never was a master with tools—so I had to use a pair of pliers.

"You don't need to do that," she said. "I can get it off."

"Susan, you seem determined to handle all these things on your own," I said, and I saw her stiffen. She crossed her arms in front of her chest, and I knew she was settling into her defensive posture and preparing to do battle.

I couldn't blame her. In the past, I would have said the very same thing as a way of launching into an assault on her pestering yen for total independence and trying to convince her that she needed me in life, if for no other reason, than to keep the house running. But this time, I followed a different tack.

"You know, guys' fathers teach them about this kind of stuff from the time they're kids. You have to give yourself time to learn," I said. "Please, call me if you need my help."

Her expression softened. It was one of the first kind offerings she had received from me through months of discord.

"Dave, thanks for saying that."

"You're welcome," I said, and as I did, I realized that I still loved Susan, always would, loved her enough to let her go, enough to play handyman until a new guy entered her life.

There are times when you view your life as a strange patchwork of experiences that at first glance seem disconnected, without apparent unity. Then, there are those flashes of insight, when you realize that everything that's come before—everything—leads you forward to the next point along a path that is uniquely yours, a path whose every twist and turn is an integral part of the person you will spend a lifetime becoming. And that the events that barely register in your consciousness and take place in the plainest possible settings are chockful of meaning. They nudge you forward in tiny imperceptible increments.

As Susan and I hovered over a broken lawnmower, I was learning to love—just as she was learning to be loved—in a whole new way. There, in the work shed, we had discovered an intimacy founded on separateness. As we did, we began defining for ourselves, and for each other, new roles that would outlast all the years of our marriage.

At that moment, I realized that we had all embarked on a new journey. My heart was still. And I knew, *I just knew,* we were all going to be all right.